A First Course in Artificial Intelligence

Authored By

Osondu Oguike
Department of Computer Science
University of Nigeria, Nsukka
Enugu State
Nigeria

A First Course in Artificial Intelligence

Author: Osondu Oguike

ISBN (Online): 978-1-68108-853-2

ISBN (Print): 978-1-68108-854-9

ISBN (Paperback): 978-1-68108-855-6

need for a court order if at any point you breach any terms of this License Agreement. In no event will any delay or failure by Bentham Science Publishers in enforcing your compliance with this License Agreement constitute a waiver of any of its rights.

3. You acknowledge that you have read this License Agreement, and agree to be bound by its terms and conditions. To the extent that any other terms and conditions presented on any website of Bentham Science Publishers conflict with, or are inconsistent with, the terms and conditions set out in this License Agreement, you acknowledge that the terms and conditions set out in this License Agreement shall prevail.

Bentham Science Publishers Ltd.
Executive Suite Y - 2
PO Box 7917, Saif Zone
Sharjah, U.A.E.
Email: subscriptions@benthamscience.net

BENTHAM SCIENCE

CONTENTS

PREFACE i
    CONSENT FOR PUBLICATION i
    CONFLICT OF INTEREST i
    ACKNOWLEDGEMENT i

CHAPTER 1 INTRODUCTION TO ARTIFICIAL INTELLIGENCE 1
  1. DEFINITION OF ARTIFICIAL INTELLIGENCE 1
    1.1. Artificial Intelligence 1
        1.1.1. Explanation of Artificial Intelligence 2
        1.1.2. Turing Test Model – Acting Like Human 2
        1.1.3. Cognitive Model – Thinking Like Human 3
        1.1.4. Rational Agent Model – Acting Rationally 3
        1.1.5. Law of Thought – Thinking Rationally 4
    1.2. Foundational Discipline in Artificial Intelligence 4
        1.2.1. Philosophy 4
        1.2.2. Mathematics 5
        1.2.3. Psychology 5
        1.2.4. Computer Engineering 5
        1.2.5. Linguistics 5
        1.2.6. Biological Science and Others 6
    1.3. Conclusion 6
    1.4. Summary 6
  2. HISTORY OF ARTIFICIAL INTELLIGENCE AND PROJECTION FOR THE
FUTURE 6
    2.1. The Birth of Artificial Intelligence 7
        2.1.1. Alan Turing (1912 – 1954) 7
        2.1.2. Other Significant Contributors Prior to Birth of AI 7
    2.2. Historical Development of Other Artificial Intelligence Systems 8
        2.2.1. Expert System (1950s – 1970s) 8
        2.2.2. First Artificial Intelligence Winter (1974 – 1980) 8
        2.2.3. Second Artificial Intelligence Winter (1987 – 1993) 8
        2.2.4. Intelligent Agent (1993 – Date) 9
    2.3. Projections into the Future of Artificial Intelligence 9
        2.3.1. Virtual Personal Assistants 9
    2.4. Conclusion 9
    2.5. Summary 10
  3. EMERGING ARTIFICIAL INTELLIGENCE APPLICATIONS 10
    3.1. Artificial Intelligence Applied Technologies 10
        3.1.1. Blockchain Technology 10
        3.1.2. Internet of Things (IoT) 13
        3.1.3. Data Science, Big Data and Data Analytic 14
    3.2. Artificial Intelligence Products 15
        3.2.1. IBM Watson 15
        3.2.2. Self-Driving/Autonomous Cars 15
        3.2.3. Face Recognition System 15
    3.3. Conclusion 16
    3.4. Summary 16
  CONCLUDING REMARKS 16
  REFERENCES 17

CHAPTER 2 EXPERT SYSTEM 18
   1. EXPERT SYSTEM BASICS 18
     1.1. Components of Expert System 18
       1.1.1. Human Expert 19
       1.1.2. Knowledge Engineer 19
       1.1.3. Knowledge Base 19
       1.1.4. Inference Engine 20
       1.1.5. User Interface 20
       1.1.6. Non-Expert User 20
     1.2. Knowledge Acquisition 20
       1.2.1. Knowledge Elicitation 20
       1.2.2. Intermediate Representation 20
       1.2.3. Executable Form Representation 21
     1.3. Characteristics of Expert System 21
     1.4. Examples of Expert System 21
       1.4.1. Medical Diagnosis System 21
       1.4.2. Game System 21
       1.4.3. Financial Forecast/Advice System 22
       1.4.4. Identification System 22
       1.4.5. Water/Oil Drilling System 22
       1.4.6. Car Engine Diagnosis System 22
     1.5. Importance of Expert Systems 22
     1.6. Conclusion 23
     1.7. Summary 23
   2. KNOWLEDGE ENGINEERING 23
     2.1. Foundations of Knowledge Engineering 23
       2.1.1. Knowledge Engineering Processes 23
       2.1.2. Sources and Types of Knowledge 25
       2.1.3. Levels and Categories of Knowledge 26
     2.2. Knowledge Acquisition Methods 27
       2.2.1. Knowledge Modelling Methods 27
     2.3. Knowledge Verification and Validation 28
     2.4. Knowledge Representation 28
       2.4.1. Production Rules 29
       2.4.2. Semantic Network 30
       2.4.3. Frames 32
     2.5. Inferencing 33
       2.5.1. Common Sense Inferencing/Reasoning 33
       2.5.2. Rule Base Inferencing/Reasoning 33
     2.6. Explanation and Meta-knowledge 34
     2.7. Inferencing with Uncertainty 35
     2.8. Expert System Development Environment 35
       2.8.1. Expert System Shells 35
       2.8.2. Programming Languages 35
       2.8.3. Hybrid Environment 35
     2.9. Conclusion 35
     2.10. Summary 36
   3. PROPOSITIONAL LOGIC 36
     3.1. Propositional Logic as Knowledge Representation Formalism 36
     3.2. Syntax of Propositional Logic Connectives 36

3.3. Semantics of Propositional Logic 37
3.4. Automating Logical Reasoning 38
3.5. Uncertainty in Logical Reasoning 43
3.6. Automating Uncertain Propositional Logic 44
3.7. Conclusion 50
3.8. Summary 50
CONCLUDING REMARKS 50
REFERENCES 50

CHAPTER 3 NATURAL LANGUAGE PROCESSING 51
  1. FUNDAMENTALS OF NATURAL LANGUAGE PROCESSING 51
    1.1. Applications of Natural Language Processing 51
    1.2. The Future of Natural Language Processing 53
    1.3. Conclusion 53
    1.4. Summary 53
  2. TEXT PRE-PROCESSING 53
    2.1. Text Normalization 54
    2.2. Tokenization 54
    2.3. Stop Words Removal 56
    2.4. Stemming 56
    2.5. Lemmatization 57
    2.6. Conclusion 57
    2.7. Summary 58
  3. TEXT REPRESENTATION 58
    3.1. Bags of Words 58
    3.2. Lookup Dictionary 58
    3.3. One-Hot Encoding 59
    3.4. Word Embedding 59
    3.5. Conclusion 59
    3.6. Summary 59
  4. PARTS OF SPEECH TAGGING 60
    4.1. Fundamentals of Parts of Speech 60
    4.2. Importance of Parts of Speech Tagging 61
      4.2.1. Word Pronunciation in Text to Speech Conversion 62
      4.2.2. Word Sense Disambiguation 62
      4.2.3. Stemming as Text Pre-processing Task 62
    4.3. Computational Methods for Parts of Speech Tagging 62
      4.3.1. Rule Based Tagging Method/Algorithm 63
      4.3.2. Stochastic Based Tagging Method/Algorithm 63
      4.3.3. Transformation Based Tagging 63
    4.4. Conclusion 65
    4.5. Summary 65
  5. TEXT TAGGING/TEXT CLASSIFICATION 65
    5.1. Approaches to Text Classification 65
      5.1.1. Rule Based Text Classification 65
      5.1.2. Machine Learning Based Text Classification 66
      5.1.3. Rule and Machine Learning Based Text Classification 66
    5.2. Machine Learning Algorithms for Text Classification 66
      5.2.1 Naïve Bayes Text Classification Machine Learning Algorithm 66
      5.2.2. Decision Tree Text Classification Machine Learning Algorithm 67
    5.3. Conclusion 68

5.4. Summary 68
6. TEXT SUMMARIZATION 68
  6.1. Brief History of Automatic Text Summarization 68
  6.2. Approaches to Text Summarization 69
    6.2.1. Extractive Text Summarization 69
    6.2.2. Abstractive Text Summarization 69
  6.3. Frequency Based Technique 69
  6.4. Feature Based Technique 71
  6.5. Text Rank Algorithm 71
  6.6. Conclusion 72
  6.7. Summary 72
7. SENTIMENT ANALYSIS 72
  7.1. Types of Sentiment Analysis 72
    7.1.1. Fine Grained Sentiment Analysis 73
    7.1.2. Emotion Detection Sentiment Analysis 73
    7.1.3. Aspects Based Sentiment Analysis 73
    7.1.4. Multi-Lingual Sentiment Analysis 73
    7.1.5. Intent Detection Sentiment Analysis 73
  7.2. Applications of Sentiment Analysis 73
    7.2.1. Social Media Sentiment Analysis 73
    7.2.2. Internet Sentiment Analysis 74
    7.2.3. Sentiment Analysis on Customer Feedback 74
    7.2.4. Sentiment Analysis on Customer Services 74
  7.3. Approaches to Sentiment Analysis 75
    7.3.1. Rule Based Approach 75
    7.3.2. Machine Learning Based Approach 75
    7.3.3. Hybrid Approach 75
  7.4. Conclusion 75
  7.5. Summary 76
8. NLP, USING PYTHON PROGRAMMING LANGUAGE 76
  8.1. Fundamentals of NLP Using Python 76
    8.1.1. Natural Language ToolKit (NLTK) 76
    8.1.2. Getting Started with NLP Using Python 77
    8.1.3. Using List in Python for NLP 79
    8.1.4. Manipulating String in Python 81
    8.1.5. Using Python Text Editor 82
  8.2. Using Control Structures in Python for NLP 83
    8.2.1. Selective Control Structure 83
    8.2.2. Repetitive/Looping Control Structure 85
  8.3. Accessing Text Corpora in Python 87
    8.3.1. Gutenberg Corpus 87
    8.3.2. Web and Chat Text 89
    8.3.3. Brown Corpus 89
    8.3.4. Reuters Corpus 90
    8.3.5. Inaugural Address Corpus 90
  8.4. Conclusion 91
  8.5. Summary 91
  CONCLUDING REMARKS 91
  REFERENCES 91

CHAPTER 4 MACHINE LEARNING 93

1. INTRODUCTION TO MACHINE LEARNING 93
   1.1. Fundamentals of Machine Learning 94
     1.1.1. Definition of Machine Learning 94
     1.1.2. Types of Learning 95
     1.1.3. Basic Terminologies in Machine Learning 96
     1.1.4. Components of a Machine Learning System 97
   1.2. Input to Machine Learning System 98
   1.3. Characteristics of Input Data 99
   1.4. Output from Machine Learning System 100
     1.4.1. Regression Equation 100
     1.4.2. Regression Trees 100
     1.4.3. Table 101
     1.4.4. Cluster Diagram 101
     1.4.5. Decision Tree 102
     1.4.6. Classification Rule 102
   1.5. Conclusion 103
   1.6. Summary 104
2. DATA PREPARATION 104
   2.1. Fundamentals of Data Preparation 104
     2.1.1. Data Selection 104
     2.1.2. Data Pre-processing 104
     2.1.3. Data Transformation 105
   2.2. Data Transformation Techniques 106
     2.2.1. Feature Engineering 106
     2.2.2. Feature Scaling 106
   2.3. Conclusion 107
   2.4. Summary 107
3. SUPERVISED MACHINE LEARNING 107
   3.1. Prediction Based Machine Learning Algorithm 107
     3.1.1. Simple Linear Regression Algorithm 108
     3.1.2. Multiple Linear Regression Algorithm 112
   3.2. Classification Based Machine Learning Algorithm 116
     3.2.1. Naïve Bayes Machine Learning Algorithm 116
     3.2.2. Decision Tree Machine Learning Algorithm 120
   3.3. Conclusion 131
   3.4. Summary 132
4. SIMPLE REGRESSION ALGORITHMS FOR NON-LINEAR RELATIONSHIPS 132
   4.1. Types of Simple Non-Linear Relationships 132
     4.1.1. Simple Non-Linear Relationships 132
     4.1.2. Polynomial of Degree 2 with Minimum Point 134
     4.1.3. Polynomial of Degree 2 with Maximum Point 134
     4.1.4. Polynomial of Degree 3 with Minimum Point on the Right 135
     4.1.5. Polynomial of Degree 3 with Maximum Point on the Right 136
   4.2. Regression Algorithm for Non Lionear Relationships 136
     4.2.1. Regression Algorithm for Simple Non-Linear Relationships 136
     4.2.2. Regression Algorithm for Polynomial of Degree 2 with Minimum Point 142
     4.2.3. Regression Algorithm for Polynomial of Degree 2, with Maximum Point 147
     4.2.4. Regression Algorithm for Polynomial of Degree 3, with Minimum Point on the Right 152
     4.2.5. Regression Algorithm for Polynomial of Degree 3, with Maximum Point on the Right 156

4.3. Conclusion 159
4.4. Summary 159
5. UNSUPERVISED MACHINE LEARNING ALGORITHMS 160
5.1. Clustering Algorithms 160
    5.1.1. K-means Clustering Algorithm 160
    5.1.2. Using K-means Algorithm to Perform Clustering on Dataset 161
    5.1.3. Choosing the Number of K Clusters 168
    5.1.4. Using WEKA to Perform K-means Clustering on Dataset 168
5.2. Data Visualization 169
    5.2.1. Visualizing Two Dimensional Linear Dataset Using Scatter Plot 170
    5.2.2. Visualizing Probability Distribution of Dataset Using Scatter Plot 171
5.3. Conclusion 186
5.4. Summary 186
6. WAIKATO ENVIRONMENT FOR KNOWLEDGE ANALYSIS, WEKA 186
6.1. Data Representation in WEKA 187
6.2. Getting Started with WEKA 189
    6.2.1. Loading CSV Files in the WEKA Explorer 191
6.2. Using WEKA to Solve Machine Learning Problems 192
6.4. Using WEKA to Solve Simple Linear Regression Problem 194
6.5. Using WEKA to Solve Linear Regression on CPU.arff Dataset 196
6.6. Using WEKA to do Naïve Bayes Classification on Norminal Weather.arff Dataset 198
6.7. Conclusion 199
6.8. Summary 200
7. NEURAL NETWORK 200
7.1. Biological Neurons 200
    7.1.1. How the Biological Neuron Works 201
7.2. Artificial Neural Network 201
    7.2.1. Feedforward Multi-Layer Perceptron 202
    7.2.2. Effect of Noise and Hardware Failure on the Artificial Neuron 203
    7.2.3. Continuous Input and Output Signals of Artificial Neuron 205
    7.2.4. Probabilistic Output Signal of Artificial Neuron 207
    7.2.5. Training the Artificial Neural Network 207
7.3. Back Propagation Algorithm 218
7.4. Using WEKA to Solve Artificial Neural Network Problem 221
7.5. Conclusion 221
7.6. Summary 222
8. DEEP LEARNING 222
8.1. Deep Feedforward Network 222
8.2. Application of Deep Feedforward Network 224
    8.2.1. Application of Deep Learning to Logic Function Evaluation 224
8.3. Deep Convolutional Neural Network 230
    8.3.1. Layers of Deep Convolutional Neural Network 231
8.4. Deep Recurrent Neural Network 233
8.5. Conclusion 234
8.6. Summary 234
9. REINFORCEMENT LEARNING 234
9.1. Introduction to Reinforcement Learning 235
9.2. Features of Reinforcement Learning 236
    9.2.1. Trade-off between Exploitation and Exploration 236
    9.2.2. Holistic Approach to Problem Solving 236
    9.2.3. Goal of Agent is Central in Reinforcement Learning 236

9.2.4. *Fruitful Interaction with Other Discipline* 236
9.2.5. *Evaluative Feedbacks* 237
9.3. Elements of Reinforcement Learning 237
9.3.1. *Agent* 237
9.3.2. *Environment* 237
9.3.3. *Action* 237
9.3.4. *Environment State* 237
9.3.5. *Policy* 238
9.3.6. *Reward Signal* 238
9.3.7. *Value Function* 238
9.3.8. *Time Step* 238
9.3.9. *Model of the Environment* 239
9.4. History of Reinforcement Learning 239
9.5. Conclusion 240
9.6. Summary 240
CONCLUDING REMARKS 240
REFERENCES 240

CHAPTER 5 MACHINE LEARNING APPLICATIONS 242
**1. ANALYZING TERRORISM DATASET USING CLASSIFICATION BASED
ALGORITHMS** 242
1.1. Introduction 242
1.2. Methodology for Collection and Analysis of Terrorism Dataset 246
1.3. Design of the Two Machine Learning Algorithms 247
1.4. Naïve Bayes Algorithm 247
1.5. The Decision Tree Algorithm 248
1.6. Simulation, Results and Discussion 248
1.7. Simulation, Results and Discussion 251
**2. ANALYZING TERRORISM DATASET USING PROBABILITY DISTRIBUTION
FUNCTIONS** 251
2.1. Methodology for Collection and Visualization of Terrorism Dataset 253
2.2. Theory of the Probability Distribution Functions 253
2.2.1. *Binomial Probability Distribution Function* 253
2.2.2. *Poisson Probability Distribution Function* 254
2.2.3. *Exponential Probability Distribution Function* 254
2.2.4. *Normal Probability Distribution Function* 255
2.3. Simulations, Results and Discussion 255
2.3.1. *Result of Simulated Models for Binomial Probability Distribution Function* 256
2.3.2. *Result of Simulated Models for Poisson Probability Distribution Function* 257
2.3.3. *Result of Simulated Models for Normal Probability Distribution Function* 257
2.4. Conclusion 259
**3. POLYNOMIAL REGRESSION ALGORITHM FOR ANALYSING COVID-19
DATASET** 259
3.1. Generalized Ordinary Least Square Method 259
3.2. Literature Review 260
3.3. Development of the Polynomial Regression Algorithm 261
3.3.1. *Polynomial of Degree 2 with Minimum Point* 261
3.3.2. *Polynomial of Degree 2 with Maximum Point* 262
3.3.3. *Polynomial Dataset, of Degree 3 with Minimum Point on the Right* 263
3.3.4. *Polynomial Dataset, of Degree 3 with Maximum Point on the Right* 265
3.3.5. *Polynomial Dataset, of Degree n with Minimum Point on the Right* 266

3.3.6. Polynomial Dataset, of Degree n with Maximum Point on the Right 268
3.4. Simulation and Discussion of Results 270
3.5. Conclusion 273
CONCLUDING REMARKS 273
REFERENCES 273

CHAPTER 6 SENSORY PERCEPTION 276
  1. COMPUTER VISION 276
    1.1. Fundamentals of Computer Vision 276
    1.2. Applications of Computer Vision 277
      1.2.1. Vehicle Driver Assistance and Traffic Management 277
      1.2.2. Eye and Head Tracker 277
      1.2.3. File and Video for Sports Analysis 277
      1.2.4. Film and Video for Sports Analysis 278
      1.2.5. Gesture Recognition 278
      1.2.6. General-Purpose Vision System 278
      1.2.7. Industrial Automation and Inspection for Electronic Industry 279
      1.2.8. Industrial Automation and Inspection for Agriculture Industry 279
    1.3. History of Computer Vision 279
    1.4. Image Formation 281
      1.4.1. Geometry of Image 281
    1.5. Image Recognition 286
      1.5.1. Object/Face Detection 287
      1.5.2. Pedestrian Detection 288
      1.5.3. Face Recognition 288
      1.5.4. Instance Recognition 289
    1.6. Use of Computer Vision in Motion 289
    1.7. Conclusion 290
    1.8. Summary 290
  2. SPEECH RECOGNITION 290
    2.1. Basics of Speech Recognition 290
    2.2. Basic Components of Speech Recognition System 291
    2.3. Signal Processing 292
    2.4. Uncertainties in Speech Recognition 293
    2.5. Historical Development of Speech Recognition 293
    2.6. Applications of Speech Recognition System 294
      2.6.1. Cloud-based Call Center/IVR (Interactive Voice Response) 294
      2.6.2. PC-Based Dictation/Command and Control 294
      2.6.3. Device-Based Embedded Command Control 294
    2.7. Conclusion 294
    2.8. Summary 295
  3. TACTILE SENSING 295
    3.1. Tactile Sensing Explained 295
    3.2. Justification for Tactile Sensing 295
    3.3. Types of Tactile Sensors 296
    3.4. Conclusion 296
    3.5. Summary 297
  CONCLUDING REMARKS 297
  REFERENCES 297

CHAPTER 7 ROBOTICS 298
  1. FOUNDATIONS OF ROBOTICS 298

1.1. Robot Explained 299
1.2. Asimov Law of Robotics 299
1.3. Characteristics of Robot 300
1.4. User Level Applications of Robot 300
1.5. Types of Robots 301
1.6. Components of Robots 302
1.7. Conclusion 303
1.8. Summary 303
2. HUMANOID ROBOTS 303
2.1. Motivations for Humanoid Robots 303
2.2. Historical Development of Humanoid Robots 304
2.3. Current Trends in Humanoid Robots 305
2.4. Locomotion in Humanoid Robots 306
2.5. Manipulation in Humanoid Robots 306
2.6. Communication in Humanoid Robots 307
2.7. Conclusion 307
2.8. Summary 308
3. AUTONOMOUS/ROBOTIC VEHICLES 308
3.1. Levels of Vehicles Automation 308
3.2. How Autonomous Vehicle Technology Works 309
3.3. History of Autonomous Vehicles 311
3.4. Benefits of Autonomous Vehicles 311
3.5. Development and Deployment of Autonomous Vehicles 312
3.6. Planning Implications for Autonomous Vehicles 313
3.7. Conclusion 314
3.8. Summary 314
4. METRICS FOR ASSESSING THE PERFORMANCE OF ROBOTS ... 314
4.1. Metrics for Navigational Tasks 315
4.2. Metrics for Perception Tasks 315
4.3. Metrics for Management Tasks 316
4.4. Metrics for Manipulation Tasks 317
4.5. Metrics for Social Tasks 317
4.6. Conclusion 318
4.7. Summary 318
CONCLUDING REMARKS 318
REFERENCES 318

SUBJECT INDEX 320

PREFACE

The importance of Artificial Intelligence cannot be over-emphasized; as a result, Artificial Intelligence occupies a central place in the curricula of Computer Science at both undergraduate and postgraduate levels. At least one or two Artificial Intelligence course(s) must be present in the curricula of Computer Science at both undergraduate and postgraduate levels. At the moment, most universities offer Artificial Intelligence as a Degree programme, leading to Bachelor Degree or Master Degree in Artificial Intelligence. This book covers all the main aspects of Artificial Intelligence, like Expert System, Natural Language Processing, Machine Learning, Machine Learning Applications, Sensory Perceptions (Computer Vision, Tactile Perception), and Robotics. The book focuses on the following areas of computer science as it relates to the specific area of Artificial Intelligence: history, applications, algorithms, and programming with relevant case studies and examples. It adopts a simplified approach so that every beginner can easily understand the contents. It assumes basic knowledge of the Java programming language. It introduces Python programming language and uses it for natural language processing. It also introduces Waikato Environment for Knowledge Analysis, WEKA, as a tool for machine learning. The book is organized into seven main chapters; each chapter is further organized into various units. In all seven chapters, there are thirty-three units.

CONSENT FOR PUBLICATION

Not applicable.

CONFLICT OF INTEREST

The author declares no conflict of interest, financial or otherwise.

ACKNOWLEDGEMENT

Declared none.

Osondu Oguike
Department of Computer Science,
University of Nigeria, Nsukka,
Enugu State, Nigeria.

CHAPTER 1

Introduction to Artificial Intelligence

Abstract: Every beginner in any subject needs a good foundation, which will help the student to understand the subject. This good foundation will be provided in a thorough and detailed definition of the subject and a detailed description of the fundamental models on which the subject is based. Artificial Intelligence needs a thorough definition and a detailed description of the fundamental models on which Artificial Intelligence is based. Furthermore, the history and applications of Artificial Intelligence will help the beginner to know where it is coming from, the journey so far, and the future development of Artificial Intelligence. On the other hand, the applications of Artificial Intelligence will help us to appreciate the use of Artificial Intelligence in our daily life. This chapter presents a detailed definition of Artificial Intelligence, its history, and emerging applications.

Keywords: Acting like a human, Acting rationally, Artificial Intelligence winter, Autonomous cars, Bitcoin, Blockchain technology, Cognitive model, Data Science, IBM Watson, Internet of things, Turing test model.

1. DEFINITION OF ARTIFICIAL INTELLIGENCE

The definition of Artificial Intelligence helps us to understand what Artificial Intelligence focuses on, the various aspects of Artificial Intelligence, and the various concepts, techniques, ideas, and viewpoints of other disciplines that Artificial Intelligence uses.

1.1. Artificial Intelligence

Many authors, in various literature, have attempted to define Artificial Intelligence from different perspectives. In this book, a broad and general definition of Artificial Intelligence will be provided. Artificial Intelligence can be defined as a field of study that deals with the design of systems that act like a human, think like a human, act rationally and think rationally [1 - 4].

This definition covers every definition of Artificial Intelligence that any literature can provide. It provides four different faces of Artificial Intelligence, which will be explained in the next section. This means that Artificial Intelligence programs/systems are programs/systems that act like a human, think like a human, act rationally and think rationally.

1.1.1. Explanation of Artificial Intelligence

Each of the four faces of Artificial Intelligence, as provided in the definition, will be explained using an appropriate model. Each model will be used to explain each of the following faces of Artificial Intelligence that are: acting like a human, thinking like a human, acting rationally, and thinking rationally.

1.1.2. Turing Test Model – Acting Like Human

The Turing test model explains what acting like human means. In 1958, Alan Turing proposed a test model that aimed at helping people to understand what acting like human means. The test that Alan Turing proposed involved interrogating a computer by a human *via* a teletype, and the computer passes the test without knowing whether the interrogator was a machine or human that answered the questions. However, in the total Turing test, there is the inclusion of video signal, which tests the perception abilities of the subject, and the exchange of physical object between the interrogator and the subject. Alan Turing, therefore, defined acting like a human as behaving intelligently. A machine/human that behaves intelligently is one that achieves human-level performance to cognitive questions. Therefore, making computers achieve human-level intelligence means that the computer will possess the following abilities or requirements [1, 3].

- The ability to communicate in natural language, like the English language, French language, *etc.*
- The ability to store information before or during the interrogation.
- The ability to use the stored information to answer questions and make a new conclusion. This is called automated reasoning in Artificial Intelligence.
- The ability to adapt to new circumstances due to new data, it discovers the pattern in the data and makes an appropriate decision.

Further more, passing the total Turing test requires additional abilities, which are:

- The ability to perceive with the sense organ of hearing, tasting, seeing, feeling, and smelling.
- The ability to move objects. This is called robotics in Artificial Intelligence.

From the above requirements or abilities of an intelligent system, we can use each requirement of an intelligent system to identify the various aspects or tasks that an Artificial Intelligence system can perform. The following are the tasks that an Artificial Intelligence system can perform.

- Natural Language Processing: This task allows an Artificial Intelligence system to communicate in natural language, like the English language.
- Knowledge Representation: This task allows an Artificial Intelligence system to use a particular method/formalism to store knowledge about a particular domain. This is called the knowledge base of an expert system.
- Automated Reasoning: This task allows an Artificial Intelligence system to query the stored knowledge with the aim of answering the user's query. This is called an inference engine in an expert system.
- Machine Learning: This task allows an Artificial Intelligence system to solve a problem using a set of data called training data.
- Sensory Perception: This task allows the Artificial Intelligence system to solve a problem, using the sensory perceptions for vision, touch, hearing, tasting, smelling, *etc.*
- Robotics: This aspect of Artificial Intelligence allows the Artificial Intelligence system to solve the problem by moving itself or objects from one place to another.

1.1.3. Cognitive Model – Thinking Like Human

If we are going to say that a given program thinks like a human, we must have some ways of determining how humans think. We need to get inside the actual workings of human minds. There are two ways to do this: through introspection — trying to catch our own thoughts as they go by — or through psychological experiments. Once we have a sufficiently precise theory of the mind, it becomes possible to express the theory as a computer program. Cognitive science brings together computer models from Artificial Intelligence and experimental techniques from psychology to try to construct precise and testable theories of the workings of the human mind [1, 5 - 8].

1.1.4. Rational Agent Model – Acting Rationally

An agent is something that perceives and acts. It acts in order to achieve its goal. Therefore, acting rationally means acting like an agent. Artificial Intelligence is therefore considered as the study and construction of rational agents. One of the ways to act rationally is to make a correct inference, using the law of thought [1].

1.1.5. Law of Thought – Thinking Rationally

The law of thought helps to explain what thinking rationally means. It means right-thinking, *i.e.*, given the correct premises (facts), it always produces the correct conclusion. The law of thought was originated by the Greet philosopher Aristotle. It marked the beginning of logic, which is very fundamental in Artificial Intelligence.

1.2. Foundational Discipline in Artificial Intelligence

Artificial Intelligence is a young field of study, but it uses many ideas, viewpoints, and techniques from various old disciplines. In this section, the various ideas, viewpoints, and techniques that Artificial Intelligence borrows from the various old disciplines will be considered. They form the foundation upon which Artificial Intelligence stands.

1.2.1. Philosophy

The theories of reasoning and learning, which Artificial Intelligence uses, emerged from the discipline of Philosophy. It started with the writings of Plato, his teacher, Socrates, and his student, Aristotle. Socrates wanted to know the characteristics of piety, so that he could be informed about standards that he could use to judges his actions and the actions of other people. In otherwords, he was asking for the algorithm that could be used to distinguish between piety and non-piety. In response, Aristotle formulated the law governing the rational part of the mind. He developed the informal system of syllogism for proper reasoning, which would allow one to generate conclusions, given initial premises. However, Aristotle did not believe all parts of the mind were governed by logical processes; he also had a notion of intuitive reasoning.

Philosophy had therefore, established the tradition that the mind was conceived of as a physical device, operating principally by reasoning and the knowledge that it contained. On the theory of knowledge, which Artificial Intelligence uses, Philosophy identified the source of knowledge with the following principles. The principle of induction, which states that general rules are acquired by exposure to repeated associations between their elements. This principle was refined with the principle of logical positivism, which states that all knowledge can be characterized by logical theories, connected ultimately to observation sentences that correspond to sensory inputs [1, 12].

Still on the philosophical picture of the mind, Philosophy also established a connection between knowledge and action. Artificial Intelligence is interested in the form the connection will take, and how can particular actions be justified ? This is because understanding how actions are justified, it will be possible to build an Artificial Intelligence agent with justifiable actions [1, 2, 13].

1.2.2. Mathematics

Artificial Intelligence uses mathematical tools as formal tool, in the following three main area of mathematics: computation, logic and probability. Computation can be expressed as a formal algorithm in Artificial Intelligence, while logic has remained a formal language for representing knowledge in Artificial Intelligence. Probability allows us to make logical reasoning and measure the level of certainty/uncertainty in ourreasoning [1, 14].

1.2.3. Psychology

The principle of cognitive psychology states that the brain possesses and processes information. The theory of human behavior in Psychology states that its valid components are beliefs, goals and reasoning steps. However, for most of the early history of Artificial Intelligence and Cognitive Science, no significant distinction was drawn between the two fields, and it was common to see Artificial Intelligence programs described as psychological results without any claim as to the exact human behavior they were modeling. In the last decade or so, however, the methodological distinctions have become clearer, and most work now falls into one field or the other [1, 15].

1.2.4. Computer Engineering

In reality, Artificial Intelligence belongs to the field of computer science or computer engineering. If it stands on itself as a discipline, thenideas, viewpoints and techniques from the discipline of computer science or computer engineering must beused for Artificial Intelligence to succeed. The Artificial Intelligence programs must bewritten to run on an appropriate architecture of computer.

1.2.5. Linguistics

Much of the early work on knowledge representation (the study of how to put knowledge into a form that a computer can reason with) was tied to language and informed by research in linguistics. Modern Linguistics and Artificial Intelligence were "born" at about the same time, so Linguistics does not play a large foundational role in the growth of Artificial Intelligence. Instead, the two grew up together, intersecting in a hybrid field called Computational Linguistics or natural language processing, which concentrates on the problem of language use [1].

1.2.6. Biological Science and Others

Since Artificial Intelligence is a field of study that deal with design of systems that act like human, and most of human actions are based on some human biological processes, therefore Artificial Intelligence uses some human biological processes to design intelligent system. Such human biological processes it uses includes: biological neurons, biological sensory perceptions (vision, touch, hearing, tasting and smelling).

In a similar manner, human actions are based on economic processes, political processes *etc.*, therefore concepts that are based on Economics, Political Science will be used to design Artificial Intelligence systems that act like man, economically and politically. In general, any discipline that determines the actions of man will be useful in developing Artificial Intelligence systems.

1.3. Conclusion

Artificial Intelligence has been defined and explained in this unit. This definition and explanation will enable us to easily identify Artificial Intelligence systems. Artificial Intelligence has been identified as an inter-disciplinary subject that has something in common with other subject areas, like Mathematics, Psychology, Philosophy, Linguistics, Computer Engineering *etc.*

1.4. Summary

Having defined and explained what Artificial Intelligence is, every chapter of this book will focus on the various aspects of Artificial Intelligence that have been identified in this unit. Furthermore, discussion on the history and applications of Artificial Intelligence will be helpful in appreciating the usefulness of Artificial Intelligence.

2. HISTORY OF ARTIFICIAL INTELLIGENCE AND PROJECTION FOR THE FUTURE

The History of Artificial Intelligence focuses on the people, significant contributions, date of their contribution, towards the development of Artificial Intelligence. This is very useful because it helps us to recognize those that made significant contributions towards the development of Artificial Intelligence. On the other hand, its future projections look into the new and future research directions of Artificial Intelligence.

2.1. The Birth of Artificial Intelligence

John McCharty, in 1956 was the first to coin the term, Artificial Intelligence, in a conference titled, Artificial Intelligence, which was held at Dartmouth College, Hanover, New Hampshire. One of the participants at the conference, who was very optimistic about the future of Artificial Intelligence was Marvin Minsky of MIT. However, before that time, several researches have taken place that contributed to the birth of Artificial Intelligence. One of such researches was undertaken by Vannevar Bush in 1945. Another research was done by Alan Turing, in 1950, which has helped to understand what intelligence system means. Alan Turing research of 1950 has led to the popular Turing test model, which helped to explain what it means to act like human. Therefore, the birth of Artificial Intelligence cannot be complete without considering the life of Alan Turing, who made significant contribution that led to the birth of Artificial Intelligence [9 - 11].

2.1.1. Alan Turing (1912 – 1954)

He was a British Mathematician, though he lived for a short period of time, but he made significant contribution towards the development of computing in general, and Artificial Intelligence in particular. In 1936, he designed a universal calculator, known as Turing machine. He proved that the calculator is capable of solving any problem as long as it can be represented and solved as an algorithm. After few decades, the first digital computer was built. Turing's electro-mechanical computer was used to unlock the code that was used by the German submarines in the Atlantic, which contributed to the British victory during world war II. In 1950, Alan Turing created a test to determine if a machine was intelligent. This test has been captioned Turing test model and it has been used by Artificial Intelligence community to explain what it means to act like human.

2.1.2. Other Significant Contributors Prior to Birth of AI

The following are other significant Artificial Intelligence systems that were made prior to the birth of Artificial Intelligence in 1956:

- EbruÍz Bin Rezzaz Al Jezeri, who is one of the pioneers of cybernetic science, made water-operated automatic controlled machines in 1206.
- Karel Capek, first introduced the robot concept in the theatre play of Rossum's Universal Robots (RUR - Rossum's Universal Robots in 1923.
- The first artificial intelligence programs for the Mark 1 device were written in 1951.

2.2. Historical Development of Other Artificial Intelligence Systems

After the birth of Artificial Intelligence in 1956, different Artificial Intelligence systems have been developed, which can be classified according to the following eras:

2.2.1. Expert System (1950s – 1970s)

Expert systems, as a subset of AI, emerged in the early 1950s when the Rand-Carnegie team developed the general problem solver to deal with theorems proof, geometric problems and chess playing [2]. About the same time, LISP, the later dominant programming language in Artificial Intelligence and Expert Systems, was invented by John McCarthy in MIT [3]. During the 1960s and 1970s, expert systems were increasingly used in industrial applications. Some of the famous applications during this period were DENDRAL (a chemical structure analyzer), XCON (a computer hardware configuration system), MYCIN (a medical diagno-sis system), and ACE (AT&T's cable maintenance system). PROLOG, as an alternative to LISP in logic programming, was created in 1972 and designed to handle computational linguistics, especially natural language processing [9 - 11].

2.2.2. First Artificial Intelligence Winter (1974 – 1980)

Due to lack of funding, there was no significant development in Artificial Intelligence research between 1974 and 1980. This period, in the history of Artificial Intelligence is regarded as the first AI winter. It ended with the introduction of expert system.

2.2.3. Second Artificial Intelligence Winter (1987 – 1993)

Between 1987 and 1993, there was significant cut in Artificial Intelligence funding, as a result, there was no significant contributions in Artificial Intelligence research, this period was regarded as the second Artificial Intelligent winter. In some literature, the first and second Artificial Intelligence winter periods were combined as Artificial Intelligence winter, which was between 1974 and 1993.

2.2.4. Intelligent Agent (1993 – Date)

At the end of the second AI winter, research in Artificial Intelligence shifted its focus to what is called intelligent agents. An agent can be regarded as anything that perceives and acts. It acts in order to achieve its goal. An agent can therefore be a piece of software application that retrieves and presents information from the internet, does online shopping *etc*. Intelligent agents can be called agents or bots and they have evolved into personal digital assistants, with the emergence of Big data programs.

2.3. Projections into the Future of Artificial Intelligence

The following are the future projections that show the directions of research in Artificial Intelligence.

2.3.1. Virtual Personal Assistants

Currently, research in Artificial Intelligence is to develop virtual personal assistants, like Facebook M, Microsoft Cortana or Apple Siri. Today and the future, Artificial Intelligence research is to develop virtual personal assistants. In the area of natural language processing, such personal assistant will be capable of communicating with the user in natural language. In robotics, it is capable of moving from place to place, providing physical personal assistant. In the area of Big Data, it will be capable of making informed business decision based on available massive data. In machine learning, it will be capable of performing complex tasks.

2.4. Conclusion

In this unit, you have learnt the historical development of Artificial Intelligence and its future direction. The historical development of Artificial Intelligence has been divided into two phase. The first phase is the development of Artificial Intelligence before the birth of Artificial Intelligence, while the second phase is the development of Artificial Intelligence after the birth of Artificial Intelligence.

2.5. Summary

The historical development of Artificial Intelligence defines the applications of Artificial Intelligence. This is because Artificial Intelligence researches in the past and present will determine the Artificial Intelligence products, which will be used for specific applications.

3. EMERGING ARTIFICIAL INTELLIGENCE APPLICATIONS

The historical development of Artificial Intelligence identified the past, present and future development of Artificial Intelligence. Artificial Intelligence depends on different technologies in order to develop appropriate applications. This unit identifies and describes emerging technologies that Artificial Intelligence depends on with the aim of developing the various Artificial Intelligence products, which can be used for different applications.

3.1. Artificial Intelligence Applied Technologies

Artificial Intelligence systems are built on different technologies. Each technology has different Artificial Intelligence systems that it supports. Some of the different technologies that apply Artificial Intelligence systems will be described in detail in this unit.

3.1.1. Blockchain Technology

A blockchain can be defined as a series of immutable records of data (block), which are time stamped, secured using cryptographic principle and managed by a collection of computers that are not owned by any single entity (chain). The cryptographic principle that are used to make the series of data (block) secured involves the process of encryption and decryption. The secured data of the blockchain technology are analysed for decision making using Artificial Intelligence systems. The blockchain technology does not have any centralized control but it is decentralized. It was the ingenuous invention of a person or group of group known asSatoshi Nakamoto. It was originally invented for the Bitcoin as a cryptocurrency, now has many uses in other areas. The collection/cluster of computers that manage the block of data form a blockchain network. The block of data is shared among all the computers in the blockchain network, which means that all the computers have access to the block of data, and they are updated across the network every ten minutes. The block of data is stored in a shared database, which is stored on each of the computers on the blockchain network.

Blockchain is a simple way of sharing information between computers in a safe and automated manner. The process is initiated by one party, who creates a block of data to be shared. The data is verified by thousands or millions of other computers on the internet. The verified data is added to a chain, which cannot easily be falsified [16 - 18].

3.1.1.1. Bitcoin: First Application of Artificial Intelligence to Blockchain

Bitcoin remains the first use of the Blockchain technology. It is a digital currency, which was created in 2009. It is a payment system that offers lower processing fee than the traditional online payment system. Bitcoin does not appear as a physical coin, but only balances that appear in a public ledger in the cloud, together with all Bitcoin transactions. Bitcoin balances are kept using public and private keys. The public and private keys are long string of numbers and letters, which are linked with the mathematical encryption algorithm that is used to create them. The public key can be likened to bank account number, which is the address that is published to the world where others will send bitcoins. On the other hand, private key can be likened to ATM PIN, which is known only by the owner of the public key. It is used to authorize Bitcoin transactions. The following terms will be useful in understanding Bitcoin [18]:

3.1.1.1.1. Bitcoin Wallet

It is a physical electronic device or software device that is used for Bitcoin trading. It allows users to track ownership of coins.

3.1.1.1.2. Peer-to-peer

This is the technology that is used to facilitate instant payments. It involves the exchange of data, information between parties without the involvement of central authority.

3.1.1.1.3. Miners

They are the individuals or companies that own the governing computing power, who participate in the Bitcoin network. Rewards and transaction fees are used to motivate them. They can be regarded as the decentralized authorities that enforce the credibility of Bitcoin network. They also make sure that Bitcoin is not duplicated. Mining therefore is the process of verifying each of the bitcoin transactions or adding a block of Bitcoin transactions into the blockchain.

3.1.1.1.4. Transaction

This is the process of making purchase or payment using Bitcoin. Each transaction forms a piece of data/record. Transactions are collected together and managed in block. Transactions in a block are secured in a network of computers (chain), using advanced cryptography. Bitcoin miners add a new block of transactions into the blockchain and the miners ensure that the transactions are accurate.

3.1.1.1.5. Earning Reward

This is the process of earning Bitcoin by Bitcoin miners, either by verifying Bitcoin transactions or by adding a block of transactions to the blockchain. The former is quite simple; it involves verifying I MB of transactions. The later involves solving a complex computational mathematical problem, called proof of work.

Therefore, Bitcoin, which is the first application of the Blockchain technology allows individuals to secure their personal information, while allowing agents to generate economic value at smaller economic scales. The data generated in the use of Bitcoin on Blockchain technology depends on Artificial Intelligence for its analysis [19].

3.1.1.2. Applications of Artificial Intelligence to Blockchain Technology

The following describes different areas where Artificial Intelligence can be applied to the blockchain technology, in particular Bitcoin technology.

3.1.1.2.1. Smart Computing Power

Operating blockchain requires generating encrypted data (blocks), which need large amount of processing power to analyse. Example, hashing algorithms will be used to mine the Bitcoin blocks (data). Such algorithm involves enumerating in a systematic manner, all the possible candidates for the solution, afterwards, checking whether each candidate satisfies the problem's statement before verifying the transaction. However, with Artificial Intelligence, the above task can easily be accomplished in an intelligent and efficient way, through the use of machine learning based algorithm with appropriate training data.

3.1.1.2.2. Analyses Diverse Data

Though Bitcoin is the first application of the blockchain technology, it is currently used in a number of industries to create decentralization of data and network. Example SingularityNET specifically uses blockchain technology to encourage broader distribution of data and algorithm. With the diverse applications of blockchain technology, it means that Artificial Intelligence can be used to analyse the diverse data that the blockchain technology generates [19].

3.1.1.2.3. Analyses Protected Data

The success of the machine learning tool of Artificial Intelligence, which is used to analyse blockchain data depends on the amount of training data. The training data of the blockchain technology are protected or secured, since blockchain allows encrypted data to be stored on distributed ledger.

3.1.1.2.4. Monetizes Data

Monetization of data is the process of allowing others to decide how data is to be sold in order to make profit for businesses. Blockchain on its own, monetizes data by first cryptographically protecting our data and use it as we want. In the same way Artificial Intelligence uses the cryptographically protected data by first buying it through data marketplaces.

3.1.1.2.5. Decision Making

Blockchain technology provides the processes for the generation of secured data, while Artificial Intelligence uses its Machine Learning tool to analyse the data for the purpose making informed decision.

3.1.2. Internet of Things (IoT)

This is another technology that depends on the application of Artificial Intelligence. Internet of Things is the collections of billions of devices all over the world, which are connected together for the purpose of collecting and sharing data. This technology is made possible by the availability of cheap and powerful microprocessor computers and wireless networks. Any object, therefore can be connected together. Connecting these objects together with sensors, which enable them to collect and communicate/share real time data, without human interference makes them intelligent devices. Any object, therefore can become an intelligent

IoT device once it can be connected to the internet with sensors for collecting and sharing information. Internets of Things devices are devices that wouldn't normally have internet connection. Therefore, personal computers, mobile devices will not be considered as Internet of Things devices. Cars, domestic electrical appliances (fridges, vending machines *etc.*) can be considered as IoT devices.

3.1.2.1. History of Internet of Things

It was in the 1980s and 1990s that the idea of adding sensors and intelligence to objects around us was first discussed. However, before this time, some of the early projects are: internet-enabled vending machine. This project was hindered based on the following reasons: the technology that the vending machine would use was not ready, the chips were too big and bulky communication between objects at that time was not possible.

3.1.3. Data Science, Big Data and Data Analytic

The amount of digital data that are created is growing every day at a high rate. It has been estimated that by the year 2020, about 1.7 Mbytes of data will be created for every human being per second. Some of these data are structured, while some are unstructured. Data Science therefore deals with the cleansing, preparation and analysis of this enormous data. Data Science combines the following disciplines: Statistics, Mathematics, Programming, problem solving, data capturing, and Artificial Intelligence with the aim of gaining insight into the large amount of data. It is an umbrella of techniques that are used when trying to obtain insight from the large amount of digital data.

Big Data refers to the enormous amount of data, which cannot be processed using the traditional applications that exist. However, Gartner Mitchell-Jones of IBM defines Big Data as "high-volume, high-velocity or high-variety information assets that demand cost-effective, innovative forms of information processing that enable insight, decision making, and process automation". It is high volume because it is enormous, it is high-velocity because of high rate of creating the data, and it is high-variety because of the various types of digital data that can be generated.

Data Analytic, on the other hand, is the process of examining datasets, using specialized systems and software in order to draw conclusion about the information they contain. It is used in commercial industries to enable organisations to make informed business decisions, and by scientists and researchers in order to verify or disprove scientific models, theories and hypothesis.

All these terms, Data Science, Big Data, Data Analytic are related to Machine Learning, which is an aspect of Artificial Intelligence that uses training data to make informed decisions.

3.2. Artificial Intelligence Products

There are many Artificial Intelligence products/systems that use the various technologies. These emerging Artificial Intelligence products/systems will be described in this section.

3.2.1. IBM Watson

This is a cognitive Artificial Intelligence platform and product, developed by IBM, named after the founder of IBM, Thomas Watson. It follows the same cognitive elements of human being and reason the way human being do. It is created as a question answering system, which applies advanced natural language processing, information retrieval, knowledge representation, automated reasoning and machine learning technologies to develop the question answering system. The capabilities of IBM Watson have evolved from question answering system to a system that combines the various aspects of an intelligent system, *i.e.* it can now see, hear, read, talk, taste, understand, reason, interpret, learn and recommend.

3.2.2. Self-Driving/Autonomous Cars

Self-driving cars or driverless cars or autonomous vehicles are terms that are used to describe cars that do not need any human being as its driver. It drives itself. It is an emerging Artificial Intelligence system that incorporates different aspect of Artificial Intelligence. It can understand natural language, when you talk to it using the appropriate interface to inform it your destination. It demonstrates all the skills of a professional driver and drives you through the road network. It employs computer vision by seeing and identifying objects on the road and knowing when to slow down and when to accelerate. It demonstrates all the skills of an expert driver with a zero tolerance to accidents. It also incorporates other systems that are provided by the vehicular network, like automatic route guidance system, cruise control system *etc*. This Artificial Intelligence product will be powered by the 5th generation (5G) network.

3.2.3. Face Recognition System

Face recognition is the process of identifying or verifying the identity of a person using the face. This method uses an Artificial Intelligence system/product, called Face Recognition System. The system can identify and verify the identity of a person in pictures, videos or in real time. It can be used by law enforcement agents to track a wanted criminal/person. It uses a computer algorithm to pick specific distinctive details about a person's face, like the distance between the eyes or shape of the chin. They are then converted into a mathematical representation and compared to data on other faces, which have been collected in a face recognition database. Some face recognition systems are designed to calculate the probability match between the unknown person and the one stored in the face recognition database.

3.3. Conclusion

This unit has explored some of the emerging technologies that Artificial Intelligence systems use. It has also considered some of the emerging Artificial Intelligence systems/products that define the various applications of Artificial Intelligence.

3.4. Summary

Most of the emerging Artificial Intelligence products, like IBM Watson, self-driving cars, face recognition systems, demonstrate the applications of the various aspects of Artificial Intelligence like natural languasge processing, machine learning, computer vision, expert system, *etc.* In the subsequent chapters, each of these areas of Artificial Intelligence will be discussed in detail.

CONCLUDING REMARKS

The broad and general definition of Artificial Intelligence has provided the knowledge of its component to the beginner of the subject. Its history and projection for the future have provided the beginner with the significant contributions of people towards the development of Artificial Intelligence and the future direction of Artificial Intelligence. Finally, emerging Artificial Intelligence applications have provided the beginner with the state of art Artificial Intelligence technologies and products.

REFERENCES

[1] S.J. Russells, and P. Norwig, "Artificial Intelligence: A Modern Approach", *Prentice Hall,* 1995.

[2] J. Copeland, "Artificial Intelligence: A Philosophical Introduction", *Oxford Blackwell,* 1993.

[3] J. McCarthy, *Review of Artificial Intelligence: A General Survey,* 2000. http://wwwformal.stan ford.edu/jmc/reviews /lighthill/lighthill.html

[4] M. Cambell, J. Hoane, and F. Hsu, "Artificial Intelligence", *Deep Blue,* vol. 134, no. 1, pp. 57-83, 2002.

[5] P.H. Winston, *Artificial Intelligence* 3rd ed. Addison Wesley: Reading, Massachusetts, 1992.

[6] M. Gindoerg, *Essentials of Artificial Intelligence* Morgan Kaufmann: Sun Mateo, California, 1993.

[7] E. Charniak, and D. McDermott, *Introduction to Artificial Intelligence* Addison-Wesley: Reading, Massachusetts, 1985.

[8] M.A. Boden, *Artificial Intelligence and Natural Man* Basic Books: New York, 1977.

[9] M.M. Mijwel, *The History of Artificial Intelligence,* 2015. https://www.researchgate.net/publication/ 322234922

[10] "AI Winter", *Wikipedia.* http://en.wikipedia.org/wiki/AI_winter

[11] R. Reddy, "Foundations and Grand Challenges of Artificial Intelligence", *AI Mag.,* p. 9, 1988.

[12] https://www.theguardian.com/technology/2016/jun/28/google-says-machine-learning-is-the-fu ure-so-i-tried-it-myself

[13] http://www.economist.com/news/briefing/21677228-technology-behind-bitcoin-lets-people-who-do-n ot-know-or-trust-each-other-build-dependable

[14] https://www.bcg.com/blockchain/thinking-outside-the-blocks.html

[15] https://www.coursera.org/learn/machine-learning

[16] https://policyreview.info/articles/analysis/invisible-politics-bitcoin-governance-crisis-decentra ised-infrastructure

[17] https://motherboard.vice.com/en_us/article/bitcoin-is-unsustainable

[18] https://www.bbvaopenmind.com/en/technology/artificial-intelligence/blockchain-and-ai-a-pe fect-match/

[19] https://www.forbes.com/sites/darrynpollock/2018/11/30/the-fourth-industrial-revolution-bui t-on-blockchain-and-advanced-with-ai/#4cb2e5d24242

CHAPTER 2

Expert System

Abstract: Knowledge representation and automated reasoning are part of the attributes of an intelligent system. These two attributes are used to form the two main components of an expert system, which are the knowledge base and inference engine. Since Artificial Intelligence deals with the study and design of a system that acts like a human, therefore, studying and designing a system that acts like a human expert in any profession qualifies to be called Artificial Intelligence.

Keywords: Explanation and justification, Inferencing, Inference engine, Knowledge acquisition, Knowledge base, Knowledge engineering, Knowledge representation, Proposition logic, Semantic network.

1. EXPERT SYSTEM BASICS

An expert system is a part of an Artificial Intelligence system, which is a computer system that emulates the decision making of a human expert. It attempts to act like a human expert in a particular area. Expert system advises non-experts in situations where human experts are not available or where it may be expensive to employ human experts or situations where it might be difficult or expensive to reach human experts. An expert system is designed based on the knowledge acquired from a human expert. Expert systems are the first systems that developed in the early days of Artificial Intelligence.

1.1. Components of Expert System

Designing and using an expert system requires the following human and non-human components: human expert, knowledge engineer, knowledge base, inference engine, user interface, and the user. The interaction between these components is shown in Fig. (**1**). The roles of each of these components in the design and use of an expert system will be explained [1 - 4].

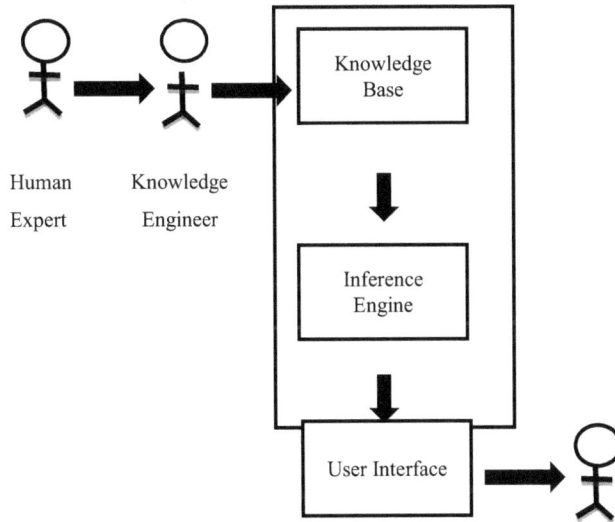

Fig. (1). Components of expert system.

1.1.1. Human Expert

The human expert provides his expertise and professional knowledge of a particular domain during the design of an expert system. The process of entering the expert knowledge into the expert system is called knowledge acquisition. In some expert systems, the human expert enters the domain knowledge directly into the expert system, while in others, the domain knowledge is not entered directly by the human expert but by the knowledge engineer.

1.1.2. Knowledge Engineer

A human engineer that designs and builds an expert system. The human expert provides the domain knowledge for the knowledge engineer, who encodes it into the expert system. However, in some expert systems, the human expert enters the domain knowledge directly into the expert system.

1.1.3. Knowledge Base

This software component of the expert system is where the domain knowledge of the human expert is stored. The domain knowledge is represented in the knowledge base using knowledge representation formalism/method. There are different knowledge representation formalisms/methods, which can be used to represent the domain knowledge in the knowledge base. The process of obtaining the domain knowledge from the human expert is called knowledge acquisition.

1.1.4. Inference Engine

It is a software component of the expert system that acts as a search engine. It can also be regarded as the brain of the expert system. It examines the knowledge base for information that matches the user's query.

1.1.5. User Interface

It is a software component of an expert system that allows a non-expert user to query or question the expert system, with the aim of receiving advice. The user interface is designed to be user friendly. It takes the user's query and passes it to the inference engine, and sends the result of the query back to the user [3].

1.1.6. Non-Expert User

It is a human user that interacts with the expert system through the user interface with the aim of obtaining advice from the expert system.

1.2. Knowledge Acquisition

Knowledge acquisition is the process of obtaining the domain knowledge from the human expert. As a process, it consists of the following sub-processes:

1.2.1. Knowledge Elicitation

This is the process whereby the knowledge engineer interacts with the human expert in order to obtain the expert knowledge in some systematic way.

1.2.2. Intermediate Representation

The knowledge that the knowledge engineer obtains will be stored in some form of the human-friendly intermediate representation. Intermediate representation, therefore, is the process of representing the knowledge obtained from a human expert in an intermediate form, which is readable by a human.

1.2.3. Executable Form Representation

The intermediate representation of knowledge is thus compiled into an executable form that the inference engine can process. Executable form representation is, therefore, the process of transforming the knowledge from its intermediate form to executable form.

1.3. Characteristics of Expert System

The following are the characteristic features of the expert system:

- Expert system simulates the human expert reasoning about the problem domain rather than simulating the domain itself.
- Expert system performs reasoning over-representation of human knowledge, in addition to doing numerical calculations or data retrieval. They have corresponding distinct modules referred to as inference engine and knowledge base. This means that reasoning is based on the domain knowledge stored in the knowledge base.
- Expert system solves problems using heuristics (rules of thumb) or approximate method, or probabilistic methods, which unlike algorithmic solutions, are not guaranteed to result in a correct or optimal solution.
- Expert system provides explanations and justifications of its solution or recommendations in order to convince the user that its reasoning is correct.

1.4. Examples of Expert System

The following are different examples of an expert system:

1.4.1. Medical Diagnosis System

The knowledge base contains medical information, which includes symptoms of a different ailment, which the patient-user will use in the query, and the advicewill be the diagnosis of the patient illness. For example, CaDet is an expert system that identifies cancer at the early stage.

1.4.2. Game System

This is a system that can be used to play strategy games, like chess against a computer. The knowledge base will contain strategies and moves. The player's move will be used as the query, while the computer expert will be the output.

1.4.3. Financial Forecast/Advice System

This is system that advices the user whether to invest in a business. The knowledge base will contain data about the performance of financial markets and businesses in the past.

1.4.4. Identification System

This is a system that helps to identify items, such as plants/animals/rocks, *etc.* The knowledge base contains characteristics of every item, the query will be the details of an unknown item, and the advice will be the identification of the unknown item.

1.4.5. Water/Oil Drilling System

This is a system that helps to discover the location to drill for water/oil. The knowledge base will contain the characteristics of likely rock formations where oil/water can be found. The query will be the details of a particular location, and the advice will be the likelihood of finding oil/water there.

1.4.6. Car Engine Diagnosis System

Similar to a medical diagnosis system, the knowledge base contains the symptoms of the various car engine faults. The query will be the signs and symptoms that the car engine is showing, while the advice is the fault that the engine has.

1.5. Importance of Expert Systems

The following are the various benefits of expert systems:

- It improves the quality of decision.
- Cuts the expense of consulting experts for problem-solving.
- It provides fast and efficient solutions to problems in a narrow area of specialization.
- It can gather scarce expertise and used it efficiently.
- Offers consistent answer for the repetitive problem
- Maintains a significant level of information
- Helps you to get fast and accurate answers
- A proper explanation of decision making
- Ability to solve complex and challenging issues
- Expert Systems can work steadily work without getting emotional, tensed or fatigued [3].

1.6. Conclusion

In this unit, you have learnt the components, characteristics, examples and importance of expert systems.

1.7. Summary

The knowledge base of an expert system is one of the important components of expert system. It stores the domain knowledge using a particular knowledge representation formalism/method. All the processes that are involved in acquiring, representing, and using the domain knowledge in the knowledge base is called knowledge engineering. This will be considered in detail in the next unit.

2. KNOWLEDGE ENGINEERING

Knowledge Engineering has been defined as the process of acquiring knowledge from an expert and building the knowledge base of an expert system. Its activities include knowledge acquisition, knowledge representation, knowledge verification and validation, inferencing, explanation and knowledge maintenance. These activities will be considered in detail in this unit. Knowledge engineering requires the cooperation of the human expert and the knowledge engineer so that the domain knowledge can be codified in a form that the computer can understand [8 - 10].

2.1. Foundations of Knowledge Engineering

A major goal of knowledge engineering is to help expert to articulate the knowledge that they possess and document it in a reusable form. The reason for this is because the knowledge that expert possesses are often unstructured and not explicitly stated.

2.1.1. Knowledge Engineering Processes

Knowledge engineering consists of the following processes or activities:

2.1.1.1. Knowledge Acquisition

This is the process of obtaining the domain knowledge from human expert, books, documents, sensors or computer files. There are different types of knowledge that knowledge engineer can obtain, they include the following: specific knowledge of a domain, general knowledge, meta-knowledge (information about how experts use their knowledge to solve problem). It has been reported that knowledge acquisition remains the bottleneck in expert system development. As a result, much theoretical and applied researches, in expert system are conducted in the area of knowledge acquisition [7].

2.1.1.2. Knowledge Representation

This is the process of organizing the acquired knowledge so that it can be ready for use. It involves preparing the knowledge map and encoding the knowledge into the knowledge base.

2.1.1.3. Knowledge Verification and Validation

This is the process of using test cases to test the knowledge base with the aim of ensuring that its quality is acceptable.

2.1.1.4. Inferencing

This is the process of designing the inference engine, which is computer software that will be used to query the knowledge base that stored the knowledge.

2.1.1.5. Explanation and Justification

This is the process of designing and programming the computer so that it will be able to state the 'why' and 'how' a particular conclusion was reached by the expert system. The relationship among the knowledge engineering processes is shown in Fig. (2), below.

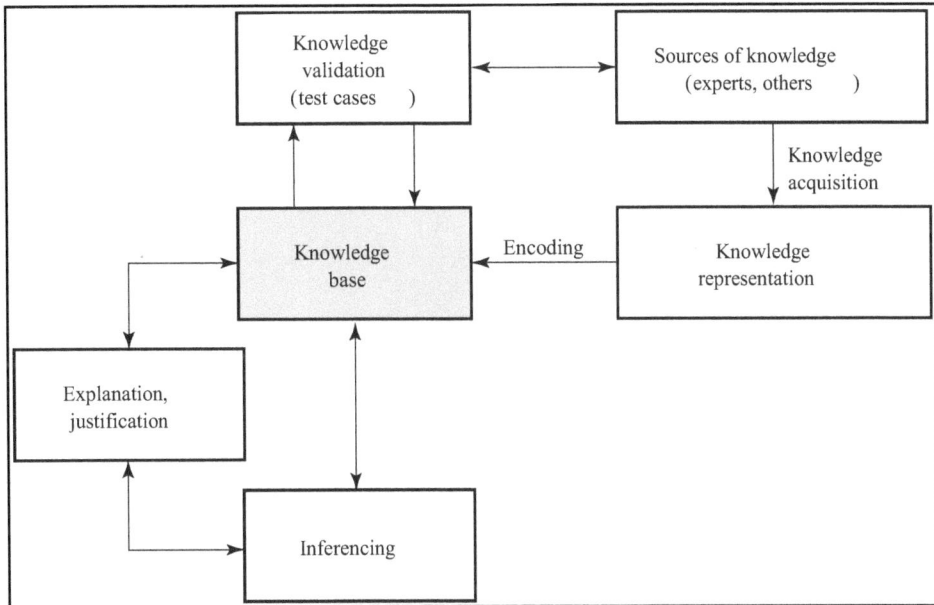

Fig. (2). Relationship between knowledge engineering processes.

2.1.2. Sources and Types of Knowledge

There are different types of knowledge that can be elicited and stored in the knowledge base of expert system. They include the following: meta-knowledge, hypothesis (theories), behaviour description and beliefs, vocabulary definitions, objects and relationships, heuristics and decision rules, typical situations, uncertain facts, processes, constraints, facts about domain, disjunctive facts, general knowledge. These different types of knowledge have been shown in Fig. (3).

In a similar manner, there are different sources where the different knowledge can be elicited from. The different sources of knowledge can be classified as: documented and undocumented sources of knowledge. The documented source of knowledge includes the following: books, films, computer databases, pictures, maps, flow diagram, sensors, radio frequency identification (RFID), songs, observed behaviours *etc*. On the other hand, undocumented source of knowledge is the source of knowledge that is resident in people's mind. The different types and sources of knowledge can be identified and collected using any of human/machine sensory perceptions. The complexity associated with knowledge acquisition is due to the various sources and types of knowledge [10].

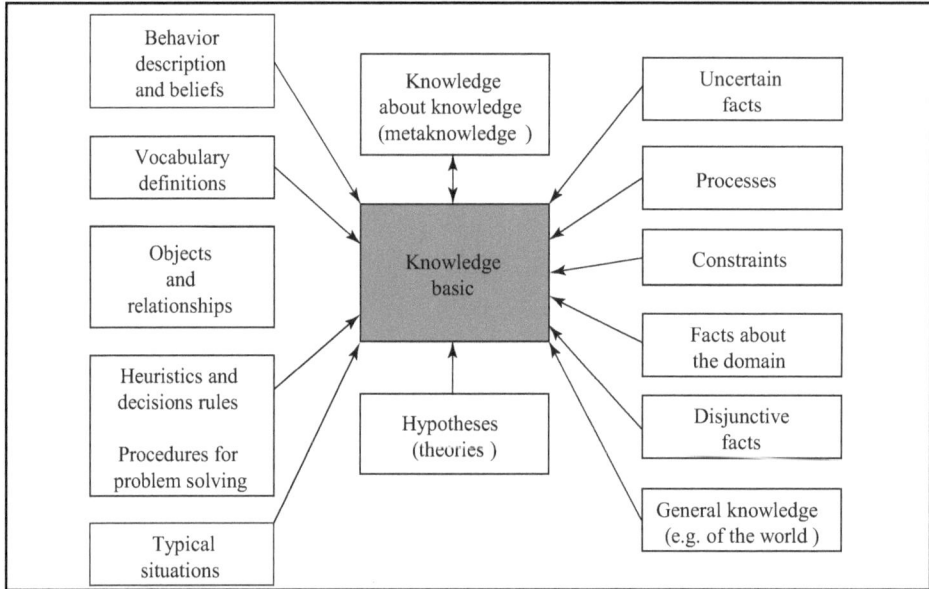

Fig. (3). Different types of knowledge.

2.1.3. Levels and Categories of Knowledge

Knowledge can be represented on the knowledge base of expert system at two different levels, which are: shallow knowledge and deep knowledge.

2.1.3.1. Shallow Level

The shallow level of representing knowledge represents knowledge at the surface level. It represents the input and output relationship of a system and it can be represented in terms of the IF THEN RULE. This level of representing knowledge is shallow because it may not be the manner in which experts view and solve problem in the domain.

2.1.3.2. Deep Level

This level of representing knowledge is the ideal level that human use to solve problem. It can be applied to different tasks and different situations and it involves interaction between the system components. Special knowledge representation formalism, like semantic network and frames are used for this level of knowledge representation.

Furthermore, knowledge can be categorized as: declarative knowledge, procedural knowledge and meta-knowledge.

2.1.3.3. Declarative Knowledge

This category of knowledge is represented in a descriptive manner. It tells us the facts about things. It is expressed in factual statement, like "This is a boy". It is considered as shallow or surface level knowledge, therefore, it is used at the initial stage of knowledge representation.

2.1.3.4. Procedural Knowledge

Procedural knowledge relates to the procedure used in the problem solving process. It includes the step-by-step sequence and the how-to types of instruction.

2.1.3.5. Meta-knowledge

This category of knowledge is knowledge about knowledge. In expert system, meta-knowledge is knowledge about the operation of knowledge based system.

2.2. Knowledge Acquisition Methods

Knowledge acquisition involves the following processes: knowledge identification, knowledge representation, knowledge structuring and knowledge transfer to machine. The participants that greatly influence these processes are knowledge engineer, human expert and the end user. Acquiring knowledge from experts has its problems, which can be overcome when the knowledge engineer has the required skills. Knowledge acquisition from an expert can be seen as a modelling process, which can be done manually or with the aid of a computer. The manual method can use some of the tools from System Analysis and Design and Psychology to elicit knowledge from the expert [5, 7. 8].

2.2.1. Knowledge Modelling Methods

Three methods can be used in knowledge modelling, which includes: manual, semi-automatic and automatic methods. The manual method of knowledge modelling consists of the following methods: interviewing (structured, semi-structured and unstructured), tracking the reasoning process of the expert and observing the expert. Because the manual method of knowledge modelling is slow, expensive and sometimes inaccurate, attempts have been made to automate the manual method.

The semi-automated method of knowledge modelling is partly manual and partly automated. It is divided into two categories, which include the following:

- Expert Support: This category supports the expert in building the knowledge base with little or no help from the knowledge engineer.
- Knowledge Engineer Support: This category supports the knowledge engineer in building the knowledge base with minimum participation from the expert.

The automatic method of knowledge modelling is fully automated. The roles of the expert and knowledge engineers are greatly minimized or completely eliminated. Example is the automatic generation of rules from a set of known cases. The following are the advantages of automatic knowledge modelling method: reduction in the productivity (cost) of knowledge engineering, reduction in the skill level required by the knowledge engineer, elimination of the expert role, elimination of the knowledge engineer role, and increase in the quality of acquired knowledge.

Apart from knowledge acquisition from expert, knowledge can be acquired from documented sources, like textbooks, films videos *etc.* However, methodologies for acquiring knowledge from documented sources are very few [10].

2.3. Knowledge Verification and Validation

Knowledge verification/validation is the process of evaluating the acquired knowledge for quality. The three terms, evaluation, verification and validation are used interchangeably; however, each of them will be explained. Evaluation is the process of assessing the expert system overall value. It assesses the acceptable performance level of the system and analyses whether the system would be usable, efficient and cost effective. Validation, though part of evaluation is the process of comparing the performance of the system with the performance of the expert. The aim of validation is to ensure that the right system is built. On the other hand, verification is the process of substantiating that the system is implemented according to specification. In knowledge acquisition, these processes ensure that the knowledge base is correct, *i.e.* we have the right knowledge base. They ensure that the knowledge base is constructed properly. Metrics are generally used to verify/validate knowledge base. Table **1** shows the various metrics for verifying/validating knowledge base [6 - 10].

2.4. Knowledge Representation

This is the process of presenting the validated knowledge in a format that human will understand the knowledge and the computer can understand it. This is done using knowledge representation formalism/methods, which include the following: production rules, Frames, decision trees, objects and logic *etc*. Each of these knowledge representation methods/formalism will be considered briefly.

Table 1. Metrics for Verifying Knowledge Base.

Metrics/Measures	Description of Metrics
Accuracy	How well the system reflects reality, how correct is the knowledge in the knowledge base
Adaptability	Possibility for future development, changes
Adequacy/Completeness	Portion of the necessary knowledge included in the knowledge base
Appeal	How well the knowledge base matches intuition and stimulates thought and practicability
Breath	How well the domain is covered
Depth	Degree of detailed knowledge
Face validity	Credibility of knowledge
Generality	Capability of a knowledge base to be used with a broad range of similar problems
Precision	Capability of the system to replicate particular system parameters, consistency of advice, coverage of variables in knowledge base
Realism	Accounting for relevant variables and relations, similarity to reality
Reliability	Fraction of the expert system predictions that are empirically correct
Robustness	Sensitivity of conclusions to model structure
Sensitivity	Impact of changes in the knowledge base on quality of outputs
Technical and operational validity	Quality of the assumed assumptions, context, constraints, andconditions, and their impact on other measures
Turing test	Ability of a human evaluator to identify whether a given conclusion is made by an expert system or by a human expert.
Usefulness	How adequate the knowledge is (in terms of parameters and relationships) for solving correctly
Validity	The knowledge base's capability of producing empirically correct predictions

*Sources:*Compiled from B. Marcot,"Testing Your Knowledge Base," *AI Expert,*August 1987; and R.M.O'Keefe, O. Balci, and E.P. Smith,"Validating Expert System Performance," *IEEE Expert,*Winter 1987.

2.4.1. Production Rules

This is the most popular method for representing knowledge in expert system. It requires that knowledge be represented in form of condition and action pair, *i.e.* IF (condition) THEN (action). The condition is called premise or antecedent, while action is called result or conclusion or consequence. Example of a production rule is as follows: IF the colour of the car is red and the driver is dark in complexion, THEN the name of the driver is Peter. Each production rule in the knowledge base implements an independent chunk of expertise, which can be developed and modified independently of other rules. All the production rules are to be combined, so that when the inference engine accesses them, it yields better results. All the production rules in the knowledge base are combined together; each of them is not independent of the other. Production rules can be regarded as a simulation of cognitive behaviour of human experts. Production rules can be in different forms, as shown below:

- IF premise THEN conclusion. Example, IF age is greater than eighteen, THEN the person is an adult.
- Conclusion, IF premise. Example, the person is an adult IF the age is greater than eighteen.
- Inclusion of OR ELSE clause. Example, IF age is greater than eighteen, THEN the person is an adult OR ELSE the person is a youth.
- Complex rule. Example, IF age is greater than eighteen AND height is above five feet, THEN the person is an adult AND can play basketball.
- Nested IF. Example, IF age is greater than eighteen, IF complexion is white THEN the person is an American adult.

In Artificial Intelligence, there are two types of rules, which are the knowledge rule and inference rule. The knowledge rule or declarative rule is used to state the facts and the relationships about the problem, while the inference rule or procedural rule is used to advise how to solve the problem. The knowledge rule is used to build the knowledge base, while the inference rule is used to build the inference engine. Production rules therefore are part of the knowledge rule.

2.4.2. Semantic Network

This is another knowledge representation formalism/method, which focuses on the relationship between different concepts. It represents knowledge as a graph that consists of nodes and links, which show hierarchical relationships between objects. The nodes of the semantic network are the objects and descriptive information about the objects, while the links show relationships between the various objects and descriptions. Nodes, which represent objects, can be any physical item, like a book, a car, a desk or a person. Nodes can also represent concepts, events or actions. Example of concept is the relationship between supply of labour and labour wage in economics, while example of event is a football match, an election *etc*. On the other hand, an action can be playing football, singing a song *etc*. Nodes of semantic network can represent attributes of objects, like colour, size, age, height *etc*. The relationship between the nodes, which the links represent can be IS-A or HAS-A relationship. The IS-A relationship is used to show that an object belongs to a larger class or category. The HAS-A relationship is used to show the characteristics and attributes of an object. The semantic network in Fig. **(4)** shows the domain knowledge of a person called, Sam. The following information can be obtained from the semantic network, about Sam. "Sam owns a car, which is a Mercedes Benz, with colour red, made in Germany".

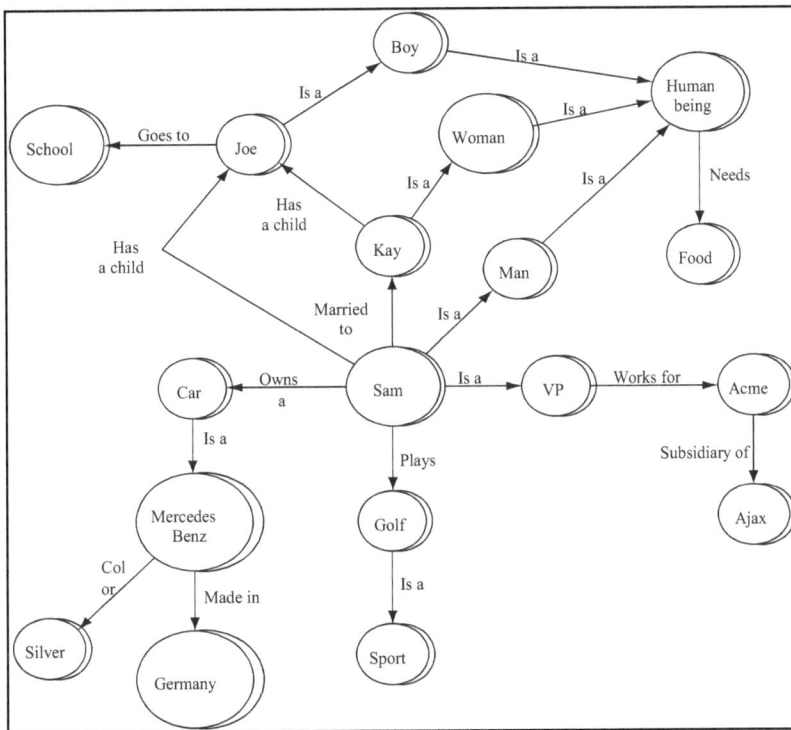

Fig. (4). Semantic network.

Semantic network can also be used to show inheritance. Inheritance allows an object to have the attributes of another object. In the above semantic network, Sam is a man, and a man is a human being, therefore, Sam can have all the attributes of a human being.

2.4.3. Frames

This is another method/formalism for representing knowledge. If you are interested in focusing on the properties of object, then frame is the ideal formalism/method. A frame can be regarded as a data structure that includes all the knowledge about a particular object. A frame organizes knowledge in slot that contains the characteristics and attributes of objects. A frame contains two basic elements, which are slots and facets. A slot is a set of attributes that describes the object represented by the frame. Each slot contains one or more facets. A facet, also called sub-slot describes the knowledge or procedural information about the attribute in the slot. Facets can take any of the following forms: values (red, blue, green etc) for a colour slot, default (The default description is used if the facet is empty), range (type of information that can appear in the slot *e.g.* integer numbers, 0 to 100), *etc.* An example of frame, which shows slots and facets has been shown in Table **2**, below.

Table 2. Example of Frame, Showing Slots and Facets.

Automobile Frame
Class of: Transportation
Name of manufacturer: Audi
Origin of manufacturer: Germany
Model: 5000 Turbo Type of car: Sedan Weight: 3300 lb.
Wheelbase: 105.8 inches
Number of doors: 4 (defaults)
Transmission: 3-speed automatic
Number of wheels: 4 (default) Engine: (Reference Engine Frame)
• Type: In-line, overhead cam
• Number of cylinders: 5
Acceleration (procedural attachment)
• 0–60: 10.4 seconds
• Quarter mile: 17.1 seconds, 85 mph
Gas mileage: 22 mpg average (procedural attachment)
Engine Frame
Cylinder bore: 3.19 inches
Cylinder stroke: 3.4 inches
Compression ratio: 7.8 to 1
Fuel system: Injection with turbocharger

(Table 2) cont.....

Automobile Frame
Horsepower: 140 hp
Torque: 160 ft/LB
Frame for an Automobile

In the above frame, weight and wheelbase are slots, while the facet for weight is 3300 Ib. and the facet for wheelbase is 105.8 inches.

2.5. Inferencing

After the knowledge has been represented in the knowledge base using a particular knowledge representation formalism/method, inferencing can commence. Inferencing can be defined as the process of reasoning about the knowledge in the knowledge base. The computer program that is used to do inferencing is called inference engine. If the program uses inference rule, it is called rule interpreter. The ability to reason is what makes the system intelligent. There are different methods of reasoning/inferencing. They include the following:

2.5.1. Common Sense Inferencing/Reasoning

This type of inferencing/reasoning deals with reasoning the way human reason. The various components of common sense reasoning include the following:

- Adequate, broad and deep common sense knowledge base.
- Reasoning methods that exhibit the features of human thinking such as ability to reason with knowledge that is true by default, ability to reason rapidly across a broad range of domain, ability to tolerate uncertainty in knowledge.
- New kind of cognitive architecture, which support multiple reasoning methods and representations.

2.5.2. Rule Base Inferencing/Reasoning

Rule based reasoning is a type of reasoning where the inference engine uses inference rule. The inference engine is called rule interpreter. The inference engine uses a process called pattern matching to search the knowledge based by applying the inference rule in the search. During the search, it decides the rule to investigate and the alternative to eliminate and which attribute to match. The two main approaches that the rule interpreter uses are: backward chaining and forward chaining. Backward chaining is a goal driven approach, where the rule interpreter starts with a goal, which is to be verified as either true or false. In order to verify the goal as either true or false, it looks for a rule that has that goal as its conclusion. If found, it matches the premise of the rule with the assertion base, otherwise, it searches for another rule that has the same conclusion as the first goal, and repeats the process again. However, if the search succeeds, the goal will be returned as true, otherwise, the goal will be returned as false.

Forward chaining is a data driven approach, the rule interpreter starts with the basic facts that are available and tries to draw conclusion. It draws conclusion by searching for the facts that matches the IF part of the IF THEN rule.

2.6. Explanation and Meta-knowledge

Explanation is the process of justifying the conclusion of an expert system. It consists of sequence of inferences that were made by the system in order to arrive at the conclusion. It provides a means of evaluating the integrity of the system when it is used by the expert. There are two basic types of explanation, which are the 'why' and the 'how'. The 'why' explanation provides justification for the conclusion, while the 'how' explanation provides the sequence of inferences that led to the conclusion. Since human experts provide justifications for their actions, therefore if an expert system is to mimic human in performing specialized tasks, it must provide justifications for its conclusion. Explanation clarifies its reasoning, recommendations and other actions. Explanation facility or justifier is the part of expert system that provides explanation. Explanation justifier serves the following objectives:

- To make the system more intelligible to the user.
- Helps in debugging of the knowledge base by the knowledge engineer. This is through the uncovering of the shortcoming of the rules and knowledge base.
- To explain situations that the user did not anticipate.
- To make the user to feel more assured of the actions of the expert system, thereby satisfying the social and psychological needs of the user.
- To clarify assumptions underlying the system operations to both the user and the knowledge engineer.

Most expert systems do not meet some of the objectives of explanation. This is because most expert systems do not effectively communicate to the user the reasoning processes that solve the problem, even though the expert system reasoning is very effective in solving the problem. Therefore, apart from storing the knowledge of the domain, expert system must store the knowledge of how the expert system reasons in order to solve the problem in the domain. This is called knowledge about knowledge or meta-knowledge. Meta-knowledge therefore is a system's knowledge about how it reasons in solving the problem.

2.7. Inferencing with Uncertainty

To err is human, but perfection is divine. Therefore, the knowledge of expert may not be perfect; it may have some measures of error. The process of representing this inexact knowledge in the knowledge base of expert system may have some errors associated with it. Therefore, the results that expert system produces are subject to error. Uncertainty therefore can be regarded as extent to which something is inexact. The most common method of measuring uncertainty is the use of probability theory. Uncertainty therefore is an important component of expert system. Uncertainty is a serious problem, avoiding it is not the solution, but the method for dealing with it must be improved [6, 10].

2.8. Expert System Development Environment

Since expert system is software that mimics the problem solving abilities of a human expert, therefore its development follows software engineering process. There are various software development environments, which can be used to develop expert system, they include the following [10]:

2.8.1. Expert System Shells

These are software with built in facilities for developing expert system. The facilities include: built in user interface, built in inference engine, an empty knowledge base. The system becomes operational after the knowledge has been entered in the knowledge base. An example of expert system shells is CORVID.

2.8.2. Programming Languages

Very high level language (fifth generation language, 5GL) can be used to build an expert system. PROLOG, LISP are examples of such programming languages.

2.8.3. Hybrid Environment

Expert system can be developed in an environment that combines different tools. Such a hybrid tool is called tool kits.

2.9. Conclusion

The various processes that are involved in knowledge engineering have been considered in detail in this unit. They include: knowledge engineering foundations, knowledge acquisition methods, knowledge verification and validation, knowledge representation, inferencing, explanation and meta-knowledge and expert system development environment.

2.10. Summary

Though some of the knowledge representation methods/formalism have been consisted in this unit, the next unit will consider in detail one of the knowledge representation method/formalism, called propositional logic.

3. PROPOSITIONAL LOGIC

Knowledge representation, using propositional logic is the process of storing knowledge of a domain with the letters of the alphabets as atomic propositional statement. The goal of knowledge representation using propositional logic is to be able to perform basic automated logical reasoning by automating the evaluation of complex propositional statement [2].

3.1. Propositional Logic as Knowledge Representation Formalism

Propositional logic is one of the fundamental knowledge representation formalism, which uses letters of the alphabets to represent the atomic statements of propositional logic. Propositional logic that is represented using letters can either be true or false. Example: Let X represent the statement, Peter is coming, and Y represents the statement, Henry has gone home. X and Y are propositional logic, because each of their values can be true or false. X and Y are called atomic statements of propositional logic. Complex propositional statements can be defined using X and Y and the various connectives of propositional logic. The connectives of propositional logic are the various operators of propositional logic.

3.2. Syntax of Propositional Logic Connectives

The syntax of propositional logic defines the rules that will be used to evaluate each of the connectives or operators of propositional logic. The symbols of propositional logic are the logical constants *True* and *False,* propositional symbols such as *P* and *Q,* the logical connectives, $\land$, $\lor$, $\Leftrightarrow$,=>, and ~, and parentheses, (). All sentences are made by putting these symbols together using the following rules:

- The logical constants *True (1)* and *False (0)* are sentences by themselves.
- A propositional symbol such as *P* or *Q* is a sentence by itself.
- Wrapping parentheses around a sentence yields a sentence, for example, (P ∧ Q).
- A sentence can be formed by combining simpler sentences with one of the five logical connectives.
- ∧ (and). A sentence whose main connective is ∧, such as A∧B, is called a conjunction logic, its parts, A and B are the conjuncts.
- V (or). A sentence using V, such as A V B is called a disjunction logic. Its parts, A and B are called disjuncts. V comes from the Latin "vel," which means "or." For most people, it is easier to remember as an upside-down, and.)
- => (implies). A sentence such as A=>B is called an implication (or conditional). Its premise or antecedent is A, and its conclusion or consequent is *B*. Implications are also known as rules or if-then statements. The implication symbol is sometimes written in other books as D or —.
- ⇔(equivalent). The sentence *A⇔B* is an equivalence (also called a biconditional).
- ~ (not). A sentence such as ~P is called the negation of P. All the other connectives combine two sentences into one; ~ is the only connective that operates on a single sentence.
- The operators/connectives, ∧, V, =>, ⇔ are binary operators, because they take two parameters/arguments. On the other hand, the operator/connective, ~ is a unary operator because it takes one parameter/argument [2].

3.3. Semantics of Propositional Logic

The semantics of propositional logic shows the meaning of each of the connectives of propositional logic, which will determine the result of the evaluation of each of connectives of propositional logic. The following show the semantics of the various connectives of propositional logic, which determines the result of the evaluations of the connectives.

The meaning of the five connectives can be stated as follows:

Based on the above semantics, complex propositional statements can be defined and evaluated easily. Example, suppose X, Y and Z are propositional logics, we can define the following complex logic sentence as:X ∧ (Y V Z).

$$X \wedge Y = \begin{cases} T, & \text{If } X = T, \quad Y = T \\ F, & \text{Otherwise} \end{cases} \tag{1}$$

$$X \vee Y = \begin{cases} F, & \text{If } X = F, \quad Y = F \\ T, & \text{Otherwise} \end{cases} \tag{2}$$

$$\sim X \quad \begin{cases} T, & \text{If } X = F \\ F, & \text{Otherwise} \end{cases} \tag{3}$$

$$X => Y = \begin{cases} F, & \text{If } X = T, \quad Y = F \\ T, & \text{Otherwise} \end{cases} \tag{4}$$

$$X <=> Y = \begin{cases} T, & \text{If } X = Y \\ F, & \text{Otherwise} \end{cases} \tag{5}$$

A truth table, which is a table that shows all the posible combinations of the values of the propositional logics can be used to perform logical reasoning, with the aim of determining if the complex logical sentence is true or false. Table **3** shows the truth table that evaluates this propositional logic, X ∧ (Y V Z).

3.4. Automating Logical Reasoning

Using truth table to evaluate complex logical sentences sometimes, can be tedious and error prone. Developing a computer program that will automate logical reasoning/inference can be regarded as an Artificial Intelligence program. The program will construct all the possible entries of a truth table and will use it to evaluate the complex logical sentence.

Table 3. Truth Table of X ∧ (Y V Z).

X	Y	Z	Y V Z	X ∧ (Y V Z)
F	F	F	F	F
F	F	T	T	F
F	T	F	T	F
F	T	T	T	F

X	Y	Z	Y V Z	X ∧ (Y V Z)
T	F	F	F	F
T	F	T	T	T
T	T	F	T	T
T	T	T	T	T

Example: Suppose P, Q and R are represented as facts using propositional logic, and we want to write an Artificial Intelligence program that will perform the following logical reasoning:

$$((P => Q) => R) \Leftrightarrow P$$

A structured approach to programming will be used, by writing the methods that will evaluate these connectives of propositional logic, => and ⇔. Since there are three propositional symbols, it means that there will be a total of 8 entries in the truth table. Three loops, each representing a propositional symbol will be used, and each loop will run two times. Each time the loops run, the various values of the propositional symbol will be used to evaluate the complex sentence, and the result is displayed as shown in the truth table. The Java program that does the logical reasoning is shown below.

```java
import java.util.*;

class truth1

{

public static void main(String args[])

{

boolean P = false, Q = false, R, result;

System.out.println("|P |Q |R |Result");

for(int i = 0; i <= 1; i++)

{

if (i == 0)

{

P = true;
```

```
}
else
{
P = false;
}
for(int j = 0; j <= 1; j++)
{
if (j == 0)
{
Q = true;
}
else
{
Q = false;
}
for(int k = 0; k <= 1; k++)
{
if (k == 0)
{
R = true;
}
else
{
R = false;
```

```
}
System.out.print("|");System.out.print(P);
if (P == true)
{
System.out.print(" |");
}
else
{
System.out.print("|");
}
System.out.print(Q);
if (Q == true)
{
System.out.print(" |");
}
else
{
System.out.print("|");
}
System.out.print(R);
if (R == true)
{
System.out.print(" |");
}
```

```
else

{

System.out.print("|");

}

result = equivalent(implies(implies(P, Q),R),P);

System.out.print(result);

if (result == true)

{

System.out.println(" |");

}

else

{

System.out.println("|");

}

}

}

}

static boolean implies(boolean a, boolean b)

{

if ((a == true) && (b == false))

{

return false;

}

else
```

```
{

return true;

}

}

static boolean equivalent(boolean a, boolean b)

{

if (a == b)

{

return true;

}

else

{

return false;

}

}

}
```

3.5. Uncertainty in Logical Reasoning

There are uncertainties in using propositional logic to represent knowledge. This is because man cannot be perfect in knowledge, what you say is true, may not be actually true, therefore, error can be associated to propositional logic. Example, if you use the following propositional logic to represent the following facts on the computer: P = Obi has gone, Q = Ada is coming. Based on certain factors, there will always be associated to P, a measure of the level of uncertainty of being false, and also associated to Q, a measure of level of uncertainty of being false. Therefore, when we make the following complex sentence, (P V Q) => Q, we can perform logical reasoning on the complex sentence and determine a measure of the degree of uncertainty that (P V Q) => Q is false. This is called logical reasoning with uncertainty. In order to do this, we follow the following steps:

- Step 1: Use truth table to make inference on the logical sentence.
- Step 2: For each value of the truth table that the sentence is false; use multiplication law of probability to determine the probability that the logical sentence is false.
- Step 3: Use addition law of probability to add all the entries in the truth table that the logical sentence is false.

Using the above example, suppose the probability that the propositional logic, P is false is 0.3, and the probability that the propositional logic, Q is false is 0.2, therefore the probability that the logical sentence, (P V Q) => Q is false or true can be obtained using Table **4**, below.

Table 4. Truth Table with Uncertainty.

P	Q	P V Q	(P V Q) => Q	P	Q	(P V Q) => Q
F	F	F	T	0.3	0.2	0.06
F	T	T	T	0.3	0.8	0.24
T	F	T	F	0.7	0.2	0.14
T	T	T	T	0.7	0.8	0.56

From Table **4**, the probability that the logical sentence, P V Q) => Q is true is 0.86, and the probability that the logical sentence, P V Q) => Q is false is 0.14. As usual, reasoning with uncertainty/certainty can be automated by writing an Artificial Intelligence program that will reason logically by using a truth table to evaluate the logical sentence and compute the probability that the logical sentence is true/false. The Java program that follows illustrates further:

Example: Consider the following complex logical sentence, ((P<=>Q)V(Q =>R)) =>(P=>R), we are to write an Artificial Intelligence program that will use a truth table and perform logical reasoning, and compute the probability that the logical sentence is true/false. The program will request the probability that the the propositional logic P, Q and R are true.

3.6. Automating Uncertain Propositional Logic

Java programming language can be used to automate the evaluation of the uncertain propositional logic, as illustrated above. The Java code that does this has been shown below. It can be copied and run on the computer with Java compiler.

import java.util.*;

```
class truth

{

public static void main(String args[])

{

double firstnum = 0.0, secondnum = 0.0, thirdnum = 0.0, pval = 1.0, resultT = 0.0,
resultF = 0.0;

boolean P = false, Q = false, R, result;

Scanner myinput = new Scanner(System.in);

System.out.print("Enter the probability for the first atomic sentence: ");

firstnum = myinput.nextDouble();

System.out.print("Enter the probability for the second atomic sentence: ");

secondnum = myinput.nextDouble();

System.out.print("Enter the probability for the third atomic sentence: ");

thirdnum = myinput.nextDouble();

System.out.println("|P |Q |R |Result|Probability");

for(int i = 0; i <= 1; i++)

{

if (i == 0)

{

P = true;

}

else

{

P = false;
```

```
}
for(int j = 0; j <= 1; j++)
{
if (j == 0)
{
Q = true;
}
else
{
Q = false;
}
for(int k = 0; k <= 1; k++)
{
if (k == 0)
{
R = true;
}
else
{
R = false;
}
System.out.print("|");System.out.print(P);
if (P == true)
{
```

```java
System.out.print(" |");

pval = pval * firstnum;

}

else

{

System.out.print("|");

pval = pval * (1.0 - firstnum);

}

System.out.print(Q);

if (Q == true)

{

System.out.print(" |");

pval = pval * secondnum;

}

else

{

System.out.print("|");

pval = pval * (1.0 - secondnum);

}

System.out.print(R);

if (R == true)

{

System.out.print(" |");

pval = pval * thirdnum;
```

```
}
else
{
System.out.print("|");
pval = pval * (1.0 - thirdnum);
}
result = implies((equivalent(P,Q) || implies(Q,R)), implies(P,R));
System.out.print(result);
if (result == true)
{
System.out.print(" |");
resultT = resultT + pval;
}
else
{
System.out.print(" |");
resultF = resultF + pval;
}
System.out.println(pval);
pval = 1.0;
}
}
}
System.out.println("The probability that the statement is true is: "+resultT);
```

```
System.out.print("The probability that the statement is false is: "+resultF);

}

static boolean implies(boolean a, boolean b)

{

if ((a == true) && (b == false))

{

return false;

}

else

{

return true;

}

}

static boolean equivalent(boolean a, boolean b)

{

if (a == b)

{

return true;

}

else

{

return false;

}

}
```

}

3.7. Conclusion

You have learned the use of propositional logic as knowledge representation formalism, and how to use propositional logic to automate logical reasoning, using Java programming language.

3.8. Summary

Propositional logic as a knowledge representation formalism has been considered in detail. The next chapter will consider another aspect of Artificial Intelligence.

CONCLUDING REMARKS

This chapter has laid a solid foundation for the expert system. It identified the knowledge base as one of the components of the expert system. It considers and explores knowledge engineering as an important process in the development of an expert system. It also focuses on propositional logic as one of the knowledge representation formalism.

REFERENCES

[1]   P.J.F. Lucas, and L.C. van der Gaag, "Principles of expert system", In: *Center for Mathematics and Computer Science* Addison-Wesley: Amsterdam, 1991.

[2]   S.J. Russells, and P. Norwig, "Artificial Intelligence: A Modern Approach", *Prentice Hall,* 1995.

[3]   https://www.guru99.com/expert-systems-with-applications.html#4

[4]   A. Hart, *Knowledge Acquisition for Expert Systems* McGraw-Hill: New York, 1992.

[5]   H. Helbig, *Knowledge Representation and the Semantics of Natural Language* Springer: New York, 2006.

[6]   P. Jackson, *Introduction to Expert Systems* 3rd ed. Addison-Wesley: Boston, MA, 1999.

[7]   D. Kuhn, and A. Zohar, *Strategies of Knowledge Acquisition* University of Chicago Press: Chicago, 1995.
      [http://dx.doi.org/10.2307/1166059]

[8]   G. Schreiber, H. Akkermans, A. Anjewierden, R. de Hong, N. Shadbolt, W. Van de Velde, and B. Wielinga, *Knowledge Engineering and Management:The Common KADS Methodology* MIT Press: Boston, 2000.

[9]   A.C. Scott, J.E. Clayton, and E.L. Gibson, *A Practical Guide to Knowledge Acquisition* Addison-Wesley: Reading, MA, 1991.

[10] http://silo.tips/download/knowledge-acquisition-representation-and-reasoning

CHAPTER 3

Natural Language Processing

Abstract: The ability to communicate in natural language remains one of the qualities of an intelligent system. The aspect of Artificial Intelligence that deals with this quality of an intelligent system is natural language processing. This chapter considers this aspect of Artificial Intelligence in detail.

Keywords: Bag of words, Lemmatization, Occurrence matrix, Parts of speech tagging, Text classification, Text normalization, Text summarization, Tokenization, Stemming.

1. FUNDAMENTALS OF NATURAL LANGUAGE PROCESSING

Natural language processing is an aspect of Artificial Intelligence that makes it possible for a computer system to read, understand and derive meaning from text or speech made in human languages, like the English language, French language, *etc*. This aspect of Artificial Intelligence becomes very relevant because it enables the intelligent system to be able to communicate in natural language. Furthermore, when combined with other aspects of Artificial Intelligence, like machine learning, it allows computers to analyse hundreds, thousands, and millions of text and word declarations of millions of people in a locality.

1.1. Applications of Natural Language Processing

Natural language processing is an interesting area of Artificial Intelligence because of its numerous areas of applications, which include the following: prediction of disease, sentiments analysis, cognitive assistant, email spam filter, identifying fake news, voice-driven assistant, recruitment exercise, litigation task, *etc*. Each of these applications of NLP will be explained briefly [1 - 6].

- **Disease Prediction:** Symptoms of some diseases can be identified when the patient talks about them. Therefore, in addition to health records, such diseases can be predicted using NLP.

- **Sentiments Analysis:** Opinions of customers about a particular service or product can be analysed and extracted from sources, like social media. This process is called sentiment analysis [1 - 6].

- **Cognitive Assistant:** It works like a personalized search engine. It learns everything about you, which can be through what you say and write, and tries to remind you of anything that you seem to forget.

- **Spam Email Filter:** Natural language processing has been used to filter spam email from entering into the inbox. This is possible by analysing the email text and identifying spam emails [1 - 6].

- **Identification of Fake News:** Natural language processing has also been used to identify if the source of news is fake.

- **Voice-Driven Assistant:** This is an application that uses audio input and audio response/output to assist users in doing anything, like finding a particular shop, weather forecast, *etc.*

- **Recruitment Exercise:** Recruitment processes, like an interview for a particular talent, can be done using natural language processing.

- **Text Summarization:** This natural language processing task involves reducing large text into a small and concise form while retaining the meaning of the text.

- **Text Categorization:** This natural language processing task involves the determination of the category of text (religion, politics, sports, *etc.*)

- **Understanding Natural Language:** One of the natural language processing tasks is the disambiguation of words. This means understanding the right meaning of text [1 - 6].

- **Question Answering (Language Output):** Understanding the correct meaning of the text will lead to language output, which is the correct answer to a question. This is useful in a question and answering system.

- **Machine Translation:** Another important task of natural language processing is the translation of text from one natural language to another natural language. This is called text translation.

1.2. The Future of Natural Language Processing

The future of natural language processing is the statistical-based natural language processing, which uses machine learning techniques to automatically learn natural language processing rules through the analysis of a large set of training data, called corpora, which are collections of different sets of documents (text or audio). Most of the data that we generate from conversations, declarations, or tweets are unstructured data, and they represent the majority of data that are available in the real world. Because of the unstructured nature of the data, it becomes difficult and messy to manipulate them. However, the emergence of machine learning has helped us not just to interpret the text or speech based on keywords but also to understand the meaning behind these words. Therefore, with machine learning, it is possible to detect figures of speech, like the irony in a speech/text, or perform sentiment analysis on collections of hundreds, thousands, or millions of texts/speech [1 - 6].

1.3. Conclusion

In this unit, you have learnt the various applications and tasks of natural language processing, together with the type of natural language processing applications that the future holds for users.

1.4. Summary

Through natural language processing, computer systems will be able to read, understand and derive meaning from text or speech. In the recent time and near future, there are myriads of natural language processing applications. Every application of natural language processing that solves a particular problem undergoes the following stages, text representation, text pre-processing, *etc.* These stages will be considered in the subsequent units.

2. TEXT PRE-PROCESSING

Text pre-processing is one of the most important tasks during natural language processing. It consists of a collection of preparatory tasks before the actual natural language processing (text normalization, tokenization, stop words removals, stemming, lemmatization, *etc.*). It can be regarded as the process of transforming raw text from human-readable form to machine-readable form for further processing. The aim of text pre-processing is to improve the result after the natural language processing task [2, 7].

2.1. Text Normalization

Text normalization forms a collection of related tasks that aims at putting all the texts in the same level playing field. It involves performing the following on text: converting all letters to upper or lower case, converting all numbers into words or removing all numbers, removing punctuations, accent marks, and other diacritics, removing white spaces, expanding abbreviations, removing stop words, sparse terms or particular words, converting text with many representations into a standard representation.

2.2. Tokenization

This is the process of splitting text into words, punctuation marks, numbers, and other discrete items. Each of the words, punctuation marks, numbers, and any discrete item that you obtain after tokenization is called token. In the English language, where white space separates two words, it can be used to split the text into tokens. Where this is the case, it can split words like San Francisco, Los Angeles, *etc.*, into two tokens, instead of one token. Illustrating with the following examples, using white space to split the text, into tokens, the following will be the tokens that will be obtained after tokenization.

Python has a function called word_tokenize(x), which can be used to tokenize any text, The function is part of the Python's Natural Language ToolKit(NLTK). The following Python codes reads text from the web with specified url address and perform tokenization on it and display the result:

```
>>>from _future_ import division

>>>import nltk, re, pprint

>>>from urllib import urlopen

>>>url = http://www.gutenberg.org/files/2554.txt

>>>raw = urlopen(url),read()

>>>type(raw)
```

```
<type 'str'>
>>>len(raw)
1176831
>>>raw[:65]
'The project Gutenberg EBook of Crime and Punishment by Fyodor Dost'
>>>token = nltk.word_tokenize(raw)
>>>type(token)
<type 'list'>
>>>len(tokens)
255809
>>>tokens[:10]
['The', 'project', 'Gutenberg', 'EBook', 'of', 'Crime']
>>>
```

Furthermore, you can read text from the keyboard and tokenize it or perform other operations on it. The following Python codes illustrate further:

```
>>>s = raw_input("Enter some text:")
Enter some text:This is an example of Python code.
>>>print "The words you typed are ", len(nltk.word_tokenize(s)), " They are."
The words you types are 8 They are
>>>nltk.word_tokenize(s)
'This is an example of Python code.
>>>
```

Finally on Python tokenization code, you can read text from a file and perform tokenization or other operations on it. The following Python codes illustrate:

```
>>>f = open('document.txt')
```

```
>>>raw = f.read()
```

```
>>>token = nltk.word_tokenize(raw)
```

```
>>>type(token)
```

```
<type 'list'>
```

```
>>>len(tokens)
```

Display Result

```
>>>tokens[:10]
```

Display Result

```
>>>
```

You need to create a file called 'document.txt', which will be in the directory as the Python IDLE. This you can do by clicking at the File menu in Python IDLE and select New Window. After typing the text in the window, save it as 'document.txt' in the same directory as the IDLE.

2.3. Stop Words Removal

This is the process of getting rid of common natural language articles, pronouns and preposition. Such common words are "and", "the", "to" *etc.* This process filters common words that do not provide any useful objectives to the natural language processing [2, 8, 9].

2.4. Stemming

This is the process of reducing words to their stem or root or base form. This involves removing the prefix or suffix in each of the words in a text of a natural language. Example, after performing stemming on the word, helpful, it becomes help. After performing stemming on the word, coeducation, it becomes education.

Python allows you to do stemming by using third party off the shelf package, like PorterStemmer or LancasterStemmer. The following Python codes illustrate the use of PorterStemmer and LancasterStemmer [9]

```
>>>porter = nltk.PorterStemmer
```

```
>>>lancaster = nltk.LancasterStemmer
```

>>>mytext = "This text is used to illustrate how to perform stemming."

>>>token = word_tokenize(mytext)

>>>[porter.stem(t) for t in token]

Display Result

>>>[lancaster.stem(t) for t in token]

Display Result

>>>

2.5. Lemmatization

Lemmatization is the process of reducing words in a text to its root or base form, but it uses a different approach to reduce the word to its root or base form. The approach that Lemmatization uses is by reducing the words to its dictionary form, known as lemma. Example, running, ran, runs are words whose lemma or dictionary root is run. Therefore, run is the result of performing the Lemmatization operation on any of the word, running, runs or ran.

Python can perform the Lemmatization task using a method in NLTK called WordNetLemmatizer. The following Python codes illustrate how to perform Lemmatization in Python [9].

>>>lemma = nltk.WordNetLemmatizer()

>>>mytext = "This piece of texts illustrate how Python does Lemmatization"

>>>token = word_tokenization(mytext)

>>>[lemma.lemmatize(t) for t in token]

Display Result

>>>

2.6. Conclusion

In this unit, you have learnt the various tasks that are involved in text pre-processing. They help to transform text into a more digestible form before applying natural language processing task.

2.7. Summary

Text pre-processing allows you to prepare your text before using it for natural language processing task. However, there are other tasks that are involved when performing a particular natural language processing task. One of such tasks is text representation.

3. TEXT REPRESENTATION

Text representation is another important task when processing natural language, using any technique. It consists of a collection of methods, which encodes/converts the text into another format that the machine can manipulate (numbers). Texts are unstructured data, therefore, there is need to convert the unstructured data into structured data. This is what text representation accomplishes [2, 8, 9].

3.1. Bags of Words

This is a model that is commonly used to count all words in a text. It uses a matrix called occurrence matrix to count the words. The rows of the matrix are the groups of text from the main text, while the columns of the matrix are the various words. Each cell of the matrix is the frequency that shows the number of times the word occurred in that group of text. This model can be very useful in some Artificial Intelligence applications.

The following example will illustrate further: Suppose you are required to develop a bag of words for this text, "This is a model that is commonly used to" The text can be grouped into two sub-text, as follows: "This is a model that", "is commonly used to". The occurrence matrix follows in Table **1**.

3.2. Lookup Dictionary

This method of text representation, first builds a dictionary of all the words that were obtained after text pre-processing. Each word in the dictionary has a corresponding ID, which is an integer number. Therefore, every word in the pre-processed word can be replaced with the corresponding integer ID by looking up the word in the dictionary of words, thus transforming the sequence of text into a sequence of integer numbers [2, 8, 9].

Table 1. Occurrence matrix.

	This	**Is**	**a**	**Model**	**That**	**Commonly**	**used**	**to**
This is a model that	1	1	1	1	1	0	0	0

(Table 1) cont.....

	This	Is	a	Model	That	Commonly	used	to
Is commonly used to	0	1	0	0	0	1	1	1

3.3. One-Hot Encoding

This is one of the simplest form of text representation. After text pre-processing, all the texts are represented in a two dimensional square vector or matrix. Each row of the vector/matrix represents a unique word. Similarly, each column of the vector/matrix represents a unique word. In each row, all the entries of the vector/matrix for that row will be filled with 0 except the entry whose column has the same word as the row. The entry is filled one hot value, 1. The following example will illustrate the One-Hot Encoding method. Suppose the following text were obtained after text pre-processing: peter mary john matthew. The one hot encoding method will produce the following representation as shown in Table **2**, below.

Table 2. One-hot encoding representation.

	Peter	**Mary**	**John**	**Matthew**
Peter	1	0	0	0
Mary	0	1	0	0
John	0	0	1	0
Matthew	0	0	0	1

3.4. Word Embedding

This is another method of representing text for natural language processing. Each text is mapped into a vector of N dimension. The dimensions of the vector will be very useful in determining the meaning of the word. This means that words/texts that have the same meaning will have similar embedding.

3.5. Conclusion

In this unit, you have learnt the various methods of representing text after the text has been pre-processed. They include: bag of words, lookup dictionary, one-hot encoding and word embedding.

3.6. Summary

Apart from text pre-processing and text representation, there are other processes that are performed on text, which will be useful for a particular natural language processing task. One of such processes is parts of speech tagging, which will be considered in the next unit.

4. PARTS OF SPEECH TAGGING

After text pre-processing, like tokenization, before using the text for some natural language processing tasks (text to speech, parsing *etc.*), each of the tokens needs to be classified according to the parts of speech that it belongs. Parts of speech tagging or POS tagging or Grammatical Tagging or Word Category Disambiguation is the process of identifying the parts of speech that each of the tokens/words in a text belongs.

4.1. Fundamentals of Parts of Speech

Parts of speech of a natural language are the collection of different classes or categories that every word/token of a text/sentence must belong to. Each part of speech or class of a natural language has a defined function and syntax. The various parts of speech of a natural language can be grouped into two main subclasses, which are: closed parts of speech and open parts of speech. In each closed part of speech, the words or tokens that belong to that part of speech remain fixed, it does not change, while in each open part of speech, the words/token that belong to that part of speech can change, they are not fixed. Example, preposition and pronoun are closed parts of speech because the words/token that belong to the classes of prepositions and pronouns as a parts of speech are fixed, new words/tokens that belong to prepositions or pronouns are hardly formed. On the other hand, nouns, adverbs, adjectives and verbs are open parts of speech because new nouns, adverbs, adjectives or verbs can easily be formed or borrowed from other languages at any time. There are eight fundamental parts of speech, which includes the following: noun, verb, pronoun, preposition, adverb, conjunction, particle and article [10, 11].

Nouns are words/tokens that include the names of people, places and things. It is further grouped into proper nouns and common nouns. Table **3** and **4** shows broad parts of speech and the subclasses, with examples in the natural language, English [10, 11].

Table 3. Subclasses and examples of different parts of speech.

Open POS	Noun	Proper Noun	*e.g.* Regina, Nigeria, IBM	
		Common Noun	Count Noun	*e.g.* goat, goats
			Mass Noun	snow, salt
	Verb	Main verb		
		Auxiliary verb	Tense	
			Aspect	
			Polarity	
			Mood	
	Adverb	Directional Adverb	*e.g.* Home, here	
		Degree Adverb	*e.g.* Very	
		Manner Adverb	*e.g.* slowly	
		Temporal Adverb	*e.g.* Today	
	Adjective	Colour Adjectives	*e.g.* Black, red	
		Age Adjectives	*e.g.* old, young	
		Value Adjectives	*e.g.* Good, bad	
Closed POS	Preposition	On, under, over, near, by, at, from		
	Determiner	Article	Definite	*e.g.* the
			Indefinite	*e.g.* a, an
		Other determiner		
	Pronoun	Personal	*e.g.* You, she	
		Possessive	*e.g.* My, your	
		wh-pronoun	*e.g.* what, who	
	Conjunction	Coordinating	*e.g.* and, or	
		Subordinating	*e.g.* That	
	Particle	*e.g.* up, down, on, off, in, out		
	Numeral	One, two, three, first, second, third		

4.2. Importance of Parts of Speech Tagging

Parts of speech tagging on itself does not solve a problem directly in natural language processing, but it solves problems indirectly in other natural language processing tasks, which includes the following:

4.2.1. Word Pronunciation in Text to Speech Conversion

A word can appear several places in a text with different meanings in each of the places that it appears. In one place it can appears as a noun with a particular meaning, while in another place, it can appear as a verb with another meaning. The pronunciation of the word based of the parts of speech of that word will differ. Therefore, text to speech systems, which convert text to speech will perform parts of speech tagging, with the aim of knowing how to pronounce the word.

4.2.2. Word Sense Disambiguation

A text, which can be a sentence can have different sequences of parts of speech, which makes it to have different meanings. The correct meaning of the sentence will depend on the context the text is being used. Therefore, in natural language processing, the computer needs to identify the appropriate meaning of the text, which can be done by identifying the correct sequence of the parts of speech of the text, based on the context the text is used [10, 11].

4.2.3. Stemming as Text Pre-processing Task

Parts of speech tagging can be very useful in stemming as a task of text pre-processing. Stemming has been defined in the previous unit as the process of reducing words to its stem by removing the prefix or suffix. However, knowing the parts of speech of a word will help to determine the prefix or suffix that the word can take [1].

4.3. Computational Methods for Parts of Speech Tagging

The computational methods for parts of speech tagging are the various methods or algorithms that can be used to automate parts of speech tagging. These algorithms or methods can be classified as follows: rule based tagging method/algorithm, stochastic based tagging method/algorithm and transformation based tagging method/algorithm. One of the main problems that a tagging method solves is how to resolve the parts of speech of ambiguous words, based on the context of its usage. In a rule based method/algorithm, it uses a large database of disambiguation rules to resolve the right parts of speech of an ambiguous word. Example, one of such rules can be that an ambiguous word is a noun rather than a verb if it follows a determiner. On the other hand, a stochastic based tagging method/algorithm uses a machine learning approach. It uses a large training data of text called corpus to compute the probability that the ambiguous word belongs to a particular parts of speech under the given context. Finally, transformation based tagging method/algorithm combines the features of rule based tagging and stochastic based tagging. On one hand, it is based on rules that determines when a given ambiguous word should have a particular tag or parts of speech, on the other hand, it has a machine learning component that induces the rules based on previously tagged large collection of text called corpus. Each of these tagging method/algorithm will be considered in detail [1].

4.3.1. Rule Based Tagging Method/Algorithm

All taggers (algorithms that perform tagging) that use rule based tagging method/algorithm have a two stage architecture. The first stage involves the use of dictionary to assign possible tags (parts of speech) to all the words in the text. The next stage uses a large list of hand written disambiguation rule to determine the tag (parts of speech), based on the given context. An example of disambiguation rule is "If the ambiguous word, X is preceded by a determiner and followed by a noun, then the tag is adjective". Defining many of these rule manually is quite difficult, hence the need for an automatic way of generating the disambiguation rules, which uses a machine learning approach. One of the most comprehensive modern rule based tagging approach is the Constraint Grammar approach, which was used to develop a tagger called EngCG tagger [1, 2].

4.3.2. Stochastic Based Tagging Method/Algorithm

The use of probabilities in tagging has been in place over the years. There are different approaches to the use of probabilities in tagging. They are as follows: word frequency approach and tag sequence probabilities approach. In the word frequency approach, the stochastic tagger disambiguates the word based on the probability that the word occurred with the tag in the training data (corpus). This approach is also called n-gram approach because the best tag for a word is determined by the probability that it occurs with the n previous words. An example of stochastic tagger is the Hidden Markov Model (HMM) tagger.

4.3.3. Transformation Based Tagging

The transformation based tagging, also called Brill tagging is a type of transformation based learning approach to machine learning. It combines the rule based tagging with the stochastic based tagging. The rule based tagging determines the rule to use for disambiguation of word, which are induced by the previous stochastic tagged approach. The disambiguation rules in this tagging method are not generated manually but automatically from the previous stochastic tagging of large set of training text [10, 11].

Table 4. Examples of english words and their respective parts of speech.

Tag	Description	Example	Tag	Description	Example
CC	Coordin.	*and, but, or one,*	SYM	Symbol	+,%, &
CD	Conjunction	*two, three a, the*	TO	"to"	*to ah,*
DT	Cardinal number	*there*	UH	Interjection	*oopseatateeatingeateneateatswhich,*
EX	Determiner	*mea culpa of, in, by*	VB	Verb, base	*thatwhat, whowhose how, where*
FW	Existential 'there'	*yellowbiggerwildest*	VBD	form	$
IN	Foreignword	*1, 2, One can,*	VBG	Verb, pasttense	#
JJ	Preposition/sub-conj	*shouldllamallamas*	VBN	Verb, gerund	' or "
JJR	Adjective	*IBM*	VBP	Verb,	' or "
JJS	Adj., comparative	*Carolinas all, both*	VBZ	pastparticiple	[, (, {, <],), }, >
LS	Adj., superlative	*'s*	WDT	Verb, non-3sg	,
MD	List item marker	*I, you, heyour,*	WP	pres	.!?
NN	Modal	*one'squickly,*	WP$	Verb, 3sg pres	: ; ... – -
NNS	Noun, sing. or mass	*neverfasterfastest*	WRB	Wh-determiner	
NNP	Noun, plural	*up, off*	$	Wh-pronoun	
NNPS	Propernoun,		#	Possessive wh-	
PDT	singular		"	Wh-adverb	
POS	Propernoun, plural		"	Dollar sign	
PRP	Predeterminer		(	Pound sign	
PRP$	Possessive ending		)	Leftquote	
RB	Personalpronoun		, .	Right quote	
RBR	Possessive pronoun		:	Leftparenthesis	
RBS	Adverb			Right parenthesis	
RP	Adverb,			Comma	
	comparative			Sentence-final punc	
	Adverb, superlative			Mid-sentence punc	
	Particle				

Python has a method in the NLTK (Natural Language ToolKit), called pos_tag(), which can be used to perform POS tagging. The following Python codes illustrate how this is done:

```
>>>import nltk

>>>mytext = nltk.word_tokenize("This example illustrates POS tagging"

>>>pos_tag(mytext)
```

Display Result

```
>>>
```

4.4. Conclusion

In this unit, you have learnt the fundamentals of parts of speech tagging, its importance and the various algorithmic approaches to parts of speech tagging.

4.5. Summary

Though parts of speech tagging does not solve its own problem, but solves the problems of other natural language processing tasks, which makes it very important and useful in natural language processing. Related in name but different in use, is text tagging or text classification, which will be considered in detail in the next unit.

5. TEXT TAGGING/TEXT CLASSIFICATION

Text, which is a collection of words is available everywhere (email, website, social media, eBooks *etc.*). The availability of sea of text requires that we devise a way of classifying them according to various categories for more insight and organisation. This is the focus of text classification or text tagging. Text classification is an important task in natural language processing because it can be used in sentiment analysis, spam detection, topic labelling *etc.*

5.1. Approaches to Text Classification

Text classification or text tagging or text categorization is the process of assigning predefined categories to various texts, based on its contents. It is one of the important tasks in natural language processing. Text classification can be done manually or automatically by the computer. The manual text classification requires a human being to read the text and understand them, afterwards classify them accordingly. Using computer to classify text, requires the computer to classify the text automatically. The manual method of classifying text is time consuming and prone to error. The use of computer in classifying text uses different approaches, which includes the following [2, 8]:

5.1.1. Rule Based Text Classification

The rule based text classification approach uses manually generated rules. The rules together with relevant elements of text, like words of the text identify the relevant category of the text. Example, suppose you want to classify some texts into two categories. The rule may be to maintain two lists; each list will contain the keywords of a particular category. Any text you want to classify will require counting the number of words that belong to each category, the category with the greater number of words means that the text belongs to that category.

5.1.2. Machine Learning Based Text Classification

The machine learning text classification approach uses collection of pre-classified texts as training data, which can be represented using bags of words. Each text in a bag of word has its corresponding category. The text classifier learns the different associations between the text and the category as represented in the bag of word. Once it is trained with enough training text with labelled category, the text classifier can begin to make accurate prediction of category of any given text. Different machine learning algorithms can be used to perform text classification [8].

5.1.3. Rule and Machine Learning Based Text Classification

This approach combines machine learning approach with rule based approach. This means that hand written rules can be used in addition to the machine learning approach with the aim of improving the accuracy of the text classification.

5.2. Machine Learning Algorithms for Text Classification

Different supervised classification based machine learning algorithms can be used for text classification. They include the following: naïve bayes algorithm, support vector machine, decision tree, deep learning. Each of these will be explained in detail.

5.2.1 Naïve Bayes Text Classification Machine Learning Algorithm

The Naïve Bayes algorithm is a supervised classification based machine learning algorithm. It can be used to perform text classification; in that case the class attribute will be the category attribute, while the non-class attributes will be the various words that have been represented in the bag of words. An understanding of the naïve bayes algorithm is very important in order to use it to perform text classification. Once you have represented the text as nominal data using the bag of words, the naïve bayes algorithm can be applied. Therefore, for an understanding of the naïve bayes algorithm, refer to the appropriate chapter and unit of this textbook for detail steps of naïve bayes algorithm. Our emphasis here is on how to represent the training data, which is a collection of non-class attributes and class attributes, using the bag of words with class attribute.

Suppose the following texts are the training data for the Naïve Bayes algorithm: "This is s model that", "is commonly used to", "model commonly". Suppose the first text has been pre-assigned the category "Poem", the second text has been pre-assigned the category "Song", while the third text has been pre-assigned the category, "Poem". Using bag of words, the three text can be represented as the Occurrence Matrix, shown in Table **5**.

Table 5. Occurrence Matrix

	This	Is	a	Model	That	Commonly	used	To
This is a model that	1	1	1	1	1	0	0	0
Is commonly used to	0	1	0	0	0	1	1	1
Model commonly	0	0	0	1	0	1	0	0

The Occurrence Matrix can be transformed into a table with eight non-class attributes and one class attribute as shown in Table **6**, below. The class attribute will be the category of the texts. Since there are two categories, we can use 0 to represent the category "Poem" and 1 to represent the category, "Song".

Table 6. of non-class attributes and a class attributes.

Category	This	Is	a	Model	That	Commonly	Used	To
0	1	1	1	1	1	0	0	0
1	0	1	0	0	0	1	1	1
0	0	0	0	1	0	1	0	0

In Table **6**, the non-class attributes are the words, This, Is, a, Model, that, commonly, used, to. On the other hand, the class attribute is Category. The Table can be used as the training data, which the naïve bayes machine learning algorithm can use to construct the tables of conditional probability for each of the non-class attributes. The tables of conditional probability can be used to determine the category of this text, "This commonly used model". Waikato Environment for Knowledge Analysis (WEKA), an open source machine learning software can be used analyse large dataset using the naïve bayes classifier.

5.2.2. Decision Tree Text Classification Machine Learning Algorithm

Similar to the naïve bayes, supervised, classification nasedmachine learning algorithm, the decision tree is another supervised classification based machine learning algorithm, which can be used to perform text classification. To understand the detail of the algorithm, refer to the relevant chapter and unit of this textbook. This aim, at the moment, is to represent the training data, using a collection of texts and bag of words to represent the text. After the training data has been represented using bag of word, the bag of words can be represented as a Table of non-class attributes and class attributes. The decision tree algorithm can be used it to classify any given text.

5.3. Conclusion

In this unit, you have learnt the various approaches to text classification and the various machine learning algorithms that can be used to perform text classification.

5.4. Summary

Having considered text classification as an important task, which can be used in different natural language processing tasks, there are other natural language processing tasks, one of them is text summarization, which will be considered in the next unit.

6. TEXT SUMMARIZATION

There are one thousand and one texts that are available for us to read *via* emails, eBooks, social media, websites, journal articles, newspapers, blogs tweets *etc.* Nobody has the time to read all these text. Any technology that reduces each of these texts to few words, while retaining the main contents on the text will help to reduce the time that will be required to read all the text that we want to read. A mobile app, called, inshorts reduces news articles into a 60 words text. Such mobile app uses a natural language processing task called text summarization. It is the process of reducing text into concise and few text, while retaining the original meaning of the main text. The reduced or concise text is called the summary of the main text [12 - 14].

6.1. Brief History of Automatic Text Summarization

The attention of the research community on natural language processing was focused in automatic text summarization in the early 1950s. Some of the important research and study made during the time were by Hans Peter Luhu and

Harold P. Edmundson. The research of Hans Peter Luhu was in late 1950, which was titled, Automatic Creation of Literature Abstract. The study used word frequency and phrase frequency to extract important sentences from the text for the purpose of summarization. The research of Harold P. Edmundson was in the late 1960s. It used cue words (words that appear in the title and in the text) and the locations of sentences where these cue words were used, to extract sentences for automatic text summarization. From that time, many studies and researches have been done in automatic text summarization [12 - 14].

6.2. Approaches to Text Summarization

There are different approaches to automatic text summarization, which can be classified using the following criteria:

- Input Types: The number of source documents, which can be single source document or multiple source documents.
- Purpose: The purpose of the text summarization, which can be any of the following: generic, domain specific or query based purpose.
- Output type: The type of summary that it will generate. This can be extractive or abstractive. Emphasis will be on the output type [12, 13].

6.2.1. Extractive Text Summarization

This approach to text summarization identifies and extracts important sentences from the document and combines them to form a summary. It uses the following techniques: frequency based technique, feature based technique and machine learning based technique [15 - 18].

6.2.2. Abstractive Text Summarization

This approach to text summarization examines the source text using some advanced natural language processing techniques with the aim of generating entirely new phrases that capture the meaning of the source text [14].

6.3. Frequency Based Technique

The frequency based technique compares the number of times or frequencies that important words of the document occur in the sentences of the documents. Therefore, the sentences that will be selected are those that the important words of the document occur in that sentence more than others. Representing the text using bag of words, the frequency based technique can use the method of word probability to compute the weight for each of the sentences in the text. The sentence with the highest weight will be selected to be part of the summary. The word probability is the probability that a word occurs in a document, which can be used to determine important words of a document. Suppose f(t) is the word probability for a token/word, t, it means that, where n(t) is the number of times that token/word t occurs in the text, and N is the number of words/token in the text. The probability f(t) can be used to determine the important tokens/words in the text. Furthermore, using bag of words to represent the text, each sentence can represent a row entry in the bag of words, while the columns of the bag of words will be the various important tokens/words. Therefore, for each sentence S_i in the bag of words, the weight of the sentence will be given in Equation (1), below:

$$\text{Weight}(S_i) = \frac{\sum_{\forall t \in Si} f(t)}{|\{t \mid t \in Si\}|} \tag{1}$$

$|\{t|t \in Si\}|$ is the count of set of all tokens/words that are in *Si* The sentence with the highest weight will be extracted as the summary. The following example illustrate further, Suppose that we want to use frequency based technique to determine the summary of a text, which consists of three sentences: "This is a model that", "is commonly used to", "Model commonly". From the bag of words, we obtain this occurrence matrix, as shown in Table 7.

Table 7. Occurrence matrix.

	This	Is	A	Model	That	Commonly	Used	To
This is a model that	1	1	1	1	1	0	0	0
Is commonly used to	0	1	0	0	0	1	1	1
Model commonly	0	0	0	1	0	1	0	0

From the bag of words, the total number of words is 11, while the words that have high frequencies of occurring are "This", "is", "a", "Model", "that", "commonly", "used", "to". These words have the following probabilities 1/11 and 2/11. Therefore, the eight words are the important words of the text.

The weight for each of the three sentences is given as:

For sentence 1, the weight is:

$$\frac{1/11+2/11+1/11+2/11+1/11}{1+1+1+1+1} = \frac{7/11}{5} = 7/55$$

For sentence 2, the weight is:

$$\frac{2/11+2/11+1/11+1/11}{1+1+1+1} = \frac{6/11}{4} = 6/44$$

For sentence 3, the weight is:

$$\frac{2/11+2/11}{1+1} = \frac{4/11}{2} = 2/11$$

The weight of third sentence is greater than the weights of the other two sentences, therefore, the summary of the text are "model commonly".

6.4. Feature Based Technique

The feature based technique of extractive text summarization tries to obtain the importance of the sentences in the text by using features of the sentence. Some of the features of the sentence that can be used to determine its importance are: title or headline word, sentence position, sentence length, term weight (word probability), proper noun in the sentence. The weight and score of each of these features of a sentence will be computed using defined algorithms. The weights and scores of all the features of a sentence is combined to determine the score of each sentence, using this formula in Equation 2.

$$Score = \sum_{i=1}^{n} w_i * f_i \qquad (2)$$

W_i is the weight of feature i for a sentence, while f_i is the feature score for feature i for a sentence. The sentence with the highest score will be considered as the most important sentence, which will be selected as the summary.

6.5. Text Rank Algorithm

Text rank algorithm is one of the extractive text summarization algorithm that is based on graph. It uses similar idea as the page rank algorithm, which is used to rank different web sites. The text rank algorithm aims at obtaining the sentence that is most similar to all other sentences in the text. This is achieved by first representing the n sentences of a text in an n square matrix. A mathematical formula, called cosine similarity function or Jaccard similarity function is used to compute the initial similarity measure between any two sentences of the text. This initial similarity measure is written in the cells of the square matrix, except the diagonal cells. Based on the initial similarity measure in the square matrix, the square matrix with the initial similarity measure is converted into a graph *i.e.* a network whose nodes are the sentences and the edges are the similarity measure. The page rank algorithm is applied iteratively with the aim of obtaining the sentence rank at each node of the graph. Select the first n sentence ranking from the highest value to the lowest value to form the n sentences that will summarize the text.

6.6. Conclusion

In this unit, you have learnt the brief history of text summarization and the various approaches to text summarization, together with the various technique/algorithms for extractive text summarization.

6.7. Summary

Having considered text summarization as an important natural language processing task, there are other natural language processing tasks. One of such tasks is sentiment analysis.

7. SENTIMENT ANALYSIS

In unit 5 of this chapter, text classification was considered in detail. It was point out that one of the applications of text classification is sentiment analysis. While text classification tries to identify the category of text, sentiment analysis tries to identify the polarity or emotion in a piece of text (positive, negative or neutral). However, the approach to sentiment analysis is similar to the approaches to sentiment analysis. Because of the wide use of sentiment analysis in businesses, it is worth treating as a separate topic in natural language processing.

7.1. Types of Sentiment Analysis

There are different types of sentiment analysis. Some focus on identifying the polarity in a piece of text (positive, negative or neutral), while others focus on identifying the feeling/emotion in a text (happy, sad, angry, *etc.*). Others may try to identify the intention in a piece of text (interested, not interested). Some of the types of sentiment analysis will be identified and discussed in this section.

7.1.1. Fine Grained Sentiment Analysis

In this type of sentiment analysis, the polarity precision in very important, therefore, the various polarity of the text can be any of the following very positive, positive, neutral, negative, very negative. It can be used for 5-star rating in a review.

7.1.2. Emotion Detection Sentiment Analysis

This type of sentiment analysis identifies the emotions expressed in a text (happiness, frustration, anger, sadness). Most emotion detection sentiment analysis use words of the natural language to indicate the emotion type. However, people can express their emotions in different ways because a word can be used to express different meaning, this remains one of the drawbacks of this type of sentiment analysis.

7.1.3. Aspects Based Sentiment Analysis

Sentiment analysis expresses the polarity about an aspect or feature of a particular thing, rather than the polarity of that particular thing as a whole. Example, sentiment analysis can be based on the duration of a particular product rather than on the product as a whole.

7.1.4. Multi-Lingual Sentiment Analysis

The text of this type of sentiment analysis can be in many languages; therefore, there is the need to perform some pre-processing on the text.

7.1.5. Intent Detection Sentiment Analysis

This type of sentiment analysis identifies the reason behind a particular opinion. This can be very helpful in detecting the area where the customer needs to be helped.

7.2. Applications of Sentiment Analysis

Sentiment analysis is widely used in the following areas:

7.2.1. Social Media Sentiment Analysis

Social media (Facebook, Twitter, Instagram) have become a veritable tool that can be used to reach millions of people about a particular thing and get their feedbacks. You can use sentiment analysis to analyse the various comments of these millions of social media users, with the aim of knowing their general comment, and acting immediately. Sentiment analysis can be done on social media in the following ways:

• Analyze tweets from Twitter, Facebook posts from a specific audience about a particular thing.

• Monitor social media posts on a particular brand and respond immediately.

• Gain insight over the general social media posts on a particular thing.

Social media sentiment analysis offers the following benefits:

• Track trend over time about the opinion of customers on a product.

• Helps to prioritize action based on the negative or positive comments.

• Helps to compete effectively with your competitors. As you monitor your social media comments, you can monitor the social media of your competitors, this will help you to know what to do at any time with the aim of competing favourably.

7.2.2. Internet Sentiment Analysis

Apart from social media, sentiment analysis can also be done across other sites on the internet, like news, bogs and forum discussion. Sentiment analysis over the internet offers similar benefits to sentiment analysis over social media, with wider audience.

7.2.3. Sentiment Analysis on Customer Feedback

Customer feedback on market survey *via* internet or social media can be analysed using sentiment analysis. The aim of the survey may be to identify customers' experience on the use of a particular product with the aim of improving service delivery.

7.2.4. Sentiment Analysis on Customer Services

Apart from customer feedback on market survey, customer service queries can be supported using sentiment analysis for effective service delivery.

7.3. Approaches to Sentiment Analysis

The various approaches that can be used to perform sentiment analysis are similar to the approaches that can be used to perform text categorization. The approaches can be classified as: rule based approach, machine learning based approach and hybrid approach.

7.3.1. Rule Based Approach

The rule based approach to sentiment analysis uses a set of hand written rules to identify the polarity of the text. The rule can involve maintaining a list for each of the polarized words. Whenever it wants to perform sentiment analysis, the number of words in each of the list of polarized words will be counted, the one that has more words in any of the polarized word will be classified as the polarized word for the text.

7.3.2. Machine Learning Based Approach

The machine learning based approach to sentiment analysis is similar to the machine learning approach to text classification. The machine learning algorithms that it uses are supervised, classification based machine learning algorithms, like naïve bayes, decision tree *etc.* The training data, which will be collection of different text, represented as bag of words. Each of the words in the bag of words will be the non-class attribute, while the class attribute will be the various polarized words (positive, neutral or negative), (happy, sad) *etc.* Each of the training data will be classified, and the machine learning algorithm will be trained using the training data. After the training, the computer should be able to predict the class of any text. Refer to the relevant unit and chapter of this book for the detail of any of the supervised classification based machine learning algorithms.

7.3.3. Hybrid Approach

The hybrid approach to sentiment analysis combines the features of the rule based approach and machine learning based approach to produce more accurate results than any of the two approaches.

7.4. Conclusion

In this unit, you have learnt the differences between text classification and sentiment analysis and why we need to consider sentiment analysis separately.

You have also learnt the various types, applications and approaches to sentiment analysis.

7.5. Summary

Python programming language contains modules that can be used to perform some of the natural language processing tasks. Therefore, writing Python codes that will perform the tasks is very important. The next unit will introduce Python programming language and its capability in perform natural language processing.

8. NLP, USING PYTHON PROGRAMMING LANGUAGE

Python programming language is an ideal programming language that can be used to perform text processing. It is an object programming language that beginners can learn. All the natural language processing tasks, like text pre-processing, text categorization, text summarization, and sentiment analysis can be done using Python programming language. Python has a module called NLTK (Natural Language ToolKit), which is exclusively for natural language processing.

8.1. Fundamentals of NLP Using Python

Python programming language is an interpreter, which means that you can interact with it by typing Python command at Python command prompt and Python interpreter responds to the command. After installing Python interpreter on your computer, you can access the Python command prompt using the simple graphical interface called Interactive DeveLopment Environment (IDLE). Once Python interpreter is running, it will display the Python command prompt, >>>, on the screen. The command prompt indicates that Python interpreter is expecting your command [4, 8, 9].

8.1.1. Natural Language ToolKit (NLTK)

The module in Python that is used to perform various natural language processing tasks is called Natural Language ToolKit, NLTK). However, there are other sub-modules in NLTK that perform specific natural language tasks. Table **8**, summarizes the sub-modules in NLTK and the tasks that they perform.

Python allows you to import any of the sub-modules that you intend to use, using the Python's import keyword. After you have installed Python, you need to install nltk module using appropriate web link.

Table 8. Modules and Sub-modules of NLTK.

Natural Language Task	NLTK Module	Specific Functions
Accessing corpora	nltk.corpus	Standard interface to corpora and lexicon
Text pre-processing	nltk.tokenize, nltk.stem	Word tokenizer, sentence tokenizer, stemmers
Discovery of collocation	nltk.collocations	t-test, chi-squared,
Parts of speech tagging	nltk.tag	n-gram, backoff
Classification	nltk.classify, nltk.cluster	Decision tree, naïve bayes, maximum entropy
Chunking	nltk.chunk	Regular expression, n-gram
Parsing	nltk.parse	Chart, feature based
Semantic interpretation	nltk.sem, nltk.inference	Lamdacalcus, first order logic
Evaluation metrics	nltk.metrics	Precision, recall, agreement coefficients
Probability and estimation	nltk.probability	Frequency distribution, smoothed probability distribution
Applications	nltk.app, nltk.chat	Graphical concordance, parsers, wordnet browser

8.1.2. Getting Started with NLP Using Python

Performing natural language processing tasks requires large text. For practice, you do not need to create these texts, rather you just download some texts that come with the NLTK. A large collection of text is called corpus, several of these corpus is called corpora. Therefore, you need to choose the corpus that you want to use. You do this by typing the following in Python command prompt [4, 8]:

>>>import nltk

>>>nltk.download()

A dialog window will appear for you to choose the corpus that you want. Once you have selected it, say book, and click download, it will download the book corpus for you. After downloading the corpus book, you can now load it and use the text that it contains. To load it, type this Python command:

>>>from nltk.book import *

To see all the texts and sentences in the imported book corpus, type this Python command:

>>>texts()

>>>sents()

Each corpus, like book corpus consists of the different titles, while each text title has many sentences. To see the specific text title, type this Python command:

>>>text4()

The Python command: >>>text1.concordance('monstrous') lists all occurrence of the word, 'monstrous' and the context it appears in the text1 title. To generate a random text from a text title, type this Python command:

>>>text3.generate()

To count the number of words and punctuation symbols in a particular text title, type this Python command:

>>>len(text2)

To obtain the list of all vocabulary in the text of a particular text title, type this Python command:

>>>set(text2)

To sort the list of the vocabulary, in a text of a particular text title, type this Python command:

>>>sorted(set(text4))

Python allows you to define function with formal parameter and call it later with the actual parameter. Function can be defined in Python as follows:

>>>from _future_ import division

>>>deflexical_diversity(text)

… return len(text) / len(set(text))

In the above code, the first import code ensures that the division is floating point division, while the second line is the definition of the function, 'def' is a keyword in Python for declaration of a function, while lexical_diversity is the name of the function, the formal parameter is 'text' The next line shows what the function returns after execution. The function divides the number of words in the text by the number of vocabulary in the text. In other words, the function lexical_diversity computes the average number of times a word appears in the text. In order to call the function, you pass the actual parameter as follows:

>>>lexical_diversity(text3)

8.1.3. Using List in Python for NLP

Text can be regarded as a sequence of words and punctuation marks, which can be regarded as a list of words and punctuation marks. Python has a very simple way of representing data (text) in a list. Python represents text in a list in an easier manner than other programming languages, like Java, Pascal *etc.* The text, 'This is my Python code on NLP.' can be represented using list in Python as follows:

>>>mytext = ['This', 'is', 'my', 'Python', 'code', 'on', 'NLP', '.']

mytext is a variable, which has been assigned to the list. The list has been enclosed in square bracket, and each item in the list is separated from the other using a comma. The '=' is the symbol for assignment.

The following Python commands can be performed on mytext:

>>>mytext

>>>lexical_diversity(mytext)

1

>>>

Python concatenates two lists by joining all the items of the two lists together, using the addition symbol as shown below:

>>>yourtext = ['Written', 'by']

>>>['This', 'is', 'my', 'Python', 'code', 'on', 'NLP', '.'] + ['Written', 'by']

['This', 'is', 'my', 'Python', 'code', 'on', 'NLP', '.', 'Written', 'by']

This can also be done using the variable names as follows:

>>>mytext = mytext + yourtext

>>>mytext

['This', 'is', 'my', 'Python', 'code', 'on', 'NLP', '.', 'Written', 'by']

>>>

Python allows you to append a word on the right hand side of a text in a list using this Python code:

```
>>>mytext.append('osondu')

>>>mytext

['This', 'is', 'my', 'Python', 'code', 'on', 'NLP', '.', 'Written', 'by', 'osondu']

>>>
```

To count the number of occurrence of a particular word in a text, use the following Python code:

```
>>>mytext.count('code')

1

>>>
```

You can identify the position or index of a word in a list using this Python code:

```
>>>mytext.index('code')

4

>>>
```

Indexing of a list starts from 0, not 1. Therefore, to know the word that occupies a particular position in a list, or the word with a particular index in a list, use this Python code:

```
>>>mytext [3]

'Python'

>>>
```

Slicing is the process of obtaining a sub-list from a main list, using range of index. Examples, if you want to obtain the sub-list from a list, starting from index 4 to 8, use this Python code:

```
>>mytext[4:8]

['code', 'on', 'NLP', '.']

>>>
```

You can omit the first index in slice command, if the slice will begin from the first word in the text. You can also omit the last index in a slice command if the slice will continue to the last item in the list. The following Python codes illustrate further:

>>mytext[:8]

['This', 'is', 'my', 'Python', 'code', 'on', 'NLP', '.']

>>>mytext[4:]

['code', 'on', 'NLP', '.', 'Written', 'by', 'osondu']

>>>

You can change the item in a list by using an assignment operator on the index of the item. Similarly, you can change the items in a slice in a similar manner. The following Python codes illustrate further:

>>>mytext [1] = 'was'

>>>mytext[2:8] = ['his', 'second', 'code']

>>>mytext

['This', 'was', 'his', 'second', 'code', 'Written', 'by', 'osondu']

8.1.4. Manipulating String in Python

A string is a collection of alpha-numeric characters, or single word. Python manipulates string in a similar way that it manipulates a list. Example, a string can be assigned to a variable, string can be indexed, sliced *etc.* The following Python codes illustrate further:

>>>mysting = 'Python'

>>>mystring

'Python'

>>>mystring [3]

'h'

>>>mystring[1:4]

'yth'

>>>mystring[0:]

'Python'

Python does not support line assignment for string, unlike in list. Example, the following is wrong Python code:

>>>mystring[0:3] = 'pyt'

However, the way some operations are performed with string is different from the way that it is performed in list of items in Python. The following codes illustrate further [7, 8]:

>>>mystring * 2

'pythonpython'

>>>mystring + 's'

'pythons'

>>>

Furthermore, the words of a list can be joined to form a single string and a string can be split to form different words of a list. The following Python codes illustrate further:

>>>' '.join(['Python', 'Programming'])

'Python Programming'

>>>'Python Programming'.split()

['Python', 'Programming']

>>>

8.1.5. Using Python Text Editor

Python Text Editor allows you to write multiple lines of Python codes, edit it and run it instead of typing the Python command in the interactive interpreter one after the other. To access the Python text editor in the Python's Independent DeveLopment Environment (IDLE), go to the file menu, select new. The file editor window appears, which allows you to enter the Python codes in the same way that you enter it in the interactive interpreter. After entering the Python codes, save it with the extension, '.py'. To execute the Python program, go to the run menu in IDLE, select the command Run module. If there is no error, the program will execute in the same way that the interactive interpreter executes it.

8.2. Using Control Structures in Python for NLP

Some of the natural language processing tasks can be performed using basic control structures. Control structures provide a way of controlling the order of execution of task through the use of logical evaluations. The logical evaluation yields a true or false value. Control structures can be classified as selective control structure or repetitive control structure. In a selective control structure, the tasks are performed by selecting between alternatives, while in a repetitive control structure, the tasks are performed in a repetitive manner. Each of these Python control structures will be used to perform natural language processing tasks.

8.2.1. Selective Control Structure

The fundamental selective control structure in Python is 'if' control structure. There are different ways of using the if control structure in Python. The following examples will illustrate the use of the 'if' control structure in Python [9].

>>>mytext = ['This', 'is', 'my', 'Python', 'code', 'on', 'NLP']

>>>[x for x in mytext if len(x) > 3]

['This', 'Python', 'code']

>>>

In the above Python code, the 'if' statement selects all the words in 'mytext', whose length is greater than 3. The result of the selection has been displayed.

Python provides some functions, which can be used to evaluate the logical conditions. They are listed below in Table **9**.

Table 9. Python functions for evaluating logical conditions.

Syntax of Logical Functions	Meaning
s.startwith(t)	Test if s starts with t

(Table 9) cont.....

Syntax of Logical Functions	Meaning
s.endswith(t)	Test if s ends with t
t in s	Test if t is contained in s
s.islower()	Test if all case characters in s are lower case.
s.isupper()	Test if all case characters in s are upper case.
s.isalpha()	Test if all characters in s are alphabetic.
s.isalnum()	Test if all characters in s are alpha-numeric.
s.isdigit()	Test if all characters in s are digits
s.istitle()	Test if all words in s have initial capitals.

The following examples illustrate how Python codes use these logical functions in an 'if' control structure.

>>>mytext = ['this', 'is', 'my', 'thesis']

>>>sorted([x for x in set(mytext) if x.startswith('th')])

['thesis', 'this']

>>>

The code first selects all the words in list of vocabulary of the text, mytext, which start with 'th', afterwards it sorts them.

>>>sorted([x for x in set(mytext) if x.endswith('is')])

['is', 'thesis', 'this']

>>>

The above Python code first select all the words in the list of vocabulary of the text, mytext that ends with 'is', afterwards it sorts them and displays the output.

>>>mytext = ['This', 'is', 'my', 'Thesis']

>>>sorted([x for x in set(mytext) if x.istitle()])

['Thesis', 'This']

>>>

The above Python code first select all the words in the list of vocabulary of the text, mytext, which are title words (*i.e.* starts with capital letter), afterwards it sorts them and displays the output.

Another usage of the 'if' statement in Python is similar to the way it is used in other programming languages, like Java and Pascal. In this type of usage, a block of statement is executed if a logical expression is true. The following example illustrate further.

>>>myword = 'python'

>>>if len(myword) == 6:

… print ('The length of the word is 6')

…

The length of the word is 6

>>>

The above usage of the 'if' control structure can have else option as follows:

>>>myword = 'python'

>>>if len(myword) == 6:

… print ('The length of the word is 6')

… elseiflen(myword) == 3:

... print ('The length of the word is 3')

… else

… print ('The length of the word is neither 6 nor 3')

…

The length of the word is 6

>>>

8.2.2. Repetitive/Looping Control Structure

This control structure is used to repeat or loop the execution of a particular task, a particular number of times, based on certain logical condition. The fundamental example of repetitive/looping control structure in Python is the 'for' control structure, which can be used in the following way [9]:

>>>myword = 'python'

>>>for myword in ['This', 'is', 'my', 'Python', 'code', 'on', 'NLP', '.']:

… print (myword)

…

This

is

my

Python

code

on

NLP

.

>>>

The above Python code executes in this manner. It executes the number of times of the items in the list, which is eight times. At each time, it assigns the appropriate item in the list to myword and prints myword, it goes through the loop again. The above 'for' control structure does not evaluate logical expression. The number of items in the list simply determines the number of times that the statement at the body of the loop will execute. If you want to incorporate logical evaluation in the 'for' control structure, you will nest an 'if' control structure inside the 'for' control structure. The following Python codes illustrate further.

>>>myword = 'python'

>>>for myword in ['This', 'is', 'my', 'Python', 'code', 'on', 'NLP', '.']:

… if 'o' in myword:

… print (myword)

…

Python

code

on

>>>

In the above example, in each iteration, an appropriate word item will be assigned to myword. A logical evaluation will be performed to determine if 'o' is in myword. If it is true, it will print myword, otherwise it will not print myword. The output is displayed as shown above.

8.3. Accessing Text Corpora in Python

Text corpora are large bodies of text that can be used for practical natural language processing. Different individual text corpus, which is large body of text make up text corpora. Each corpus is made of different text files or text titles, while each text file or text title is made of different sentences, and each sentence is made of different words. Natural Language ToolKit, NLTK come with different text corpora, and it allows you to access them in your Python code. The following are the different text corpus that comes with the NLTK: Gutenberg corpus, web and chat text, brown corpus, reuters corpus, inaugural address corpus, automated text corpora, corpora in other languages *etc*. This section will consider how to access and manipulate the texts in these corpora in Python [9].

8.3.1. Gutenberg Corpus

The Gutenberg corpus can be accessed by first loading the NLTK package/module. The following Python codes load NLTK and list all the file identifiers of the Gutenberg corpus.

>>>import nltk

>>>nltk.corpus.gutenberg.fileids()

['austen-emma.txt', 'austen-persuasion.txt', 'austen-sense.txt', 'bible-kjv.txt', 'blake-poem.txt',…]

>>>

Some of the Python codes learnt in the previous sections can be used to display the number of words in any of the listed text file in Gutenberg corpus, as shown below:

```
>>>mybible = nltk.scopus.gutenberg.words('bible-kjv.txt')

>>>len(mybible)

6354823456

>>>
```

Instead of typing this long path, nltk.scopus.gutenberg anytime that you want to call any of the functions that will access the Gutenberg corpus, you can import the Gutenberg corpus once and write the functions without specifying the paths. This is illustrated in the Python code below:

```
>>>from nltk import nltk.corpus.gutenberg

>>>gutenberg.fields()

['austen-emma.txt', 'austen-persuasion.txt', 'austen-sense.txt', 'bible-kjv.txt', 'blake-poem.txt',...]

>>>mybible = gutenberg.words('bible-kjv.txt')

>>>len(mybible)

6354823456

>>>
```

The following Python codes list all the text titles or text files in the Gutenberg corpus. For a text title, it lists all the sentences. For a sentence it lists all the words [9]:

```
>>>from nltk import nltk.corpus.gutenberg

>>>gutenberg.texts()
```

Display Results

```
>>>mybible = gutenberg.sents('bible-kjv.txt')

>>>mybible
```

Display Results

>>>Gutenberg.words(sent4)

Display Result

>>>

8.3.2. Web and Chat Text

This is another corpus that comes with Python's NLTK. The collection of texts consists of web texts, which consists of contents from Firefox discussion forum, conversations overheard in New York, movie scripts, personal advertisement. It can be accessed in the similar way of accessing the Gutenberg corpus, using the following Python codes:

>>>from nltk import nltk.corpus.webtext

>>>webchat.fields()

Display Results

>>>

In addition, there is another corpus of instant messaging chat session, which was compiled by the Naval Postgraduate School. It consists of about 10,000 posts, organized into 15 files. The files of this corpus can be accessed using the following Python codes:

>>>from nltk import nltk.corpus.nps_chat

>>>nps_chat.fields()

Display Results

>>>

8.3.3. Brown Corpus

This corpus was created in 1961 at Brown University. It contains texts from 500 sources, which has been categorized into news, editorials, reviews, religion, hobbies *etc*. The Python codes below access the corpus and list its various categories [9]:

```
>>>from nltk import nltk.corpus.brown
```

```
>>>brown.categories()
```

Display Results

```
>>>
```

8.3.4. Reuters Corpus

This consists of a collection of 10,788 news documents, the documents have been classified into 90 topics and grouped into two sets: training and test sets. The following Python codes will be used to access the corpus and list the various groups and categories/classes of the documents of the corpus:

```
>>>from nltk import nltk.corpus.reuters
```

```
>>>reuters.fileids()
```

Display Results

```
>>>reuters.categories()
```

Display Results

```
>>>
```

8.3.5. Inaugural Address Corpus

The corpus is a collection of 55 texts, one for each of the presidential address. Each inaugural address has a time dimension, which is the year the inaugural address was delivered. The following Python codes can be used to access the corpus and display the field identifiers of the various inaugural addresses [9]:

```
>>>from nltk import nltk.corpus.inaugural
```

```
>>>inaugural.fileids()
```

['1789-Washington-txt', 1793-Washington-txt', 1797-Adams-txt'....]

```
>>>[fileid[:4] for fileid in inaugural.fileids()]
```

['1789', '1793', '1797'...]

```
>>>
```

8.4. Conclusion

In this unit, you have learnt the fundamentals of using Python programming in performing basic natural language processing. This includes the use of lists and strings in natural language processing, the use of the basic control structures in Python, and how they can be used to perform some text processing tasks. The various text corpora have been considered and how they can be accessed using the Python programming language.

8.5. Summary

Most of the tasks in natural language processing, like text categorization, text summarization, and sentiment analysis, use machine learning algorithms to perform the task; therefore, it is necessary that a separate chapter should be devoted to machine learning.

CONCLUDING REMARKS

This unit has focused on various aspects of natural language processing, like text pre-processing, text categorization, sentiment analysis, parts of speech tagging, text summarization, *etc.* Most of these aspects of natural language processing can be automated using Python programming language.

REFERENCES

[1]   D. Jurafsky, and J.H. Martin, *Speech and Language Processing: An introduction to speech recognition, computational linguistics and natural language processing,* 2006. https://www1.essex. ac.uk/linguistics/research/resgroups/clgroup/papers/tmp/5.pdf

[2]   G.J. Carbonell, *A tutorial on natural-languageprocessing,* 1981. https://www.researchgate.net /publication/234796788

[3]   T. Winograde, *Understanding Natural Language.* Academic Press: New York, 1972. [http://dx.doi.org/10.1016/0010-0285(72)90002-3]

[4]   J. D. Booth, "Natural Language Processing Succinctly", *Succinctly eBook Series, Syncfusion.*

[5]   R. Kibble, *Introduction to Natural Language Processing.* University of London, 2013.

[6]   Michael Walker, Introduction to Natural Language Processing: Concepts and Fundamentals for Beginners.*Createspace Independent Publishing Platform,* 2017.

[7]   G.G. Hendrix, and J.G. Carbonell, *A Tutorial on Natural-Language Processing.* ACM, 1981. [http://dx.doi.org/10.1145/800175.809820]

[8]   D. Mertz, *Text Processing in Python.* Addison-Wesley: Boston, 2003.

[9]   Daniel Jurafsky, and James H. Martin, *Speech and Language Processing: An introduction to speech recognition, computational linguistics and natural language processing,* 2013.

[10]   B. Santorini, *Part-of-speech tagging guidelines for the Penn Tree bank project* 3rd revision, 2nd printing. , 1990.

[11]   P. Schachter, "Parts-of-speech systems", In: *LanguageTypology and Syntactic Description.,* T. Shopen, Ed., vol. Vol. 1. Cambridge University Press, 1985, pp. 3-61.

[12]   E. Hovy, "Text Summarization", In: *The Oxford Handbook of Computational Linguistics.*, R. Mitkov, Ed., OUP Oxford, 2005.

[13]   H. Saggion, and T. Poibeau, "Automatic Text Summarization: Past, Present and Future", [http://dx.doi.org/10.1007/978-3-642-28569-1_1]

[14]   M.E. Hannah, and S. Mukherjee, "A Classification-based Summarization model for Summarizing text documents", *Int. J. Inf. Commun. Technol.,* vol. 6, pp. 292-308, 2014. [http://dx.doi.org/10.1504/IJICT.2014.063217]

[15]   D.R. Roddy, *Speech Understanding Systems: A Summary of Results of the Five Year Research effort*, 1977.

[16]   R. Mitkov, Ed., *Oxford Handbook on Computational Lingustics.* Oxford University Press, 2002.

[17]   Y.J. Kumar, O.S. Goh, H. Basiron, N.H. Choon, and P.C. Suppiah, "A Review on Automatic Text Summarization Approaches", *J. Comput. Sci.,* 2009.

[18]   S. Bird, E. Klein, and E. Loper, *Natural Language Processing with Python.*

CHAPTER 4

Machine Learning

Abstract: All discoveries made by man in any discipline, like physical sciences, biological sciences, social sciences, engineering, *etc.*, are based on past experiences or collected data. This means that human beings solve the problem by using past experiences or collected data. Therefore, since one aspect of Artificial Intelligence, as pointed out in chapter 1, unit 1, is to design systems that act like man, it becomes necessary that computer systems should be designed to solve the problem the way human beings solve a problem. This means that computer systems should be designed to solve the problem using past experience or previously stored data. The data are called training data because they are used to train the computer to learn the trend or pattern of the training data. Learning the pattern or trend of the training data as a rule, it uses the learnt rule to solve a subsequent problem using test data that has the same structure as the training data. The vast amount of data in machine learning is divided into two sets, which are the training set and the test set. The training set is used to develop a model, while the test set is used to evaluate the performance of the model. Data splitting technique in machine learning refers to the technique used to split the data into a training set and test set. The aim is to avoid poor generalization, *i.e.*, overfitting or overtraining. Using more training sets improves the accuracy of the model, while using more test data improves the accuracy of the error estimate. An appropriate training/test set ratio of 70:30 is considered appropriate. Machine learning, therefore, is an aspect of Artificial Intelligence that deals with the design of systems that uses a large set of data called training data to solve a particular problem. Machine learning is a broad area in Artificial Intelligence, which will be considered in the various units of this chapter.

Keywords: Classification algorithm, Data pre-processing, Decision tree algorithm, Feature engineering, K-means clustering algorithm, Learner's input, Learner's output, Naive Bayes algorithm, Regression algorithm.

1. INTRODUCTION TO MACHINE LEARNING

Human beings possess the ability to adapt, *i.e.*, convert experience (data) into knowledge (output). In this context, data refers to the basic facts, while knowledge refers to the ability to use the basic fact to solve problems. God created human beings with a well-developed ability to turn experience (data) into knowledge. Therefore, in order to program computers to convert experience (data) into knowledge, you need to understand some fundamental concepts involved in converting data into knowledge. These fundamental learning concepts are discussed in this unit.

1.1. Fundamentals of Machine Learning

A formal definition of machine learning is very important for a thorough understanding of machine learning. In addition to the definition of machine learning, some of the fundamental terminologies and the various components of a machine learning system will be very useful in providing a good foundation of machine learning.

1.1.1. Definition of Machine Learning

Learning can be defined as the process of using past experiences to acquire knowledge. The past experience varies depending on the object that is performing the machine learning. Knowledge is the basis of the action that the object has performed based on past experience. Therefore, machine learning is the process by which the computer turns experience (data) into knowledge. As a discipline, machine learning is an aspect of Artificial Intelligence that deals with the design of a computer system that turns experience (data) into knowledge. These examples will be used to illustrate the learning process.

• Bait Shyness by Rats Learning to Avoid Poisonous Baits

When rats encounter a food item with a new look or smell, they will first eat very small amounts. Subsequent feeding will depend on the flavour of the food and its physiological effect. If the food produces an ill effect on the rat, the food will always be associated with the illness. If the rat encounters the food that smells and tastes like it again, it will not eat it. A learning mechanism is in place here. This is because the rat has used past experience, which is the illness that is associated with eating the food, to acquire knowledge of food safety. This means that if past experience with the eating of the food was negatively labelled, the rat predicts that it will also have the same negative effect when consumed in the future.

• Spam Email Filtering

Suppose you are to program a computer to learn how to filter spam emails. A typical solution, which is similar to the way rats avoid poisonous baits, is to memorize all previous emails that have been labelled as spam emails by the human user. When a new email arrives, your program compares it with the set of all previous spam emails. If it is very similar to one of them, you will tag it as spam email and put it in the spam folder; otherwise, it stays in the user inbox folder [1 - 4].

1.1.2. Types of Learning

The following are the various types of learning

• **Learning by Memorization**

This is a type of learning where the learner does not have the ability to identify an unseen item, except the exact item that it has identified before. This is not a good approach to learning because a learner will not have the ability to identify an item that he has not seen before. An example of this type of learning is the way kindergarten children learn, by rote learning whereby they continuously repeat the same set of alphabets.

• **Inductive Learning Inference**

A successful learner progresses from individual example to broader generalization. This is called inductive reasoning or inductive inference. In the bait shyness example, when the rat encounters a food item for the first time, it uses the smell and taste of the food to determine whether similar food that it encounters in the future is poisoned or not. In the spam filtering example, generalization can be achieved by extracting a set of words in the previous emails that the user has tagged as a spam email. Whenever a new email arrives, the computer searches for any of the words in the email, to tag the email as spam email or genuine.

• **Useful Learning and Superstition**

Inductive learning can sometimes lead to false conclusions or superstition, generally called over-generalization. Learning that leads to a true conclusion is called useful learning. What distinguishes a learning mechanism that leads to superstition from useful learning? This question is very important in the development of automated learning systems. Human beings use common sense to filter meaningless and false conclusions. When you are programming a computer to learn, you must provide well-defined principles that will protect the computer from reaching a meaningless or useless conclusion. The development of such principles is one of the central goals of the theory of learning [1 - 3, 5].

1.1.3. Basic Terminologies in Machine Learning

The spam detection learning task will be used to describe the use of the following basic terminologies in machine learning:

• Instances

These are example records of data used for learning or evaluation. In the spam detection problem, an instance corresponds to an email message that can be used for training and testing.

• Attributes

These are the set of features or characteristics, which are usually represented as a vector. In the email detection example, some important attributes may include the length of the message, the name of the sender, various characteristics of the header, relative frequency of certain keywords, *etc.* An attribute varies from one machine learning task to another. This means that the attributes of a particular machine learning task from the same data may be different from the attributes used in another machine learning task.

• Class Labels

Class labels, or classes, are values or identities assigned to examples. In the spam detection machine learning problem, the class of each email is either SPAM or NON-SPAM.

• Hyper-parameters

These are free parameters that are not determined by the learning algorithm, but they are specified as inputs to the learning algorithm.

• Training Set

They are the instances that are used to train a learning algorithm. In the spam detection problem, the training set (or dataset) is the collection of email instances along with their associated labels. The training sample varies for different scenarios.

• **Test Set**

These are instances used to evaluate the performance of a learning algorithm. This is different from the training set. In the spam detection problem, the test set is a collection of email instances for which the learning algorithm will predict class labels based on the attributes. In order to measure the performance of the learning algorithm, the predictions will be compared with the class labels of the test sample.

1.1.4. Components of a Machine Learning System

Every machine learning system can be modelled to consist of the following components:

• **The Learner's Input**

This can be any or combination of the following: instances or domain set, class labels, training set and test set. They all form input into the machine learning algorithm/program.

• **The Learner's Output**

The learning system is expected to output a prediction rule, which is a function called predictor, a hypothesis or a classifier. The predictor will be used to predict the class of a new test instance. In the spam detector problem, it can be a rule that will be used to determine if an email is a spam or not.

• **A Simple Data Generating Model**

Each instance of the training data will be generated by a particular probability distribution that represents the environment. The learner may not know anything about the probability distribution for generating the training data. However, we assume that there is a correct labelling function, which labels the training data.

• **Measures of Success**

This measures the extent to which the learning process is successful. A measure called error of classifier is defined as the probability of predicting wrong result.

Fig. (**1**) illustrates the model that shows the various component of a machine learning system.

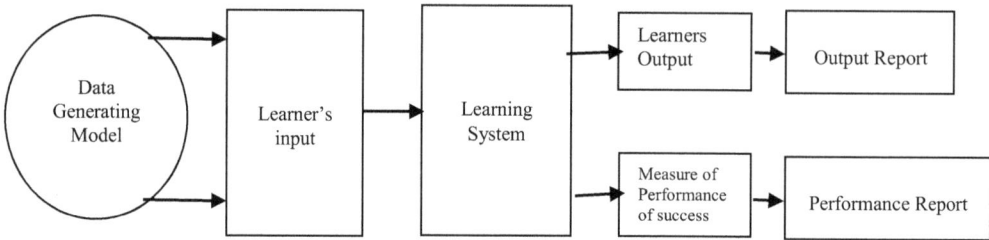

Fig. (1). A model showing the various component of machine learning system.

1.2. Input to Machine Learning System

Learner's input can be any of the following: instances from the domain, class labels and training set. The input to a learner is an important aspect of machine learning system. Some literature try to classify machine learning problems based on the type of data that the learner uses. This is because problems with similar data are likely to be solved using similar techniques. Different structures can be used to represent data in a machine learning system, which include the following [1 - 3]:

• Vectors

Vectors are the most basic structures that can be used to represent data in machine learning. A vector of attributes of an instance can be stored in this form: (blood pressure, height, weight, cholesterol level, smoker, gender *etc.*). This vector can be useful to a life insurance company, who can use the various attribute values in the vector to predict the life expectancy of a potential customer. However, another vector of attributes can be of the form: (name, size, weight, spectral data). This can be useful to a farmer, who can use the attribute values in the vector to predict how ripe a fruit is. The unit and scale of the various attributes can vary, *e.g.* you can measure the weight in kilograms, pounds, grams, tons, stones *etc.* This indeed is a challenge, but an automatic approach can be used to normalize the data.

• Lists

Lists are structures, which can be used to represent input data in a machine learning system. Lists are ideal when you have a collection of features. Suppose the life insurance company maintains the following attributes of a collection of customers, (blood pressure, heart rate, height, weight, cholesterol level, smoker, gender). List will be an ideal structure that will be used to represent the data. Therefore, list can be regarded as a collection of vectors.

• Matrices

Matrices represent pair-wise relationship conveniently. If you are interested in representing the relationship between customers and the products they use, matrices can be used to do that, where the customers can be in the rows of the matrices and the products can be in the columns of the matrices.

• Trees

If you are interested in maintaining the order of the input data in a machine learning algorithm, then tree (binary) tree will be the ideal structure to be used in representing the data. Tree can also be used to represent relationship between collections of items of the same type.

• Graphs

Graphs can also be used to represent relationship between collections of items that are of the same type. Graphs are ideal when such relationships can be shown as a network diagram.

1.3. Characteristics of Input Data

The quality of machine learning prediction, to a large extent depends on the quality of the input data to the learner. Data quality therefore is an important aspect of machine learning. The characteristics of input data are those factors that make for high data quality, which are shown in Table **1**, below.

Table 1. Characteristics of input data to machine learning system.

S/N	Characteristics of Input Data	Definitions
1	Accessibility	Data should be available or easily and quickly retrievable.
2.	Appropriate amount of data	The volume of data should be appropriate for the task at hand.
3.	Believability	Data should be regarded as true and credible.
4.	Completeness	Data should be regarded as true and credible.
5.	Concise representation	Data should be compactly represented.
6.	Consistent representation	Data should be presented in the same format.
7.	Ease of manipulation	Data should be easy to manipulate and apply to different tasks.
8.	Free of error	Data should be correct and reliable.
9.	Interpretability	Data should be in appropriate languages, symbols and units and the definitions are clear.

(Table 1) cont.....

S/N	Characteristics of Input Data	Definitions
10	Objectivity	Data should be unbiased, unprejudiced and impartial.
11	Relevancy	Data should be applicable and helpful for the task at hand.
12.	Reputation	Data should be highly regarded in terms of its source and content.
13	Security	Access to data should be restricted appropriately
14.	Timeliness	Data should be sufficiently up-to-date for the task at hand.
15	Understandability	Data should be easy to comprehend.
16	Value-Added	Data should be beneficial and provide advantage from its use.

1.4. Output from Machine Learning System

Output from machine learning system defines the rule that the learning algorithm will use to solve the problem. Another form of output from a machine learning system is the output report that the algorithm will produce. Each of the different machine learning algorithms will have its own learner's output and its own output report.

1.4.1. Regression Equation

The regression equation, which is the learner's output from regression based machine learning algorithm can be linear regression equation. In linear regression equation, the maximum number of exponent is 1.

The number of variables in linear regression equation ranges from 2 to any number n. If the number of variables in a linear regression equation is 2, the linear regression equation will be of the form, $Y = A + BX$. The attribute of the training data that will not be predicted is X and the attribute of the training data that will be predicted is Y. The regression constants are A and B. If the number of variables is 3, the regression equation will be of the form, $Y = A + BX + CW$. The attributes of the training data that will not be predicted are X and W, while the attribute of the training data that will be predicted is Y. The regression constants are A, B and C. The machine learning algorithm uses the method of least square to determine the various regression constants.

1.4.2. Regression Trees

The regression tree is another structure, which can be used to represent the acquired knowledge or the rule that linear regression machine learning uses to make prediction. It is a tree like structure, where the nodes are the attributes of the data set and the leaf is the predicted value. The branches of each node are the possible values of the attribute of the node can assume. The path from a node to a leaf shows all the instances of a particular data set and the predicted value [1 - 3].

1.4.3. Table

Since memorization based learning does not perform any training, therefore it does not have any output. This means that the input dataset is the same as the output. In some machine learning algorithm, some attributes of the input table can be selected as the output. Therefore, Table is an output to some machine learning algorithm.

1.4.4. Cluster Diagram

The structure that is used to represent the acquired knowledge is the diagram, which shows the various clusters and all the instances of the data set that belong to the various clusters. Some clustering algorithm allow an instance of the training data to belong to more than one clusters, while others use probability of each instance of the data set belonging to each of clusters. Table **2** show the outputs of clustering algorithm, based on probability clustering. Fig. (**2**) illustrates the output from clustering based machine learning algorithm [1].

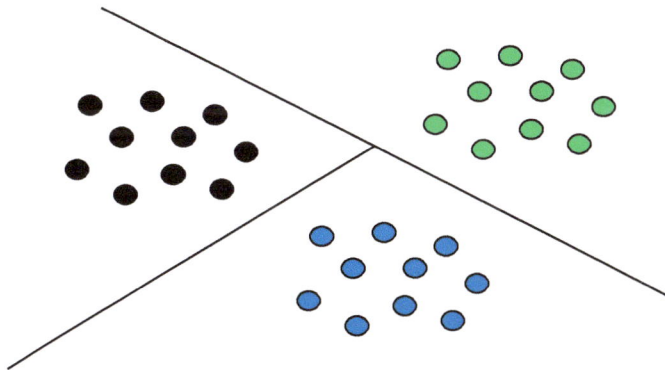

Fig. (2). Visualization of clustering.

Table 2. Probabilities of instances of dataset belonging to various clusters.

Instances	Cluster 1	Cluster 2	Cluster 3
A	0.4	0.1	0.5
B	0.1	0.8	0.1

(Table 2) cont.....

Instances	Cluster 1	Cluster 2	Cluster 3
C	0.3	0.3	0.4
D	0.1	0.1	0.8
E	0.4	0.2	0.4
F	0.1	0.4	0.5

1.4.5. Decision Tree

Like the regression tree, the nodes of the tree are the attributes, which are tested with a constant. The leaves of the tree are the various classes, which the decision tree determines for various instances of input attributes. In order to classify an unknown instance of attributes, it is routed down the tree through the various nodes, based on the values of the various nodes tested. If the attribute at the node that is tested is a numeric value, the test is usually whether the attribute is greater than or equal to a predetermined constant value. This test usually give result to a two or three way split, each split will be represented as an edge or link from the node. A two way split means that there are two possibilities, while a three-way test means that there are three possibilities. For a three-way test, where the attribute is a numeric value, a three way split can be the following: less than, equal to and greater than.

1.4.6. Classification Rule

This can be regarded as an alternative to decision tree, because a decision tree can be transformed into a classification rule. Classification rule consists of two parts, which are the antecedents or preconditions, and consequent or conclusion. The antecedents or precondition are the series of test, which is similar to the tests that are performed at the nodes of the decision tree. The consequents or conclusions are the results of the tests. This is similar to the class that the leaf of the decision tree determines. All the tests are ANDed together, and they must be successful before the conclusion will be fired. Each leaf of a decision tree is a conclusion, which is derived by combination of different antecedents at the node of the decision tree. Therefore, each path from the root of the tree to the leaf consists of a rule that consists the antecedents and the conclusion. Fig. (**3**), shows an example of decision tree.

From the decision tree, there are four leaves, which means that there are four classification rules. Each classification rule has its own antecedents and conclusion. A path from the root of the tree to the leaf is a rule. The following are the various classification rules [2]:

IF x = 1 and Y = 1 the class = A

IF X = 1 and Y <> 1 then class = B

IF X <> 1 and Y =1 then class = C

IF X <> 1 and Y <> 1 then class = D

One major advantage of classification rule over decision tree is that new rules can easily be added to existing rules without disturbing existing rules, whereas adding to the tree structure will require reshaping the whole tree.

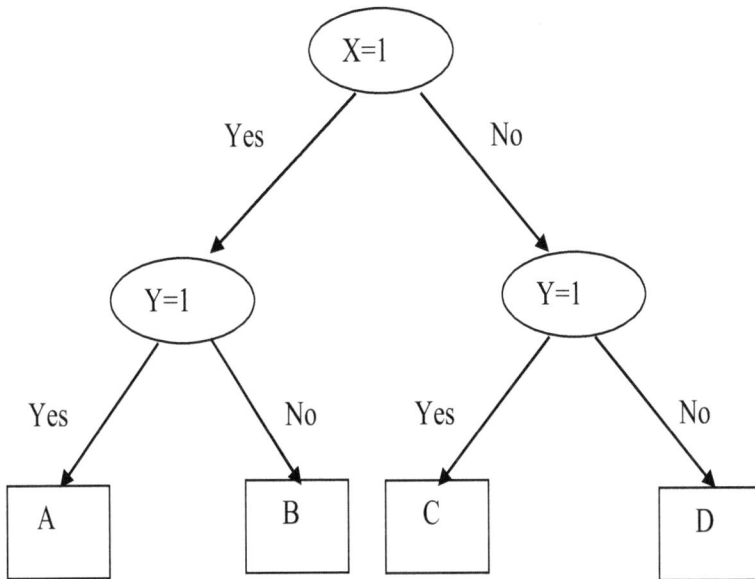

Fig. (3). An example of a decision tree.

1.5. Conclusion

This unit has explained what machine learning is, as an aspect of Artificial Intelligence, together with some fundamental concepts of machine learning. It has also identified and explained the various components of a machine learning system.

1.6. Summary

Having introduced machine learning, the subsequent units will consider the various aspects of machine learning and the various tools and algorithms that they use in order to train the system.

2. DATA PREPARATION

Before a dataset can be analyse using a particular machine learning tool, the dataset needs to be prepared. Data preparation consists of different activities that are aimed at making the data suitable for analysis, using a specific machine learning tool.

2.1. Fundamentals of Data Preparation

Data preparation is the process of making the input data (domain set, instances, training and test sets) suitable for machine learning. It consists of three main activities, which are: data selection, data pre-processing and data transformation [7].

2.1.1. Data Selection

Data selection is the process of choosing part of the available dataset for the machine learning algorithm. This stage is necessary because there is large volume of data available for a machine learning problem, which may not all be used. The chosen sample should be an accurate representation of the available data. The selection process will require excluding the data that are not relevant to the problem at hand.

2.1.2. Data Pre-processing

After the data has been selected, the data needs to be pre-processed. Data pre-processing is the process of manipulating the data so that it will be suitable for the machine learning algorithm. The following three steps are necessary during data pre-processing [7].

• **Data Formatting**

This step formats the data so that it will be in a suitable format for machine learning (structured format).

• Data Cleaning

This step removes all incomplete variables. This involves filtering the data based on the following variables:

a. Insufficient Data: If the machine learning algorithm requires large dataset, and the available dataset is small, then, more instances of the dataset will need to be added.

b. Non-Representative Data: Those data that do not represent the entire data must be removed. This is because non-representative data might lead to making wrong prediction on test data.

c. Substandard Data: Outliers, errors and noise are data that can cause the machine learning algorithm/program to produce wrong model, therefore such data must be filtered.

• Data Sampling

This step chooses the appropriate data from the selected data so that running time and memory requirements for the machine learning algorithm will be reduced. Choosing the right size of the sample is an important step in data preparation. This is because too large or too small sample may produce skewed results. Too small sample can cause sampling noise, which is the wrong effect of choosing non-representative data. An example is checking voter remarks from a very small subset of voters. Furthermore, large samples are good, provided that there is no sample bias, *i.e.* when the right data are picked. An example of sampling bias would occur when checking voter sentiment only from a part of the voters, without considering others [7].

2.1.3. Data Transformation

Data transformation is the process of changing the selected and pre-processed data using any of the following methods:

• Scaling

This involves selecting the right feature scale for the selected and pre-processed data.

• Aggregation

This is the process of collating a collection of data feature into a single data feature.

The data transformation stage in data preparation uses the following important techniques: feature engineering and feature scaling. These will be discussed in detail.

2.2. Data Transformation Techniques

The following are two important data transformation techniques: feature engineering and feature scaling.

2.2.1. Feature Engineering

You will recall that a feature is the same as a set of attributes, which is usually represented as a vector. Sometimes, not all the attributes are required, and at other times, the available attributes may not be adequate, depending on the machine learning problem. Therefore, feature engineering is the process of selecting and extracting the right attributes from the data, which are relevant to the machine learning task and model under consideration. There are different aspects of feature engineering, which include the following:

- **Feature Selection:** This is the process of selecting the most useful and relevant features from the data.
- **Feature Extraction:** This is the process of combining existing features to define more useful ones.
- **Feature Addition:** This is the process of creating more features by gathering new data.
- **Feature Filtering:** This is the process of removing irrelevant features from a particular feature.

2.2.2. Feature Scaling

This is another important step of data transformation stage in data preparation. It is the process of standardizing independent attributes. This process is very important because sometimes the values of attributes may have different range of values that will make it difficult to solve a problem. This means that converting the values of these attributes to the same scale will make it easy to use them to solve the intended problem. Feature scaling uses two methods, which are known as: Standardization and Normalization [7].

• Standardization

This is a popular feature scaling method, which gives the value of a particular attribute or collection of attributes of a feature, a standard normal distribution, called Gaussian distribution.

• Normalization

This is another feature scaling method, which rescale the value of the attribute or collection of attributes of a feature to a uniform scale.

2.3. Conclusion

This unit has explained some of the processes that are involved in preparing data for machine learning.

2.4. Summary

Having introduced data preparation processes, the next thing to do after the data has been prepared is to apply the specific machine learning algorithm to the prepared data. The machine learning algorithms can be classified as: supervised and unsupervised machine learning algorithm. The next unit will focus on supervised machine learning algorithms.

3. SUPERVISED MACHINE LEARNING

Supervised machine learning is one of the types of machine learning where the identity or category or class of the training data is known. The algorithms that it uses are generally called supervised machine learning algorithms and the problems that it solves are generally called supervised machine learning problem. Supervised machine learning problems can be any of the following: prediction problem, classification problem *etc.*

3.1. Prediction Based Machine Learning Algorithm

The dataset of a prediction based machine learning algorithm is in form of a table with rows and columns. The columns are the attributes of the dataset, while the rows are the instances of the dataset. One of the attributes of the dataset will be the prediction attribute, while the others are the non-prediction attributes. With the dataset, the computer system will be trained with the aim of learning the prediction rule. Once it learns the prediction rule, it can use it to make prediction *i.e.* determine the prediction attribute when given the non-prediction attribute as the test data. The dataset of most prediction based machine learning algorithms are numeric values. Examples of prediction based machine learning algorithms are simple linear regression, multiple linear regression, Poisson regression [6, 8].

3.1.1. Simple Linear Regression Algorithm

The dataset of a simple linear regression algorithm is a table with only two columns. One of the columns is the prediction attribute, while the other column is the non-prediction attribute. The rows are the instances of the dataset. Using the dataset to train the system means that the system will use the dataset to identify the prediction rule, which is the learners output that is of the form:

$$Y = A + BX \tag{1}$$

A and B are the regression parameters, which the system determines from the dataset. Once the values of A and B are determined, it means that the computer system has been trained. After the training, with a test data of the non-prediction attribute, X, the computer system can predict the value of the prediction attribute Y. The statistical method of least square is commonly used to determine the regression parameters, A and B. One of the assumptions of the simple linear regression algorithm is that the dataset represents a linear model. Therefore, in order to ensure that the assumption holds, a scatter plot of Y is plotted against X. If the scatter plot does not show linear plot, the simple linear regression algorithm will not be the ideal algorithm to use.

3.1.1.1. Least Square Method of Simple Linear Regression

The least method is a statistical method of obtaining the values of the regression parameters, A and B. The least square statistical formula for A and B are given in Equation 2 and Equation 3, as:

$$B = \frac{\left(\displaystyle\sum_{i=1}^{n} X_i Y_i - \frac{\left(\displaystyle\sum_{i=1}^{n} X_i \right)\left(\displaystyle\sum_{i=1}^{n} Y_i \right)}{n} \right)}{\left(\displaystyle\sum_{i=1}^{n} X^2_i - \frac{\left(\displaystyle\sum_{i=1}^{n} X_i \right)^2}{n} \right)} \qquad (2)$$

$$A = \frac{\displaystyle\sum_{i=1}^{n} Y_i}{n} - B \frac{\displaystyle\sum_{i=1}^{n} X_i}{n} \qquad (3)$$

3.1.1.2. Simple Linear Regression Algorithm Based on Least Square Method

The algorithm that computes the values of A and B using the training data, (X_i, Y_i) and afterwards predicts the value of Y_0, given test data X_0 can be formally stated as:

1. Read Data

1.1 Read n

1.2 Read X_0

2 Predict Y_0

2.1 count = 0

2.2 count = count + 1

2.3 Read X, Y

2.4 sumxy = sumxy + X * Y

2.5 sumsqx = sumsqx + X * X

2.6 sumx = sumx + X

2.7 sumy = sumy + Y

2.8 Repeat 2.2, 2.3, 2.4, 2.5, 2.6, 2.7 until count = n

2.9 B = (sumxy − (sumy * sumx)/n)/(sumsqx − (sumx * sumx)/n)

2.10 A = sumy/n − B*sumx/n

2.11 $Y_0 = A + B*X_0$

3 Display Y_0

The algorithm can be converted into Java program as shown below:

import java.util.Scanner;

class pattern

{ public static void main(String args[])

{

Scanner myinput = new Scanner(System.in);

double n = 0.0, x = 0.0, x0 = 0.0, t0 = 0.0, y = 0.0, sumx = 0.0, sumy = 0.0,

sumxy = 0.0, sumsqx = 0.0, b = 0.0, a = 0.0;

System.out.print("Enter the number of pairs of training data: ");

n = myinput.nextDouble();

System.out.print("Enter the value of test data, x that you want to predict its Y value");

x_0 = myinput.nextDouble();

for(int i = 1; i <= n; i++)

{

System.out.print("Enter a pair of training data: ");

x = myinput.nextDouble();

y = myinput.nextDouble();

sumx = sumx + x;

sumy = sumy + y;

sumxy = sumxy + (x *y);

sumsqx = sumsqx + (x * x);

}

b = (sumxy - ((sumx * sumy)/n))/(sumsqx - ((sumx *sumx)/n));

a = (sumy/n) - (b * (sumx/n));

y_0 = b * x_0 + alpha;

System.out.println("The predicted value is "+y0);

}

}

3.1.1.3. Illustrating the Use of Linear Regression Algorithm

The example that follows will illustrate the use of the above algorithm.

Example:

Suppose the dataset in Table **3**, below represents a linear relationship between X and Y, use an appropriate regression based supervised machine learning algorithm to predict the category of test data, X_0 = 18.

Table 3. An example of linear dataset.

X	2	4	6	8	10	12	14
Y	5	10	15	20	25	30	35

The manual simulation of the algorithm is presented in Table **4**.

Table 4. Manual simulation using the dataset in table 3.

Count	X	Y	Sumx	Sumy	Sumsqx	Sumxy
0			0	0	0	0
1	2	5	2	5	4	10
2	4	10	6	15	20	50

(Table 4) cont.....

Count	X	Y	Sumx	Sumy	Sumsqx	Sumxy
3	6	15	12	30	56	140
4	8	20	20	50	120	300
5	10	25	30	75	220	550
6	12	30	42	105	364	910
7	14	35	56	140	560	1400

From the algorithm:

$$B = \frac{1400 - \dfrac{56*140}{7}}{560 - \dfrac{56*56}{7}} = \frac{280}{112} = 2.5$$

From the algorithm:

$$A = \frac{140}{7} - 2.5*\frac{56}{7} = 20 - 20 = 0$$

From the algorithm:

$$Yo = 2.5*18 + 0 = 45$$

3.1.2. Multiple Linear Regression Algorithm

Like simple linear regression algorithm, the dataset of a multiple linear regression algorithm is a table with three or more columns. One of the columns is the prediction attribute (dependent attribute), while others are the non-prediction attributes (independent attributes). The rows are the instances of the dataset. Using the dataset to train the system means that the system will use the dataset to identify the prediction rule, which is the learners output is in Equation 4.

$$Z = A + BX + CY \qquad (4)$$

A, B and C are the regression parameters, which the system uses the dataset to determine the values. Once the values of A, B and C are determined, it means that the computer system has been trained. After the training, with a test data of the non-prediction attributes (independent attributes), X and Y, the computer system can predict the value of the prediction attribute (dependent attribute) Y. The statistical method of least square is commonly used to determine the regression parameters, A, B and C.

3.1.2.1. Least Square Method for Linear Multiple Regression

The least method is a statistical method of obtaining the values of the regression parameters, A, B and C. The least square statistical formula for A, B and C are given in Equation 5, Equation 6 and Equation 7, as:

$$B = \frac{\left(\sum_{i=1}^{n} Y_i^2\right)\left(\sum_{i=1}^{n} X_i Z_i\right) - \left(\sum_{i=1}^{n} X_i Y_i\right)\left(\sum_{i=1}^{n} Y_i Z_i\right)}{\left(\sum_{i=1}^{n} X_i^2\right)\left(\sum_{i=1}^{n} Y_i^2\right) - \left(\sum_{i=1}^{n} X_i Y_i\right)^2} \tag{5}$$

$$C = \frac{\left(\sum_{i=1}^{n} X_i^2\right)\left(\sum_{i=1}^{n} Y_i Z_i\right) - \left(\sum_{i=1}^{n} X_i Y_i\right)\left(\sum_{i=1}^{n} X_i Z_i\right)}{\left(\sum_{i=1}^{n} X_i^2\right)\left(\sum_{i=1}^{n} Y_i^2\right) - \left(\sum_{i=1}^{n} X_i Y_i\right)^2} \tag{6}$$

$$A = \frac{\sum_{i=1}^{n} Z_i}{n} - B \frac{\sum_{i=1}^{n} X_i}{n} - C \frac{\sum_{i=1}^{n} Y_i}{n} \tag{7}$$

3.1.2.2. Multiple Linear Regression Algorithm Based on Least Square Method

The algorithm that computes the values of A, B and C using the training data, (X_i, Y_i, Z_i) and afterwards predicts the value of Z_0, given test data X_0, Y_0 can be formally stated as:

1 Read Data

1.1 Read n

1.2 Read X_0

1.3 Read Y_0

2 Predict Z_0

2.1 count = 0

2.2 count = count + 1

2.3 Read X, Y, Z

2.4 sumyy = sumyy + Y * Y

2.5 sumxz = sumxz + X * Z

2.6 sumxy = sumxy + X * Y

2.7 sumyz = sumyz + Y * Z

2.8 sumxx = sumxx + X * X

2.9 Repeat 2.2, 2.3, 2.4, 2.5, 2.6, 2.7 and 2.8 until count

= n

2.10 B = ((sumyy*sumxz) − (sumxy * sumyz))/((sumxx *sumyy − (sumxy * sumxy))

2.11 C = ((sumxx*sumyz) − (sumxy * sumxz))/((sumxx *sumyy − (sumxy * sumxy))

2.12 A = sumz/n − B*sumx/n− C*sumy/n

2.13 Z_0 = A + B*X_0+ C*Y_0

3 Display Z_0

The algorithm can be converted into Java program as shown below:

import java.util.Scanner;

class pattern

{ public static void main(String args[])

{

Scanner myinput = new Scanner(System.in);

double n = 0.0, x = 0.0, x0 = 0.0, y = 0.0, y0 = 0.0, z = 0.0, sumyy = 0.0, sumxz = 0.0, sumxy = 0.0, sumyz = 0.0, sumxx = 0.0, b = 0.0, a = 0.0, c = 0.0;

System.out.print("Enter the number of pairs of training data: ");

```
n = myinput.nextDouble();

for(int i = 1; i <= n; i++)

{

System.out.print("Enter a pair of training data: ");

x = myinput.nextDouble();

y = myinput.nextDouble();

z = myinput.nextDouble();

sumyy = sumyy + (y * y);

sumxz = sumxz + (x * z);

sumxy = sumxy + (x * y);

sumyz = sumyz + (y * z);

sumxx = sumxx + (x * x);

}

b = ((sumyy * sumxz) - (sumxy * sumyz))/((sumxx * sumyy) - (sumxy *sumxy));

c = ((sumxx * sumyz) - (sumxy * sumxz))/((sumxx * sumyy) - (sumxy *sumxy));

a = (sumz/n) - (b * (sumx/n)) - (c * (sumy/n));

System.out.print("Enter the pair of x and y that you want to predict ");

x0 = myinput.nextDouble();

y0 = myinput.nextDouble();

z0 = a + b * x0 + c * y0;

System.out.println("The predicted value is "+z0);

}

}
```

Finally, for multiple linear regression algorithm with more than two non-prediction attributes (independent attributes), knowledge of matrices will be required to obtain the least square estimate. Moreover, WEKA, which is a machine learning environment can be used to automate the prediction algorithms.

3.2. Classification Based Machine Learning Algorithm

This is another example of supervised machine learning algorithm. The dataset of classification based machine learning algorithms takes the form of a table, where one of the columns of the table is a class attributes that specifies the class or category of an instance of the dataset. The other columns of the dataset are non-class attributes. This means that before applying the algorithm to the dataset, each instance of the dataset will be classified. After the machine has been trained with the dataset, it will learn the rule that it will use to determine the class of a non-class test data. The dataset of classification based machine learning algorithm may not contain numeric data. If the dataset does not contain numeric data, before applying the classification algorithm on the dataset, the dataset will be categorized using numeric values. Examples of classification based machine learning algorithms are naïve bayes algorithm, decision tree algorithm *etc.*

3.2.1. Naïve Bayes Machine Learning Algorithm

The naïve bayes algorithm is a simple classification algorithm that uses Bayesian theorem of conditional probability as the learner's output rule. The algorithm assumes that the attributes of the training data are independent. It begins by identifying the input attributes and the output attribute, which is the class attribute to be determined, given the input attributes. It also identifies the various classes of both the input attributes and the output attributes to be predicted, and categorizes the training data, where necessary. It proceeds by computing the probability that the output attribute belongs to each of the identified output class, called class probabilities. The algorithm proceeds by computing the conditional probability of each value of the input attribute given each value of the output attribute/class, called conditional probabilities. It then uses the Bayesian theorem as the decision rule for determining the class of input data. The naïve bayes algorithms can be formally stated as follows [2]:

1. Identify the input attribute and the output attribute/class
2. Categorize the training data, where necessary.
3. Compute the class probabilities.
4. Compute the conditional probabilities.
5. Use Baye's theorem to determine decision rule for each instance of input data.

3.2.1.1. Bayes Theorem

This is an important theorem in probability theory, which is used to compute the conditional probability. The naïve bayes algorithm is based on this theorem. Equation 8 states Bayes theorem as:

$$P(h|d) = P(d|h) * P(h)/P(d) \qquad\qquad (8)$$

Each of the probabilities in the above Bayesian theorem means the following:

$P(h|d)$ is the probability of hypothesis h given the data d. It is called the posterior probability.

$P(d|h)$ is the probability of data d given the hypothesis h is true.

$P(h)$ is the probability that hypothesis h is true regardless of the data. It is called the prior probability of h.

$P(d)$ is probability of the data regardless of the hypothesis h.

3.2.1.2. Illustrating the Use of Naïve Bayes Algorithm to Solve Classification Problem

The following example illustrates the use of naïve bayes algorithm in solving classification machine learning problem. The dataset in Table **5** shows ten training data; each has three attributes.

Table 5. Example dataset for naïve bayes algorithm.

Weather	Car	Class
sunny	working	go-out
rainy	broken	go-out
sunny	working	go-out
sunny	working	go-out
sunny	working	go-out
rainy	broken	stay-home
rainy	broken	stay-home
sunny	working	stay-home
sunny	broken	stay-home
rainy	broken	stay-home

The task is to use the naïve bayes algorithm to classify any input data.

1. Identify the input attributes and the output class. From the training data, the input attributes are Weather and Car, while the output class is Class.
2. Categorize the training data where necessary. For the input attribute, Weather, the only values it can take are: sunny or rainy,therefore 1 can be used for sunny, while 0 be used for rainy. For the input attribute, Car, the only value that it can take are working or broken, therefore 1 can be used for working, while 0 be used for broken. Finally, for the output class, Class, the two values are go-out and stay-home, therefore 1 can be used for go-out, while 0 used for stay-home. Using these representations, the training data can be categorized in the Table **6**.

Table 6. Example dataset after categorization.

Weather	Car	Class
1	1	1
0	0	1
1	1	1
1	1	1
1	1	1
0	0	0
0	0	0
1	1	0
1	0	0
0	0	0

3. Compute the class probabilities. Since the class can only be 1 or 0, therefore the probability of a 1 is $5/10 = \frac{1}{2}$. Similarly, the probability of a 0 is $5/10 = \frac{1}{2}$.
4. Compute the conditional probabilities. For attribute, Weather, you compute the probability that it is 1 given that Class is 1. You also compute the probability that it 0 given that Class is 1. Furthermore, you compute the probability that it is 1 given that the Class is 0, and finally you compute the probability that it is 0, given that Class is 0.

From the table above, there are 5 instances of the training data that are in Class 1, the number of instances of training data that are in Class 1 and Weather is 1, is 4. Therefore, the probability that Weather is 1, given that Class is 1 is $4/5 = 0.8$.

Similarly, the number of instances of the training data that are in Class 1 and Weather is 0 is 1. Therefore, the probability that Weather is 0 given that Class is 1 is 0.2.

Similarly, there are 5 instances of the training data that are in Class 0, the number of instances of training data that are in Class 0 and Weather is 1, is 2. Therefore, the probability that Weather is 1, given that Class is 0 is 2/5 = 0.4. Similarly, the number of instances of the training data that are in Class 0 and Weather is 0 is 3. Therefore, the probability that Weather is 0 given that Class is 0 is 0.6.

For the attribute, Car, you compute the probability that it is 1 given that Class is 1. You also compute the probability that Car is 0 given that Class is 1. Furthermore, you compute the probability that Car is 1, given that Class is 0 and the probability that Car is 0 given that Class is 0.

As usual, from the table above, the probability that Car is 1 given that Class is 1 is 0.8, the probability that Car is 0 given that Class is 1 is 0.2. Furthermore, the probability that Car is 1, given that Class is 0 is 0.2, and the probability that Car is 0, given that Class is 0 is 0.8.

These conditional probabilities can be represented in Table 7.

Table 7. Conditional probabilities.

-	-	Class	
-	-	1	0
Weather	1	0.8	0.4
	0	0.2	0.6
Car	1	0.8	0.2
	0	0.2	0.8

5. Use Baye's theorem to determine decision rule for each instance of input data. In order to use the Bayesian theorem to determine the class an input data belongs to, you proceed as follows:

Suppose you want to determine the class that this input data belongs to:

Weather = sunny, Car = working

You will compute the conditional probabilities for the two Classes, and compare their results. The one that has the highest probability will be the class that the input data belongs to.

For Class = go-out (1), you compute the conditional probability that Weather = sunny (1), given that Class = go-out (1), multiply by the conditional probability that Car = working (1), given that Class = go-out (1) multiply by the probability that Class = go-out (1).

For Class = stay-home (0), you will compute the conditional probability that Weather = sunny (1), given that Class = stay-home (0) multiply by the conditional probability that Car = working (1), given that Class = stay-home (0) multiply by the probability that Class = stay-home (0).

When you compute the two conditional probabilities as describe above, you obtain the following:

For Class = go-out (1), the conditional probability is $0.8 * 0.8 * 0.5 - 0.32$

For Class = stay-home (0), the conditional probability is $0.4 * 0.2 * 0.5 = 0.04$

When you compare the two conditional probabilities, you can see that 0.32 is greater than 0.04, therefore, the class that the input data, Weather = sunny, Car = working belongs to is Class = go-out (1).

3.2.2. Decision Tree Machine Learning Algorithm

This is one of the most important supervised machine learning algorithms. Decision Tree algorithm tries to identify ways of splitting a dataset based on certain conditions. The learners' output, which is the goal of the algorithm, is to create a model in form a rule, which is represented as a tree that predicts the value of a target variable by learning simple decision rules inferred from the data features. The decision rules are generally in form of if-then-else statements. The decision tree is a tree-like graph, where the nodes represent the attributes and places where we ask a question. The edges represent the answer to the question and the leaves represent the actual outputs or class labels. A node of the decision tree, therefore acts like a test case of some attributes, while the edges descending from the node are the possible answers to the test case [2].

3.2.2.1. Basic Terminologies Used in Decision Tree Algorithm

The following are the basic terminologies of the decision tree algorithm.

• **Instances:** They are the vectors of features or attributes that define the input space.

- **Attribute:** A quantity describing an instance
- **Concept:** The function that maps input to output
- **Target Concept:** The function that we are trying to find, *i.e.*, the actual answer
- **Hypothesis Class:** Set of all the possible functions
- **Sample:** A set of inputs paired with a label, which is the correct output (also known as the Training Set)
- **Candidate Concept:** A concept which we think is the target concept
- **Testing Set:** Similar to the training set and is used to test the candidate concept and determine its performance

3.2.2.2. Outline of the Decision Tree Algorithm

A general algorithm for a decision tree can be described as follows:

1. Pick the best attribute/feature. The best attribute is one which best splits or separates the data. It is also the attribute that has the most information gain. The most information gain is a measure that shows the attribute that best splits the data set.
2. Ask the relevant question.
3. Follow the answer path.
4. Go to step 1 until you arrive to the answer.

The best split is one which separates two different labels into two sets.

3.2.2.3. Determining the Most Information Gain of Attributes by Visualization

The attribute that best splits the dataset based on the class label of the data set is the attribute that split the dataset in the most uneven way, based on the class label. This is because such a split with that attribute will be very easy to reach a decision that the one that evenly splits the dataset according to the class label. The diagram in Figs. (**4** and **5**) illustrate further.

Table **8** shows sample dataset that will be used to illustrate how to determine the Information Gain by observation.

Table 8. Sample dataset for decision tree algorithm.

Outlook	Temperature	Humidity	Wind	Pay
Sunny	Hot	High	Weak	No
Sunny	Hot	High	Strong	No

(Table 8) cont.....

Outlook	Temperature	Humidity	Wind	Pay
Cloudy	Hot	High	Weak	Yes
Rainy	Mild	High	Weak	Yes
Rainy	Cool	Normal	Weak	Yes
Rainy	Cool	Normal	Strong	No
Cloudy	Cool	Normal	Strong	Yes
Sunny	Mild	High	Weak	No
Sunny	Cool	Normal	Weak	Yes
Rainy	Mild	Normal	Weak	Yes
Sunny	Mild	Normal	Strong	Yes
Cloudy	Mild	High	Strong	Yes
Cloudy	Hot	Normal	Weak	Yes
Rainy	Mild	High	Strong	No

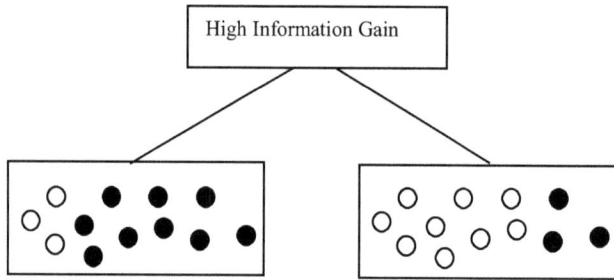

Fig. (4). High information gain.

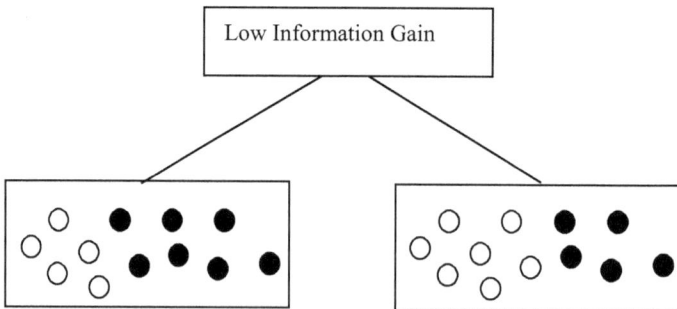

Fig. (5). Low information gain.

The task is to determine the attribute with the most information gain. Table **9** Table **10**, Table **11** and Table **12**, below show the way the attributes distribute the dataset among the class attribute, Play.

Table 9 . Dataset split using attribute, Outlook.

Outlook	Yes	No
Sunny	2	3
Cloudy	4	0
Rainy	3	2

Tabel 10. Dataset split using attribute, Temperature.

Temperature	Yes	No
Hot	2	2
Mild	4	2
Cool	3	1

Table 11. Dataset split using attribute, Humidity.

Humidity	Yes	No
High	3	4
Normal	6	1

Table 12. Dataset Split using Attribute, Wind.

Wind	Yes	No
Weak	6	2
Strong	3	3

From the distribution of the data items among the class play by the various values of the attributes, it is clear that Outlook is the most information gain.

3.2.2.4. Illustrating with Example

Table **13** shows sample dataset that will be used to illustrate how to split training data to determine the attribute that best splits the data among the class attribute.

Table **14** and Table **15** illustrate how each of the attributes, weather and car splits the dataset among the various class categories.

From the two tables, it can be seen that the attribute that best split the data among the various values of the class attribute is Car attribute.

Table 13. Sample data Set for the example.

Weather	Car	Class
sunny	working	go-out
rainy	broken	go-out
sunny	working	go-out
sunny	working	go-out
sunny	working	go-out
rainy	broken	stay-home
rainy	broken	stay-home
sunny	working	stay-home
sunny	broken	stay-home
rainy	broken	stay-home

Table 14. Dataset split using attribute, Weather.

Weather	Go-out	Stay-home
Sunny	4	2
Rainy	1	3

Table 15. Dataset split using attribute, Car.

Car	Go-out	Stay-home
Working	4	1
Broken	1	4

3.2.2.5. Computation of the Information Gain of Attribute by Formula

The above example determines the most information gain of attributes of a dataset is by observation. It may be confusing sometimes to determine the most information gain by observation, therefore, there is a mathematical formula that can be used to determine the information gain of any attribute of a dataset. Suppose k is the number of alternatives of an attribute, the mathematical formula that computes the information gain of an attribute is given in Equation 9 [2].

$$IG = Entropy(parent) - Weighted(Entropy(Children)) \qquad (9)$$

$$Entropy(attribute) = \sum_{i=1}^{k} - p_i \log_2 p_i \qquad (10)$$

P_i is the proportion of class I in the dataset.

Therefore, the most information gain is attribute with the highest IG (Information Gain). The following example will illustrate the use of the formula. Suppose an attribute Weather splits the instances of a dataset as shown in Table **16**, below.

Table 16. Illustrating the use of ig formula.

Weather	Sunny	Rainy	Grand Total
Go-out	12	4	16
Stay-home	1	13	14
Total	13	17	30

This means that the attribute, Weather has two links (children).

For child 1(Sunny): $P_1 = 12/13 = 0.92$, $P_2 = 1/13 = 0.08$

For child 2(Rainy): $P_1 = 4/17 = 0.24$, $P_2 = 13/17 = 0.76$

For Parent $P_1 = 16/30 = 0.53$, $P_2 = 14/30 = 0.47$

Therefore, Entropy(Child 1) = $-0.92*\log_2 0.92 - 0.08 * \log_2 0.08 = 0.391$

Entropy(Child 2) = $0.24*\log_2 0.24 - 0.76 * \log_2 0.76 = 0.787$

Entropy(Parent) = $-0.53* \log_2 0.53 - 0.47 * \log_2 0.47 = 0.996$

Weighted Enthropy(Children) = $(13/30)*0.391 +(17/30)*0.787 = 0.615$

Therefore, IG = $0.996 - 0.615 = 0.38$

The Most Information Gain among all the attributes is the IG with the highest numeric value.

3.2.2.6. Illustrating the Computation of Information Gain with Example

Table **17** shows another sample dataset that will be used to illustrates how to compute the Information Gain of an attribute using the formula.

Consider the dataset below, you are to determine the IG for attribute X.

Table 17. Sample Dataset.

X	Y	Z	C
1	1	1	I

(Table 17) cont.....

1	1	0	I
0	0	1	II
1	0	0	II

The computation of IG for attribute X can be tabulated in the Table **18**, below:

Table 18. Computation of the IG using dataset in table 17.

X	1	0	Parent
I	2	0	2
II	1	1	2
Total	3	1	4
P1	2/3=0.67	0	0.5
P2	1/3= 0.33	1	0.5
E1	$-0.67\log_2(0.67)$	$-0\log_2(0)$	$-0.5\log_2(0.5)$
E2	$-0.33\log_2(0.33)$	$--1\log_2(1)$	$-0.5\log_2(0.5)$

From the table above:

Child 1 Entropy = $-0.67\log_2(0.67) -0.33\log_2(0.33) = 0.5284 + 0.39 = 0.9184$

Child 2 Entropy = $-0\log_2(0) --1\log_2(1) = 0$

Parent Entropy = $-0.5\log_2(0.5) -0.5\log_2(0.5) = 1$

Weighted Children Entropy = $\{\frac{3}{4}\}*0.9184 + (1/4)*0 = 0.688$

IG for attribute X = $1- 0.688 = 0.3112$

3.2.2.7. Using Decision Tree to Solve Classification Problem

Table **19** is a sample dataset that will be used to illustrates the use of Decision Tree algorithm in solving practical classification problem.

The task is to use the Decision Tree algorithm to determine the class Play. Given that Outlook is Rainy, Temperature is Hot, Humidity is Normal and Wind is Weak. We have seen earlier that the most information gain attribute is Outlook, followed by wind, followed by humidity, and the last is temperature.

You can also use the mathematical formula for determining the IG (information gain) of the following attributes: Outlook, Temperature, Humidity and Wind, as shown in Tables **20 - 22** below.

Table 19. Sample dataset for decision tree algorithm.

Outlook	Temperature	Humidity	Wind	Pay
Sunny	Hot	High	Weak	No
Sunny	Hot	High	Strong	No
Cloudy	Hot	High	Weak	Yes
Rainy	Mild	High	Weak	Yes
Rainy	Cool	Normal	Weak	Yes
Rainy	Cool	Normal	Strong	No
Cloudy	Cool	Normal	Strong	Yes
Sunny	Mild	High	Weak	No
Sunny	Cool	Normal	Weak	Yes
Rainy	Mild	Normal	Weak	Yes
Sunny	Mild	Normal	Strong	Yes
Cloudy	Mild	High	Strong	Yes
Cloudy	Hot	Normal	Weak	Yes
Rainy	Mild	High	Strong	No

Table 20. Computation of ig for attribute, outlook.

Outlook	Sunny	Cloudy	Rainy	Parents
Yes	2	4	3	9
No	3	0	2	5
Total	5	4	5	14
P1	2/5	4/4	3/5	9/14
P2	3/5	0/4	2/5	5/14
Entropy	0.971	0	0.971	0.9403

$$\text{Weighted children entropy} = \frac{5}{14}*0.971+\frac{4}{14}*0+\frac{5}{14}*0.971 = 0.6936$$

Information Gain (IG) = 0.9403 − 0.6936 = 0.2467

Table 21. Computation of IG for attribute, temperature.

Temperature	Hot	Mild	Cool	Parent
Yes	2	4	3	9
No	2	2	1	5
Total	4	6	4	14
P1	2/4	4/6	¾	9/14
P2	2/4	2/6	¼	5/14
Entropy	1	0.9183	0.8113	0.9403

Weighted children entropy = $\dfrac{4}{14}*1+\dfrac{6}{14}*0.9183+\dfrac{4}{14}*0.8113=0.9111$

Information Gain (IG) = 0.9403 − 0.9111 = 0.0292

Table 22. Computation of IG for attribute, humidity.

Humidity	High	Normal	Parent
Yes	3	6	9
No	4	1	5
Total	7	7	14
P1	3/7	6/7	9/14
P2	4/7	1/7	5/14
Entropy	0.9852	0.5917	0.9403

Weighted children entropy = $\dfrac{7}{14}*0.9852+\dfrac{7}{14}*0.5917=0.7885$

Information Gain (IG) = 0.9403 − 0.7885 = 0.1518

Table 23. Computation of IG for attribute, wind.

Wind	Weak	Strong	Parent
Yes	6	3	9
No	2	3	5
Total	8	6	14
P1	6/8	3/6	9/14
P2	2/8	3/6	5/14
Entropy	0.8113	1	0.9403

Weighted children entropy $= \dfrac{8}{14} * 0.8113 + \dfrac{6}{14} * 1 = 0.8922$

Information Gain (IG) = 0.9403 − 0.8922 = 0.0481

Therefore, from the computations in the above tables, the information gain of each of the attributes is:

Outlook = 0.247

Temperature = 0.029

Humidity = 0.152

Wind = 0.048

The most information gain is Outlook. Therefore, the root of the decision tree will be Outlook, with the three children as shown in Fig. (**6**) [2]:

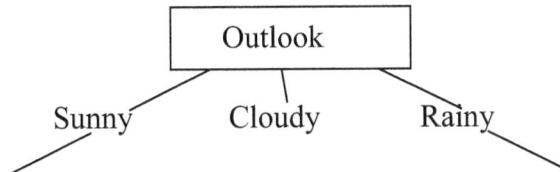

Fig. (6). Using outlook as the root of the decision tree.

When the Outlook is Sunny or Cloudy or Rainy, you need to determine the attribute that will be at the nodes of each of the child's tree. To do that, you repeat the process again. Illustrating when the Outlook is Sunny, you determine the attribute that will be at the node of the child's tree by computing the new information gain for the attributes, Temperature, Humidity and Wind. In order to compute the new information gain for Temperature, Humidity and Wind, you need to see how each of the attributes splits the data when Outlook is Sunny, as shown in Figs. (**7 - 9**).

When you use the new distribution of the dataset to compute new information gain, Humidity will have the most information gain. The process will terminate when each child has only one data item. The derived decision tree is shown in Fig. (**10**).

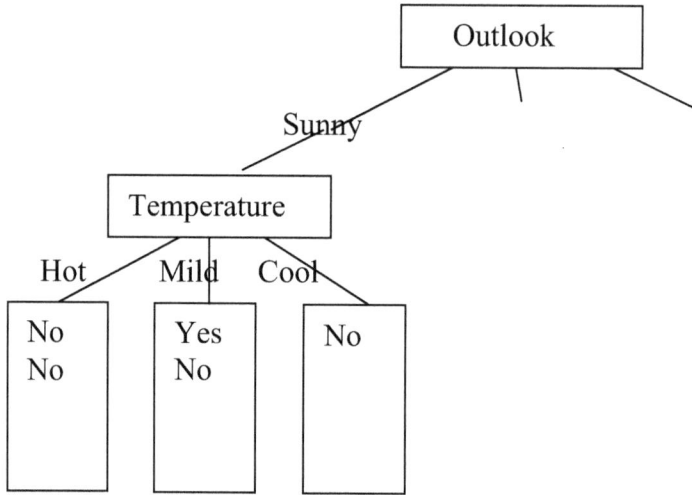

Fig. (7). How temperature splits the dataset when outlook is sunny [2].

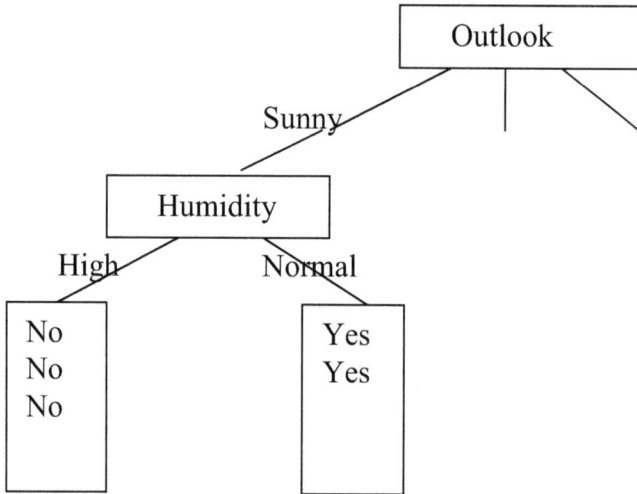

Fig. (8). How humidity splits the dataset when outlook is sunny [2].

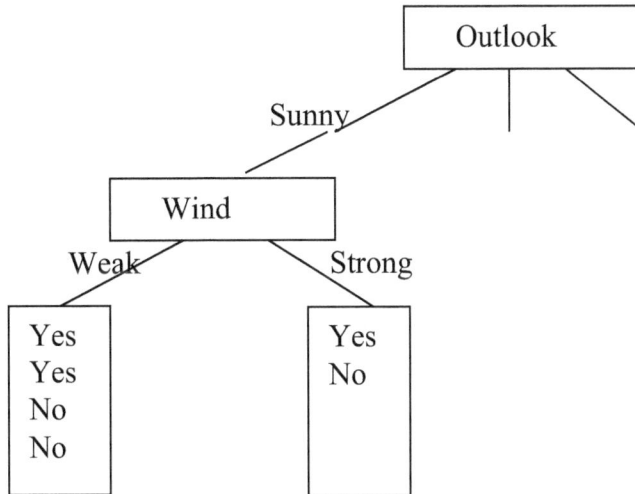

Fig. (9). How wind splits the dataset when outlook is sunny [2].

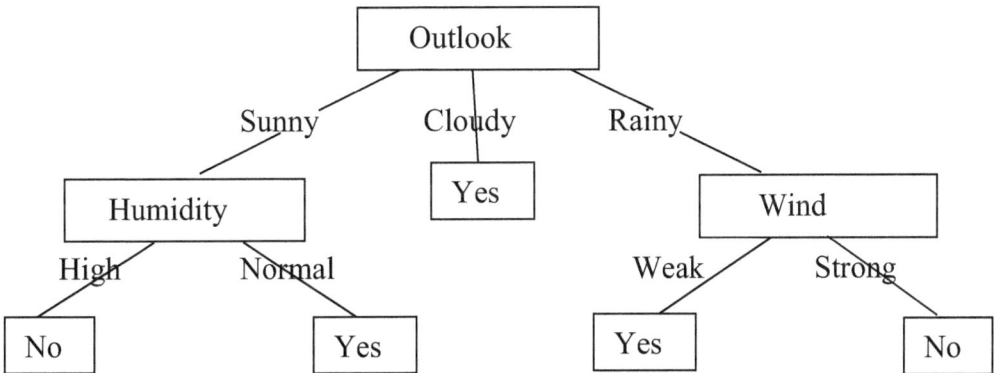

Fig. (10). Decision tree of the dataset.

3.3. Conclusion

Regression based and classification based machine learning algorithms have been considered in detail with examples of sample dataset and how to use the various algorithms to predict or classify a text data.

3.4. Summary

One of the assumptions made in this unit on the use of simple linear regression algorithm is that there must exist a linear relationship between the non-predictive attribute (independent attribute) and the predictive attribute (dependent attribute). If this condition does not hold, using the simple linear regression algorithm will not be the ideal thing. There are some non-linear regression algorithms that can be used in that situation. The next unit will consider in detail some of the simple non-linear regression algorithms.

4. SIMPLE REGRESSION ALGORITHMS FOR NON-LINEAR RELATIONSHIPS

Simple regression algorithms for non-linear relationship between the non-prediction attribute (independent attribute) and the prediction attribute (dependent attribute) are important because sometimes the dataset shows non-linear relationship between the attributes. However, there are different types of simple non-linear relationships that can exist between the independent attribute and the dependent attribute. Each of these relationships requires separate regression algorithm. The type of relationship can be detected by making a scatter plot of the dependent attribute against the independent attribute.

4.1. Types of Simple Non-Linear Relationships

There are different types of simple non-linear relationships between dependent attribute and independent attribute. These simple non-linear relationships can be classified as follows: simple non-linear relationships, polynomial of degree 2 with minimum point, polynomial with degree 2 with maximum point, polynomial of degree 3 with minimum point on the right, polynomial with degree 3 with maximum point on the right.

4.1.1. Simple Non-Linear Relationships

This class of simple non-linear relationship between an independent variable and a dependent variable can be regarded as two linear relationships that intersect at a point. This class of non-linear relationship can take any of the following forms, as shown in Figs. (11 - 14):

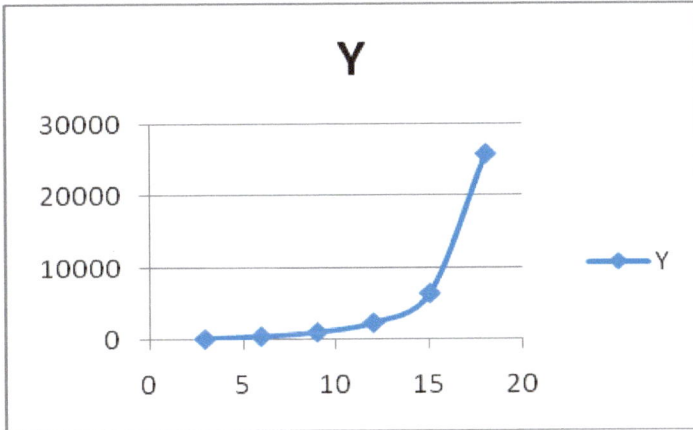

Fig. (11). A form of non linear relationship.

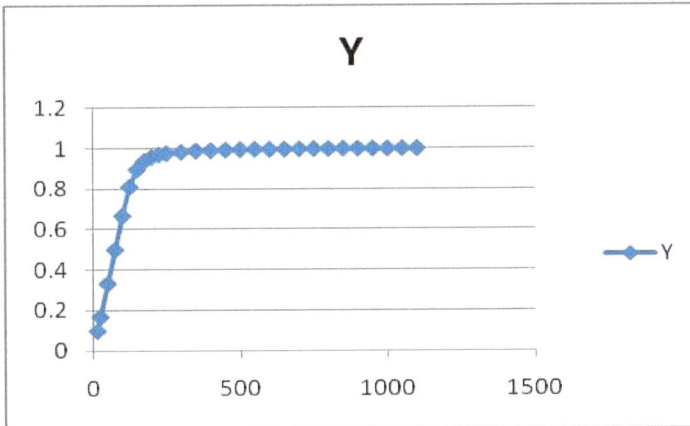

Fig. (12). A form of non linear relationship.

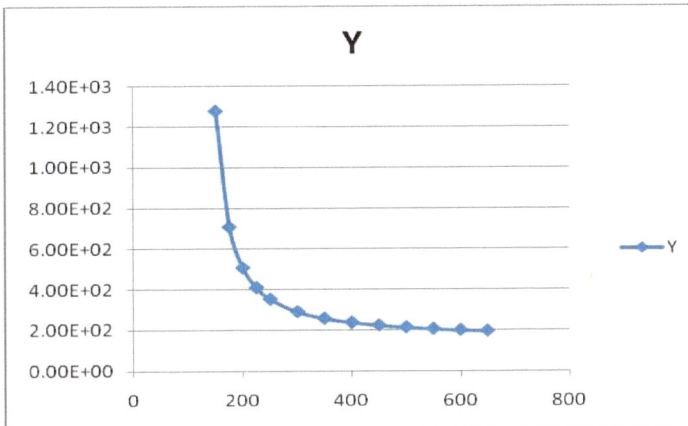

Fig. (13). A form of non linear relationship.

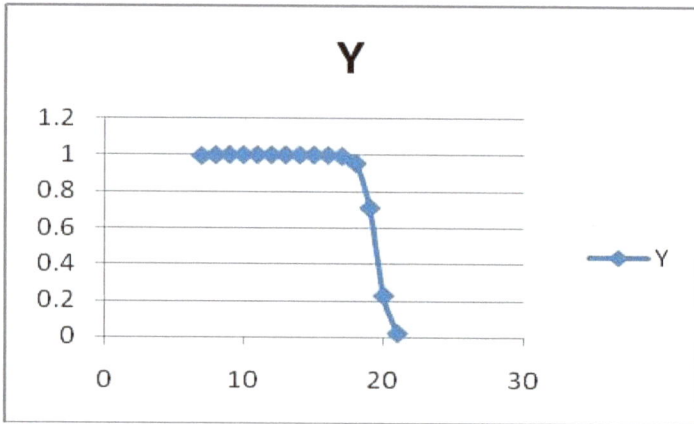

Fig. (14). A form of non linear relationship.

4.1.2. Polynomial of Degree 2 with Minimum Point

This type of simple non-linear relationship is in form of a polynomial of degree 2 with a minimum point, which can be visualize in Fig. (**15**).

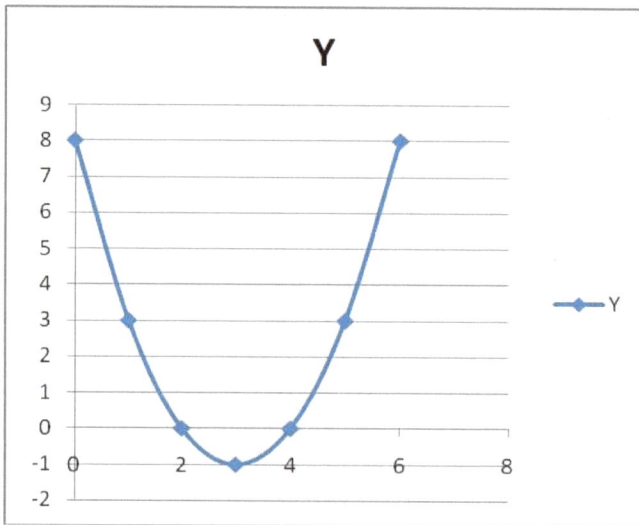

Fig. (15). Polynomial of degree 2, with minimum point.

4.1.3. Polynomial of Degree 2 with Maximum Point

This type of simple non-linear relationship is in form of a polynomial of degree 2 with a maximum point, which can be visualize in Fig. (**16**).

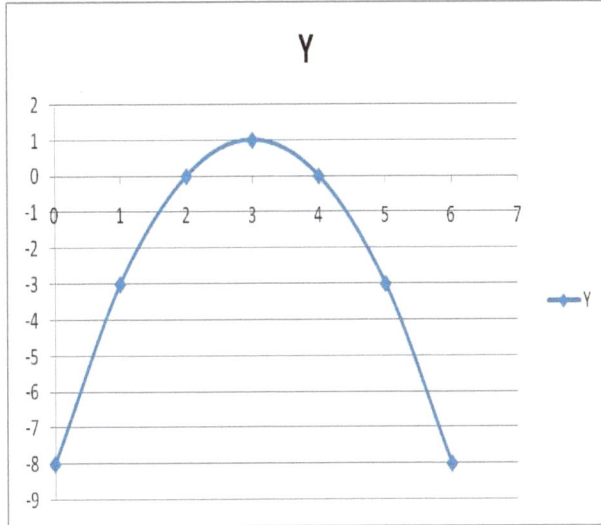

Fig. (16). Polynomial of degree 2 with maximum point.

4.1.4. Polynomial of Degree 3 with Minimum Point on the Right

This type of simple non-linear relationship can be visualize in Fig. (**17**):

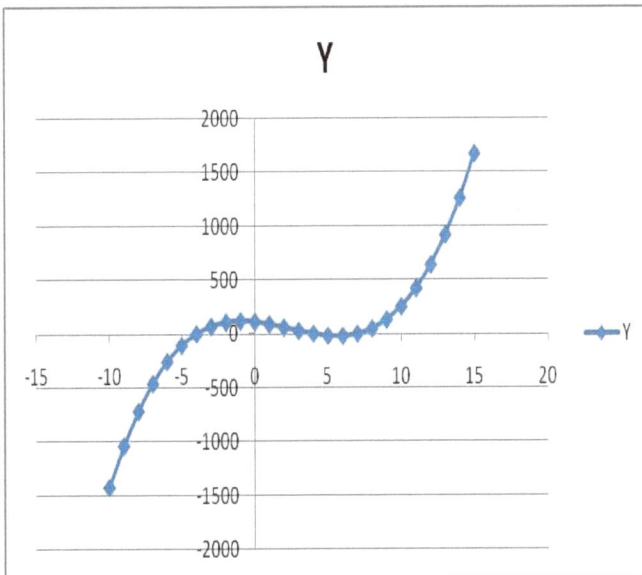

Fig. (17). Polynomial of degree 3, with minimum point on the right.

4.1.5. Polynomial of Degree 3 with Maximum Point on the Right

This type of simple non-linear relationship can be visualized in Fig. (18):

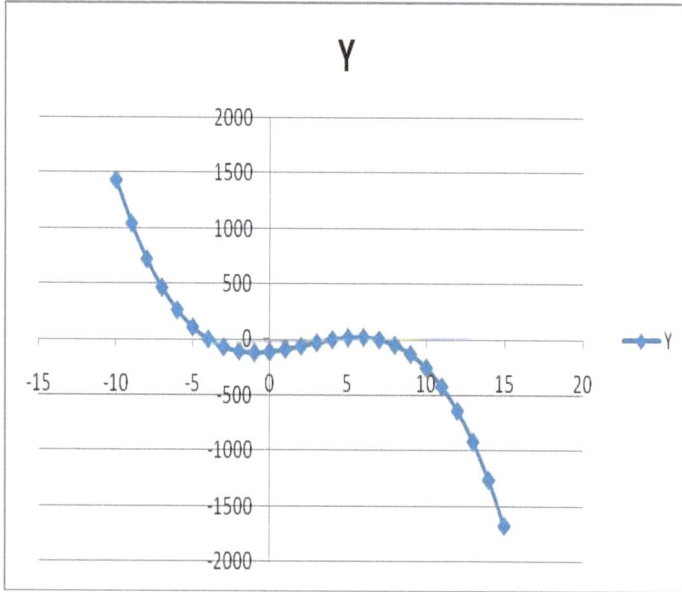

Fig. (18). Polynomial of degree 3, with maximum point on the right.

4.2. Regression Algorithm for Non Lionear Relationships

Each of the simple non-linear relationships will use its own non-linear regression algorithm to train the computer system with the training data. with the aim of identifying the prediction model/rule that will be used to make prediction.

4.2.1. Regression Algorithm for Simple Non-Linear Relationships

The regression algorithm for this type of non-linear relationships, which were shown in Figs (**11 - 14**) will split the training data into two, the first part will be from top, while the second part will be from bottom. The algorithm will use the simple linear regression algorithm to determine the parameters for the linear models of the first and second dataset. Furthermore, it determines the point of intersection of the two linear models. The decision rule that it learns will be thus: If the independent attribute test data is less than the independent value point of intersection, the first linear regression model will be used to predict the dependent attribute, otherwise, the second linear regression model will be used to predict the dependent attribute.

Illustrating further, suppose the independent attribute is represented as X, while the dependent attribute is represented as Y. The simple linear models of the dataset that has been split into two are:

Y = A1 + B1X

Y = A2 + B2X

The point of intersection at X is:

$$intercept \ = \frac{A2 - A1}{B1 - B2} \qquad \textbf{(11)}$$

Therefore, the decision rule that will be used to predict the prediction attribute (label) of a test data X_0 is as follows: IF $X_0 <$ intercept, $Y_0 = A1 + B1X_0$, otherwise, $Y_0 = A2 + B2X_0$. This rule can be stated as a model, as follows:

$$Y_0 = \begin{cases} A1 + B1X_0, X_0 < int\, ercept \\ A2 + B2X_0, \quad otherwise \end{cases} \qquad \textbf{(12)}$$

The algorithm that uses this model to make prediction can be stated formally as follows:

1 Read

1.1 Read n

1.2 Read x0

2 Determine y0

2.1 count = 0

2.2 count = count + 1

2.3 Read x1, y1, x2, y2

2.4 sumx1 = sumx1 + x1

2.5 sumy1 = sumt1 + y1

2.6 sumx1y1 = sumx1y1 + (x1 * y1)

2.7 sumsqx1 = sumsqx1 + (x1 * x1)

2.8 sumx2 = sumx2 + x2

2.9 sumy2 = sumy2 + y2

2.10 sumx2y2 = sumx2y2 + (x2 * y2)

2.11 sumsqx2 = sumsqx2 + (x2 * x2)

2.12 Repeat 2.2, 2.3, 2.4, 2.5, 2.6, 2.7, 2.8, 2.9, 2.10, 2.11 until count = n

2.13 beta1 = (sumx1y1 – sumx1 * sumt1/n)/(sumsqx1 – sumx1 * sumx1/n)

2.14 alpha1 = sumy1/n – beta1 * sumx1/n

2.15 beta2 = (sumx2y2 – sumx2 * sumy2/n)/(sumsqx2 – sumx2 * sumx2/n)

2.16 alpha2 = sumy2/n – beta2 * sumx2/n

2.17 intersect = (alpha2 – alpha1)/(beta1 – beta2)

2.18 IF x0 < intersect THEN

2.18.1 y0 = beta1 *x0 + alpha1

ELSE

2.18.1 y0 = beta2 * x0 + alpha2

3 Display y0

The algorithm can be converted into Java codes as shown below:

```
import java.util.Scanner;

class twolinear
{ public static void main(String args[])
{
Scanner myinput = new Scanner(System.in);
double n = 0.0, x1 = 0.0, x2 = 0.0, x0 = 0.0, y0 = 0.0, y1 = 0.0, y2 = 0.0, sumx1 = 0.0, sumx2 = 0.0;
double sumy1 = 0.0, sumy2 = 0.0, sumx1y1 = 0.0, sumx2y2 = 0.0, sumsqx1 = 0.0, sumsqx2 = 0.0;
```

```
double beta1 = 0.0, beta2 = 0.0, alpha1 = 0.0, alpha2 = 0.0,intersect = 0.0;

System.out.print("Enter the value of x that you want to predict ");

x0 = myinput.nextDouble();

System.out.print("Enter the number of pairs of training data: ");

n = myinput.nextDouble();

for(int i = 1; i <= n; i++)

{

System.out.print("Enter two pairs of training data: ");

x1 = myinput.nextDouble();

y1 = myinput.nextDouble();

x2 = myinput.nextDouble();

y2 = myinput.nextDouble();

sumx1 = sumx1 + x1;

sumy1 = sumt1 + y1;

sumx1y1 = sumx1y1 + (x1 * y1);

sumsqx1 = sumsqx1 + (x1 * x1);

sumx2 = sumx2 + x2;

sumy2 = sumy2 + y2;

sumx2y2 = sumx2y2 + (x2 * y2);

sumsqx2 = sumsqx2 + (x2 * x2);

}

beta1 = (sumx1y1 - ((sumx1 * sumy1)/n))/(sumsqx1 - ((sumx1

*sumx1)/n));

alpha1 = (sumy1/n) - (beta1 * (sumx1/n));
```

beta2 = (sumx2y2 - ((sumx2 * sumy2)/n))/(sumsqx2 - ((sumx2

*sumx2)/n));

alpha2 = (sumy2/n) - (beta2 * (sumx2/n));

intersect = (alpha2 - alpha1)/(beta1 - beta2);

if (x0 < intersect)

{

y0 = alpha1 + beta1 * x0;

}

else

{

y0 = alpha2 + beta2 * x0;

}

System.out.println("The predicted value of Y0 is: "+y0);

}

}

4.2.1.1. Example Illustrating the Use of the Regression Algorithm for Simple Non-Linear Relationship

The following example will illustrate the use of the above algorithm:

Table **24** is a sample dataset, which shows a two attribute dataset, X and Y. When visualized, it can be regarded as two straight lines that intercept at a point. The task is to use the above algorithm to predict the values of Y, when X = 2, and when X = 23.

The first four and the last four data can be used for the two straight lines. Table **25** and Table **26** show the computations for the sample data in Table **24**.

Table 24. Sample dataset.

X	3	6	9	12	15	18	21	24
Y	0.8	0.6	0.4	0.2	0.15	0.14	0.13	0.12

Table 25. Computation for the sample dataset in table 24.

Count	X1	Y1	SX1	SY1	SX1X1	SX1Y1
0			0	0	0	0
1	3	0.8	3	0.8	9	2.4
2	6	0.6	9	1.4	45	6
3	9	0.4	18	1.8	126	9.6
4	12	0.2	30	2	270	12

Table 26 . Computation for the sample dataset in table 24.

Count	X2	Y2	SX2	SY2	SX2X2	SX2Y2
0			0	0	0	0
1	15	0.15	15	0.15	225	2.25
2	18	0.14	33	0.29	549	4.77
3	21	0.13	54	0.42	990	7.5
4	24	0.12	78	0.54	1566	10.38

From the algorithm, $beta1 = \dfrac{12 - \dfrac{30*2}{4}}{270 - \dfrac{30*30}{4}} = \dfrac{-3}{45} = -0.067$

From the algorithm: $alpha1 = \dfrac{2}{4} - \left(-0.067 * \dfrac{30}{4} \right) = 1.00$

From the algorithm: $beta2 = \dfrac{10.38 - \dfrac{78*0.54}{4}}{1566 - \dfrac{78*78}{4}} = \dfrac{-0.15}{45} = -0.003$

From the algorithm: $alpha2 = \dfrac{0.54}{4} - \left(-0.003 * \dfrac{78}{4} \right) = 0.1935$

From the algorithm, the intercept of the two lines is at point

$$intercept = \frac{0.1935 - 1}{-0.067 - (-0.003)} = 12.6$$

From the algorithm, since Xo = 2 is less than the intercept, 12.6, we use the first model to predict the category of the test data.

Therefore, Yo = $-0.067 * 2 + 1 = 0.866$

From the algorithm, since Xo = 23 is greater than the intercept, 12.6, we use the second model to predict the category of the test data.

Therefore, Yo = $-0.003 * 23 + 0.1935 = 0.1245$

4.2.2. Regression Algorithm for Polynomial of Degree 2 with Minimum Point

Suppose X is the non-class or non-prediction or independent attribute, while Y is the class or prediction or dependent attribute. The training data is assumed to represent a simple polynomial of degree 2 with minimum point. The polynomial can be assumed to be two straight lines that cut the X-axis at point X1, X2, which will be the roots of the polynomial. Therefore, the regression algorithm for degree 2 polynomial with minimum point will split the training data into two. The first part of the training data will start from the top, while the second part will start from the bottom. Each of the two parts of the training data will represent a simple linear model. Suppose the two simple linear models are shown below as:

Y = A1 + B1X

Y = A2 + B2X

It means that the roots of the polynomial, *i.e.* where the two straight lines cut the X-axis are given as:

root1 = -A1/B1

root2 = -A2/B2

Therefore, the roots of the simple polynomial can be used to form the polynomial model as:

$$Y = (X - root1)(X - root2) \tag{13}$$

During the training session, the computer will use the training data with the aim of determining the parameters of the polynomial model as shown above. This polynomial model will be used to predict the value of Y, given the value of X.

This can be formalized in the algorithm below:

1 Read Data

1.1 Read n

1.2 Read x0

2 Determine y0

2.1 count = 0

2.2 count = count + 1

2.3 Read x1, y1, x2, y2

2.4 sumx1 = sumx1 + x1

2.5 sumy1 = sumy1 + y1

2.6 sumx1y1 = sumx1y1 + (x1 * y1)

2.7 sumsqx1 = sumsqx1 + (x1 * x1)

2.8 sumx2 = sumx2 + x2

2.9 sumy2 = sumy2 + y2

2.10 sumx2y2 = sumx2y2 + (x2 * y2)

2.11 sumsqx2 = sumsqx2 + (x2 * x2)

2.12 Repeat 2.2, 2.3, 2.4, 2.5, 2.6, 2.7, 2.8, 2.9, 2.10, 2.11 until count = n

2.13 beta1 = (sumx1y1 – sumx1 * sumy1/n)/(sumsqx1 – sumx1 * sumx1/n)

2.14 alpha1 = sumy1/n – beta1 * sumx1/n

2.15 beta2 = (sumx2y2 – sumx2 * sumy2/n)/(sumsqx2 – sumx2 * sumx2/n)

2.16 alpha2 = sumy2/n – beta2 * sumx2/n

2.17 root1 = -alpha1/beta1

2.18 root2 = -alpha2/beta2

2.19 y0 = (x0 – root1) * (x0 – root2)

3 Display y0

The Java program for the above machine learning algorithm follows below:

```
import java.util.Scanner;

class poly
{ public static void main(String args[])

{

Scanner myinput = new Scanner(System.in);

double n = 0.0, x1 = 0.0, x2 = 0.0, x0 = 0.0, y0 = 0.0, y1 = 0.0, y2 = 0.0, sumx1 =
0.0, sumx2 = 0.0;

double sumy1 = 0.0, sumy2 = 0.0, sumx1t1 = 0.0, sumx2y2 = 0.0, sumsqx1 = 0.0,
sumsqx2 = 0.0;

double beta1 = 0.0, beta2 = 0.0, alpha1 = 0.0, alpha2 = 0.0,root1 = 0.0, root2 =
0.0;

System.out.print("Enter the number of pairs of training data: ");

n = myinput.nextDouble();

System.out.print("Enter the value of x that you want to predict ");

x0 = myinput.nextDouble();

for(int i = 1; i <= n; i++)

{

System.out.print("Enter two pairs of training data: ");

x1 = myinput.nextDouble();

y1 = myinput.nextDouble();

x2 = myinput.nextDouble();
```

```
y2 = myinput.nextDouble();

sumx1 = sumx1 + x1;

sumy1 = sumy1 + y1;

sumx1y1 = sumx1y1 + (x1 * y1);

sumsqx1 = sumsqx1 + (x1 * x1);

sumx2 = sumx2 + x2;

sumy2 = sumy2 + y2;

sumx2y2 = sumx2y2 + (x2 * y2);

sumsqx2 = sumsqx2 + (x2 * x2);

}

beta1 = (sumx1y1 - ((sumx1 * sumy1)/n))/(sumsqx1 - ((sumx1 *sumx1)/n));

alpha1 = (sumt1/n) - (beta1 * (sumx1/n));

root1 = -alpha1/beta1;

beta2 = (sumx2y2 - ((sumx2 * sumy2)/n))/(sumsqx2 - ((sumx2 *sumx2)/n));

alpha2 = (sumt2/n) - (beta2 * (sumx2/n));

root2 = -alpha2/beta2;

y0 = (x0 - root1)*(x0 - root2);

System.out.println("The predicted value of To is: "+y0);

}

}
```

4.2.2.1. Example Illustrating the Use of Regression Algorithm for Polynomial of Degree 2 with Minimum Point

The following example illustrates the use of the algorithm, which is shown above.

Consider the two attribute dataset, X, Y, which is shown in Table **27**.

Table 27. Sample dataset.

X	Y
0	8
1	3
2	0
3	-1
4	0
5	3
6	8

When visualized, the dataset represents a polynomial of degree 2, with minimum point. The task is to use the above algorithm to predict the values of Y, when X are 4.5 and 3.

After feature extraction, the set of training data can be reduced to the dataset in Table **28**.

Table 28. Transformed sample dataset.

X1	Y1	X2	Y2
0	8	4	0
1	3	5	3
2	0	6	8

Table 29. Computation for the transformed dataset in Table 28.

Count	X1	Y1	SX1	SY1	SX1X1	SX1Y1
0			0	0	0	0
1	0	8	0	8	0	0
2	1	3	1	11	1	3
3	2	0	3	11	5	3

Table 30. Computation for the transformed dataset in Table 28.

Count	X2	Y2	SX2	SY2	SX2X2	SX2Y2
0			0	0	0	0
1	4	0	4	0	16	0
2	5	3	9	3	41	15
3	6	8	15	11	77	63

From the algorithm, $beta1 = \dfrac{3 - \dfrac{3*11}{3}}{5 - \dfrac{3*3}{3}} = \dfrac{-8}{2} = -4$

From the algorithm: $alpha1 = \dfrac{11}{3} - \left(-4 * \dfrac{3}{3}\right) = 7.67$

From the algorithm: $beta2 = \dfrac{63 - \dfrac{15*11}{3}}{77 - \dfrac{15*15}{3}} = \dfrac{8}{2} = 4$

From the algorithm: $alpha2 = \dfrac{11}{3} - \left(4 * \dfrac{15}{3}\right) = -16.3$

From the algorithm, we obtain the following:

root1 = -7.67/-4 = 1.918

root2 = -(-16.3)/4 = 4.075

When X0 = 4.5, y0 = (4.5 – 1.918) * (4.5 – 4.075)= 2.582*0.425 = 1.097

When X0 = 3, y0 = (3 – 1.918) * (3 – 4.075)= 1.082*(-1.075) = -1.16

4.2.3. Regression Algorithm for Polynomial of Degree 2, with Maximum Point

This regression algorithm is similar to the regression algorithm for polynomial of degree 2, with minimum point. The difference between them is the steps that determines the polynomial model after determining the two roots. The algorithm can be stated below:

1 Read Data

1.1 Read n

1.2 Read x0

2 Determine y0

2.1 count = 0

2.2 count = count + 1

2.3 Read x1, y1, x2, y2

2.4 sumx1 = sumx1 + x1

2.5 sumy1 = sumy1 + y1

2.6 sumx1y1 = sumx1y1 + (x1 * y1)

2.7 sumsqx1 = sumsqx1 + (x1 * x1)

2.8 sumx2 = sumx2 + x2

2.9 sumy2 = sumy2 + y2

2.10 sumx2y2 = sumx2y2 + (x2 * y2)

2.11 sumsqx2 = sumsqx2 + (x2 * x2)

2.12 Repeat 2.2, 2.3, 2.4, 2.5, 2.6, 2.7, 2.8, 2.9, 2.10 until

count = n

2.13 beta1 = (sumx1y1 – sumx1 * sumy1/n)/(sumsqx1 – sumx1 * sumx1/n)

2.14 alpha1 = sumy1/n – beta1 * sumx1/n

2.15 beta2 = (sumx2y2 – sumx2 * sumy2/n)/(sumsqx2 – sumx2 * sumx2/n)

2.16 alpha2 = sumy2/n – beta2 * sumx2/n

2.17 root1 = -alpha1/beta1

2.18 root2 = -alpha2/beta2

2.19 y0 = -(x0 – root1) * (x0 – root2)

3 Display y0

The Java program for the above machine learning algorithm follows below:

import java.util.Scanner;

class poly

```
{ public static void main(String args[])

{

Scanner myinput = new Scanner(System.in);

double n = 0.0, x1 = 0.0, x2 = 0.0, x0 = 0.0, y0 = 0.0, y1 = 0.0, y2 = 0.0, sumx1 =
0.0, sumx2 = 0.0;

double sumy1 = 0.0, sumy2 = 0.0, sumx1t1 = 0.0, sumx2y2 = 0.0, sumsqx1 = 0.0,

sumsqx2 = 0.0;

double beta1 = 0.0, beta2 = 0.0, alpha1 = 0.0, alpha2 = 0.0,root1 = 0.0, root2 =
0.0;

System.out.print("Enter the number of pairs of training data: ");

n = myinput.nextDouble();

System.out.print("Enter the value of x that you want to predict ");

x0 = myinput.nextDouble();

for(int i = 1; i <= n; i++)

{

System.out.print("Enter two pairs of training data: ");

x1 = myinput.nextDouble();

y1 = myinput.nextDouble();

x2 = myinput.nextDouble();

y2 = myinput.nextDouble();

sumx1 = sumx1 + x1;

sumy1 = sumy1 + y1;

sumx1y1 = sumx1y1 + (x1 * y1);

sumsqx1 = sumsqx1 + (x1 * x1);

sumx2 = sumx2 + x2;
```

sumy2 = sumy2 + y2;

sumx2y2 = sumx2y2 + (x2 * y2);

sumsqx2 = sumsqx2 + (x2 * x2);

}

beta1 = (sumx1y1 - ((sumx1 * sumy1)/n))/(sumsqx1 - ((sumx1 *sumx1)/n));

alpha1 = (sumt1/n) - (beta1 * (sumx1/n));

root1 = -alpha1/beta1;

beta2 = (sumx2y2 - ((sumx2 * sumy2)/n))/(sumsqx2 - ((sumx2 *sumx2)/n));

alpha2 = (sumt2/n) - (beta2 * (sumx2/n));

root2 = -alpha2/beta2;

y0 = -(x0 - root1)*(x0 - root2);

System.out.println("The predicted value of To is: "+y0);

}

}

4.2.3.1. Example Illustrating the Use of Regression Algorithm for Polynomial of Degree 2 with Maximum Point

The following example will illustrate the use of the above algorithm.

Consider the two attribute dataset, X, Y, which is shown in Table **31**.

Table 31. Sample dataset.

X	Y
0	-8
1	-3
2	0
3	1
4	0
5	-3

6	-8

When visualized, the dataset represents a polynomial of degree 2, with maximum point. The task is to use the above algorithm to predict the values of Y, when X are 4.5 and 3.

After feature extraction, the set of training data can to the dataset in Table **32**, below.

Table 32. Transformed sample dataset.

X1	Y1	X2	Y2
0	-8	4	0
1	-3	5	-3
2	0	6	-8

Using the algorithm, the following computations in Table **33** and Table **34** follow:

Table 33. Computation of the transformed dataset in Table 32.

Count	X1	Y1	SX1	SY1	SX1X1	SX1Y1
0			0	0	0	0
1	0	-8	0	-8	0	0
2	1	-3	1	-11	1	-3
3	2	0	3	-11	5	-3

Table 34. Computation of the transformed dataset in Table 32.

Count	X2	Y2	SX2	SY2	SX2X2	SX2Y2
0			0	0	0	0
1	4	0	4	0	16	0
2	5	-3	9	-3	41	-15
3	6	-8	15	-11	77	-63

From the algorithm, $beta1 = \dfrac{-3 - \dfrac{3*(-11)}{3}}{5 - \dfrac{3*3}{3}} = \dfrac{8}{2} = 4$

From the algorithm: $alpha1 = \dfrac{-11}{3} - \left(4 * \dfrac{3}{3}\right) = -7.67$

From the algorithm: $beta2 = \dfrac{-63 - \dfrac{15*(-11)}{3}}{77 - \dfrac{15*15}{3}} = \dfrac{-8}{2} = -4$

From the algorithm: $alpha2 = \dfrac{-11}{3} - \left(-4 * \dfrac{15}{3}\right) = 16.3$

From the algorithm, we obtain the following:

root1 = -(-7.67)/4 = 1.918

root2 = (-16.3)/-4 = 4.075

When X0 = 4.5, y0 = -(4.5 − 1.918) * (4.5 − 4.075)= -2.582*0.425 = -1.097

When X0 = 3, y0 = -(3 − 1.918) * (3 − 4.075)= -1.082*(-1.075) = 1.16

4.2.4. Regression Algorithm for Polynomial of Degree 3, with Minimum Point on the Right

Since simple polynomial of degree 3 is expected to have three roots, therefore the training data will be split into three parts. Each of the parts will represent a linear model. The machine learning algorithm will request for three pairs of n data, of the form: X1, Y1, X2, Y2, X3, Y3. The algorithm will computer beta1, alpha1, beta2, alpha2, beta3 and alpha3. Furthermore, the machine learning algorithm will compute the three roots of the polynomial, which will be used to determine the polynomial model. The machine learning algorithm is shown below:

1 Read Data

1.1 Read n

1.2 Read x0

2 Determine y0

2.1 count = 0

2.2 count = count + 1

2.3 Read x1, y1, x2, y2, x3, y3

2.4 sumx1 = sumx1 + x1

2.5 sumy1 = sumy1 + y1

2.6 sumx1y1 = sumx1y1 + (x1 * y1)

2.7 sumsqx1 = sumsqx1 + (x1 * x1)

2.8 sumx2 = sumx2 + x2

2.9 sumy2 = sumy2 + y2

2.10 sumx2y2 = sumx2y2 + (x2 * y2)

2.11 sumsqx2 = sumsqx2 + (x2 * x2)

2.12 sumx3 = sumx3 + x3

2.13 sumy3 = sumy3 + y3

2.14 sumx3y3 = sumx3y3 + (x3 * y3)

2.15 sumsqx3 = sumsqx3 + (x3 * x3)

2.16 Repeat 2.2, 2.3, 2.4, 2.5, 2.6, 2.7, 2.8, 2.9, 2.10, 2.11, 2.12, 2.13, 2.14, 2.15 until count = n

2.17 beta1 = (sumx1y1 – sumx1 * sumy1/n)/(sumsqx1 – sumx1 * sumx1/n)

2.18 alpha1 = sumy1/n – beta1 * sumx1/n

2.19 beta2 = (sumx2y2 – sumx2 * sumy2/n)/(sumsqx2 – sumx2 * sumx2/n)

2.20 alpha2 = sumy2/n – beta2 * sumx2/n

2.21 beta3 = (sumx3y3 – sumx3 * sumy3/n)/(sumsqx3 – sumx3 * sumx3/n)

2.22 alpha3 = sumy3/n – beta3 * sumx3/n

2.23 root1 = -alpha1/beta1

2.24 root2 = -alpha2/beta2

2.25 root3 = -alpha3/beta3

2.26 y0 = (x0 – root1) * (x0 – root2)*(x0 – root3)

3. Display y0

The Java program for the above machine learning algorithm follows below:

```
import java.util.Scanner;

class poly
{ public static void main(String args[])

{

Scanner myinput = new Scanner(System.in);

double n = 0.0, x1 = 0.0, x2 = 0.0, x3 = 0.0, x0 = 0.0, y0 = 0.0, y1 = 0.0, y2 = 0.0,
y3 =0.0, sumx1 = 0.0, sumx2 = 0.0, sumx3 = 0.0;

double sumy1 = 0.0, sumy2 = 0.0, sumy3 = 0.0, sumx1y1 = 0.0, sumx2y2 = 0.0,
sumx3y3 = 0.0, sumsqx1 = 0.0, sumsqx2 = 0.0, sumsqx3 = 0.0;

double beta1 = 0.0, beta2 = 0.0, beta3 = 0.0, alpha1 = 0.0, alpha2 = 0.0, alpha3 =
0.0, root1 = 0.0, root2 = 0.0, root3 = 0.0;

System.out.print("Enter the number of pairs of training data: ");

n = myinput.nextDouble();

System.out.print("Enter the value of x that you want to predict ");

x0 = myinput.nextDouble();

for(int i = 1; i <= n; i++)

{

System.out.print("Enter two pairs of training data: ");

x1 = myinput.nextDouble();

y1 = myinput.nextDouble();

x2 = myinput.nextDouble();
```

```
y2 = myinput.nextDouble();

x3 = myinput.nextDouble();

y3 = myinput.nextDouble();

sumx1 = sumx1 + x1;

sumy1 = sumy1 + y1;

sumx1y1 = sumx1y1 + (x1 * y1);

sumsqx1 = sumsqx1 + (x1 * x1);

sumx2 = sumx2 + x2;

sumy2 = sumy2 + y2;

sumx2y2 = sumx2y2 + (x2 * y2);

sumsqx2 = sumsqx2 + (x2 * x2);

sumx3 = sumx3 + x3;

sumy3 = sumy3 + y3;

sumx3y3 = sumx3y3 + (x3 * y3);

sumsqx3 = sumsqx3 + (x3 * x3);

}

beta1 = (sumx1y1 - ((sumx1 * sumy1)/n))/(sumsqx1 - ((sumx1 *sumx1)/n));

alpha1 = (sumt1/n) - (beta1 * (sumx1/n));

root1 = -alpha1/beta1;

beta2 = (sumx2y2 - ((sumx2 * sumy2)/n))/(sumsqx2 - ((sumx2 *sumx2)/n));

alpha2 = (sumt2/n) - (beta2 * (sumx2/n));

root2 = -alpha2/beta2;

beta3 = (sumx3y3 - ((sumx3 * sumy3)/n))/(sumsqx3 - ((sumx3 *sumx3)/n));

alpha3 = (sumy3/n) - (beta3 * (sumx3/n));
```

root3 = -alpha3/beta3;

y0 = (x0 - root1)*(x0 - root2)*(x0-root3);

System.out.println("The predicted value of Yo is: "+y0);

}

}

4.2.5. Regression Algorithm for Polynomial of Degree 3, with Maximum Point on the Right

This is similar to the regression algorithm for polynomial of degree 3, with minimum point on the right. The minor difference is the step that determines the polynomial that will be used for the prediction. The algorithm is stated below.

1 Read Data

1.3 Read n

1.4 Read x0

2 Determine y0

2.1 count = 0

2.2 count = count + 1

2.3 Read x1, y1, x2, y2, x3, y3

2.4 sumx1 = sumx1 + x1

2.5 sumy1 = sumy1 + y1

2.6 sumx1y1 = sumx1y1 + (x1 * y1)

2.7 sumsqx1 = sumsqx1 + (x1 * x1)

2.8 sumx2 = sumx2 + x2

2.9 sumy2 = sumy2 + y2

2.10 sumx2y2 = sumx2y2 + (x2 * y2)

2.11 sumsqx2 = sumsqx2 + (x2 * x2)

2.12 sumx3 = sumx3 + x3

2.13 sumy3 = sumy3 + y3

2.14 sumx3y3 = sumx3y3 + (x3 * y3)

2.15 sumsqx3 = sumsqx3 + (x3 * x3)

2.16 Repeat 2.2, 2.3, 2.4, 2.5, 2.6, 2.7, 2.8, 2.9, 2.10, 2.11, 2.12, 2.13, 2.14, 2.15 until count = n

2.17 beta1 = (sumx1y1 – sumx1 * sumy1/n)/(sumsqx1 – sumx1 * sumx1/n)

2.18 alpha1 = sumy1/n – beta1 * sumx1/n

2.19 beta2 = (sumx2y2 – sumx2 * sumy2/n)/(sumsqx2 – sumx2 * sumx2/n)

2.20 alpha2 = sumy2/n – beta2 * sumx2/n

2.21 beta3 = (sumx3y3 – sumx3 * sumy3/n)/(sumsqx3 – sumx3 * sumx3/n)

2.27 alpha3 = sumy3/n – beta3 * sumx3/n

2.28 root1 = -alpha1/beta1

2.29 root2 = -alpha2/beta2

2.30 root3 = -alpha3/beta3

2.31 y0 = -(x0 – root1) * (x0 – root2)*(x0 – root3)

3. Display y0

The Java program for the above machine learning algorithm follows below:

import java.util.Scanner;

class poly

{ public static void main(String args[])

{

Scanner myinput = new Scanner(System.in);

double n = 0.0, x1 = 0.0, x2 = 0.0, x3 = 0.0, x0 = 0.0, y0 = 0.0, y1 = 0.0, y2 = 0.0, y3 =0.0, sumx1 = 0.0, sumx2 = 0.0, sumx3 = 0.0;

double sumy1 = 0.0, sumy2 = 0.0, sumy3 = 0.0, sumx1y1 = 0.0, sumx2y2 = 0.0, sumx3y3 = 0.0, sumsqx1 = 0.0, sumsqx2 = 0.0, sumsqx3 = 0.0;

double beta1 = 0.0, beta2 = 0.0, beta3 = 0.0, alpha1 = 0.0, alpha2 = 0.0, alpha3 = 0.0, root1 = 0.0, root2 = 0.0, root3 = 0.0;

System.out.print("Enter the number of pairs of training data: ");

n = myinput.nextDouble();

System.out.print("Enter the value of x that you want to predict ");

x0 = myinput.nextDouble();

for(int i = 1; i <= n; i++)

{

System.out.print("Enter two pairs of training data: ");

x1 = myinput.nextDouble();

y1 = myinput.nextDouble();

x2 = myinput.nextDouble();

y2 = myinput.nextDouble();

x3 = myinput.nextDouble();

y3 = myinput.nextDouble();

sumx1 = sumx1 + x1;

sumy1 = sumy1 + y1;

sumx1y1 = sumx1y1 + (x1 * y1);

sumsqx1 = sumsqx1 + (x1 * x1);

sumx2 = sumx2 + x2;

sumy2 = sumy2 + y2;

sumx2y2 = sumx2y2 + (x2 * y2);

sumsqx2 = sumsqx2 + (x2 * x2);

```
sumx3 = sumx3 + x3;

sumy3 = sumy3 + y3;

sumx3y3 = sumx3y3 + (x3 * y3);

sumsqx3 = sumsqx3 + (x3 * x3);

}

beta1 = (sumx1y1 - ((sumx1 * sumy1)/n))/(sumsqx1 - ((sumx1 *sumx1)/n));

alpha1 = (sumt1/n) - (beta1 * (sumx1/n));

root1 = -alpha1/beta1;

beta2 = (sumx2y2 - ((sumx2 * sumy2)/n))/(sumsqx2 - ((sumx2 *sumx2)/n));

alpha2 = (sumt2/n) - (beta2 * (sumx2/n));

root2 = -alpha2/beta2;

beta3 = (sumx3y3 - ((sumx3 * sumy3)/n))/(sumsqx3 - ((sumx3 *sumx3)/n));

alpha3 = (sumy3/n) - (beta3 * (sumx3/n));

root3 = -alpha3/beta3;

y0 = -(x0 - root1)*(x0 - root2)*(x0-root3);

System.out.println("The predicted value of Yo is: "+y0);

}

}
```

4.3. Conclusion

This unit has considered in detail the various regression algorithms that predicts a dependent attribute, given the independent attribute for different types of non-linear regression models.

4.4. Summary

All the machine learning algorithms that have been considered in this unit are supervised machine learning algorithms. This means that the identities or categories or values of the training data are known. However, there are some machine learning algorithms that the identities or categories or values of the training data are not known. They are called unsupervised machine learning algorithms, which will form the focus of the next unit.

5. UNSUPERVISED MACHINE LEARNING ALGORITHMS

Unlike supervised machine learning algorithm, there is no distinction between the non-class attributes and the class attribute in the training data. This means that unsupervised machine learning algorithm does not have class and non-class attributes in the training data. It can be put in this way, that in unsupervised machine learning algorithm, the identity or category or class of the training data is not known. The type of problem that unsupervised machine learning algorithms solve includes: clustering (grouping of similar data item), density extraction, visualization *etc.*

5.1. Clustering Algorithms

Clustering algorithms are collections of machine learning algorithm that identify groups of similar data in dataset, which can be visualized in order to gain more insight in the dataset. Clustering algorithms can be used to identify the cluster of age groups that patronize a particular brand of product. Clustering dataset into various groups of similar data can take any of the following form [1, 2]:

• Exclusive clustering: Any instance of the dataset belongs to only one group.
• Overlapping Clustering: Any instance of the dataset can belong to more than one group.
• Probabilistic Clustering: Any instance of the dataset belongs to any group with a known probability.
• Hierarchical Clustering: The dataset is split into groups of similar data in a hierarchical manner. Example, the dataset can be split into two main groups, male and female. In each main group, it is refined into subgroups, like age groups, and each age group can be split into smaller subgroups *etc.*

One of classic clustering algorithm is the K-means clustering algorithm.

5.1.1. K-means Clustering Algorithm

The K-means clustering algorithm splits the dataset into K different clusters, hence the letter, K. The choice of the K clusters can be chosen arbitrarily, and the choice of initial central value (centroid) for each cluster can be picked from the dataset arbitrarily. Afterwards, each of the instances of the dataset will be assigned to one of the clusters, based on the cluster that has the minimum Euclidean distance to the instance of the dataset. After the initial assignments of the instances of the dataset to the various clusters, the mean of each of the clusters will be computed, hence the word, means. Each of the means of the clusters will represent the central data (centroid) of the cluster. The centroids or means will be used to reassign each of the instances of the dataset to the clusters, based on the cluster (centroid/mean) with the minimum Euclidean distance to the instance of the dataset. The iteration continues until the current assignment of instances of the dataset to clusters is the same as the previous assignment. The algorithm can be formally stated as follows [1, 2]:

Each instance of the dataset is assigned to a cluster, based on the cluster with the minimum Euclidean distance from the centroid to the instance of the dataset.

1. Data Assignment Step
2. Re-compute the mean (centroid) of each cluster.
3. Repeat step 1 and 2 until the current cluster assignment is the same as the previous cluster assignment.

5.1.2. Using K-means Algorithm to Perform Clustering on Dataset

Table **35** shows a sample dataset that will be used to illustrates the use of K-means clustering algorithm on a dataset of sixty scores, which is shown below.

Table 35. Sample dataset of sixty scores.

77	62	46	53	78	67	71	37	65	60
45	81	46	62	53	50	72	62	75	77
46	52	23	42	51	42	29	34	52	38
50	61	54	50	47	68	50	43	46	45
72	85	47	70	62	46	40	56	46	82
16	45	27	50	39	48	19	23	30	40

Step 1.

I arbitrarily choose K = 4 clusters, and arbitrarily choose the following means (centroids) for the four clusters: 40, 50, 60 and 70. Initial assignments of instances of the dataset to the clusters as shown in Tables **36 - 42**.

Table 36. Initial clustering.

40	50	60	70
37	46	62	77
45	53	65	78
23	46	60	67
42	53	62	71
42	50	62	81
29	46	61	72
34	52	62	75
38	51	56	77
43	52	**61.3**	68
45	50	-	72
47	54	-	85
40	50	-	70
16	47	-	82
45	50	-	**75**
27	46	-	-
39	46	-	-
19	46	-	-
23	50	-	-
30	48	-	-
40	**49.3**	-	-
35.2	-	-	-

Table 37. First iteration clustering.

35.2	49.3	61.3	75
37	46	62	77
23	53	67	78
42	45	65	71
42	46	60	81
29	53	62	72
34	50	62	75
38	46	61	77
40	52	68	72
16	51	62	85

(Table 37) cont.....

27	52	56	70
39	50	**62.5**	82
19	54	-	**76.4**
23	50	-	-
30	47	-	-
40	50	-	-
31.9	43	-	-
-	46	-	-
-	45	-	-
-	47	-	-
-	46	-	-
-	46	-	-
-	45	-	-
-	50	-	-
-	48	-	-
-	**48.3**	-	-

Table 38. Second iteration.

31.9	**48.3**	**62.5**	**76.4**
37	46	62	77
23	53	67	78
29	45	65	71
34	46	60	81
38	53	62	72
40	50	62	75
16	46	61	77
27	52	68	72
39	42	62	85
19	51	56	70
23	42	**62.5**	82
30	52	-	**76.4**
40	50	-	-
30.4	54	-	-
-	50	-	-
-	47	-	-

(Table 38) cont.....

-	50	-	-
-	43	-	-
-	46	-	-
-	45	-	-
-	47	-	-
-	46	-	-
-	46	-	-
-	45	-	-
-	50	-	-
-	48	-	-
-	**47.4**	-	-
-	-	-	-
-	-	-	-

Table 39. Third iteration.

30.4	**47.4**	**62.5**	**76.4**
37	46	62	77
23	53	67	78
29	45	65	71
34	46	60	81
38	53	62	72
16	50	62	75
27	46	61	77
39	52	62	72
19	42	56	85
23	51	68	70
30	42	**62.5**	82
28.6	52	-	**76.4**
-	50	-	-
-	54	-	-
-	50	-	-
-	43	-	-
-	46	-	-
-	50	-	-
-	47	-	-

(Table 39) cont.....

-	45	-	-
-	47	-	-
-	46	-	-
-	40	-	-
-	46	-	-
-	45	-	-
-	50	-	-
-	48	-	-
-	40	-	-
-	**47.3**	-	-

Table 40. Fifth iteration.

28.6	**47.3**	**62.5**	**76.4**
37	46	62	77
23	53	67	78
29	45	65	71
34	46	60	81
16	53	62	72
27	50	62	75
19	46	61	77
23	52	68	72
30	42	62	85
26.4	52	56	70
-	38	**62.5**	82
-	50	-	**76.4**
-	54	-	-
-	50	-	-
-	47	-	-
-	50	-	-
-	43	-	-
-	46	-	-
-	45	-	-
-	47	-	-
-	46	-	-
-	40	-	-

(Table 40) cont.....

-	46	-	-
-	45	-	-
-	42	-	-
-	51	-	-
-	50	-	-
-	39	-	-
-	48	-	-
-	40	-	-
-	**46.7**	-	-

Table 41. Sixth iteration.

26.4	**46.7**	**62.5**	**76.4**
37	46	62	77
23	53	67	78
29	45	65	71
34	46	60	81
16	53	62	72
27	50	62	75
19	46	61	77
23	52	68	72
30	42	62	85
26.4	52	56	70
-	38	**62.5**	82
-	50	-	**76.4**
-	54	-	-
-	50	-	-
-	47	-	-
-	50	-	-
-	43	-	-
-	46	-	-
-	45	-	-
-	47	-	-
-	46	-	-
-	40	-	-
-	46	-	-

(Table 41) cont.....

-	45	-	-
-	42	-	-
-	51	-	-
-	50	-	-
-	39	-	-
-	48	-	-
-	40	-	-
-	**46.7**	-	-

Table 42. Seventh Iteration Clustering.

26.4	**46.7**	**62.5**	**76.4**
37	46	62	77
23	53	67	78
29	45	65	71
34	46	60	81
16	53	62	72
27	50	62	75
19	46	61	77
23	52	68	72
30	42	62	85
	52	56	70
-	38		82
-	50	-	
-	54	-	-
-	50	-	-
-	47	-	-
-	50	-	-
-	43	-	-
-	46	-	-
-	45	-	-
-	47	-	-
-	46	-	-
-	40	-	-
-	46	-	-
-	45	-	-

(Table 42) cont.....

-	42	-	-
-	51	-	-
-	50	-	-
-	39	-	-
-	48	-	-
-	40	-	-

Observe that the seventh iteration clustering is the same as the sixth iteration clustering, therefore, the seventh iteration clustering is the final cluster.

5.1.3. Choosing the Number of K Clusters

The algorithm described above arbitrarily chooses the number of clusters, K that will be used to split the dataset into various clusters. To find the best number of clusters, K, different values of K can be chosen arbitrarily to spilt the dataset, and comparing the values of the total squared Euclidean distance of all the instances of the dataset to their centroids/means, for all the clusters. The best value of K is the one that has the minimum total squared Euclidean distance of the instances of the dataset to the centroid/mean, for all the clusters. Choosing K to be close of the number of instances of the dataset will yield minimum total squared Euclidean distance of instances of the dataset to the centroid/mean for all the clusters. However, this approach may not help much in gaining insight into the dataset [1, 2].

Another approach to determine the best number of K clusters is to start with very small value of K = 2. After performing clustering with K = 2, try to perform another clustering with K = 2 for each of the clusters you obtained before. Continue this process until it is no longer possible to obtain any further cluster. The total number of clusters will be the best value of K clusters.

5.1.4. Using WEKA to Perform K-means Clustering on Dataset

Table **43** shows the dataset of sixty scores in an examination. The dataset was entered as a single column data in MS Excel. It was converted into CSV file format and opened in WEKA Explorer.

Table 43. Sample dataset of sixty scores.

77	62	46	53	78	67	71	37	65	60
45	81	46	62	53	50	72	62	75	77

(Table 43) cont.....

46	52	23	42	51	42	29	34	52	38
50	61	54	50	47	68	50	43	46	45
72	85	47	70	62	46	40	56	46	82
16	45	27	50	39	48	19	23	30	40

WEKA was used to perform K-means clustering on the dataset, with 4 clusters. The result obtained from WEKA is shown below in Fig. (**19**). It must be observed the difference between the result obtain with the use of WEKA and the manual computation of the algorithm is the arbitrarily choice of the 4 centroids for the four clusters.

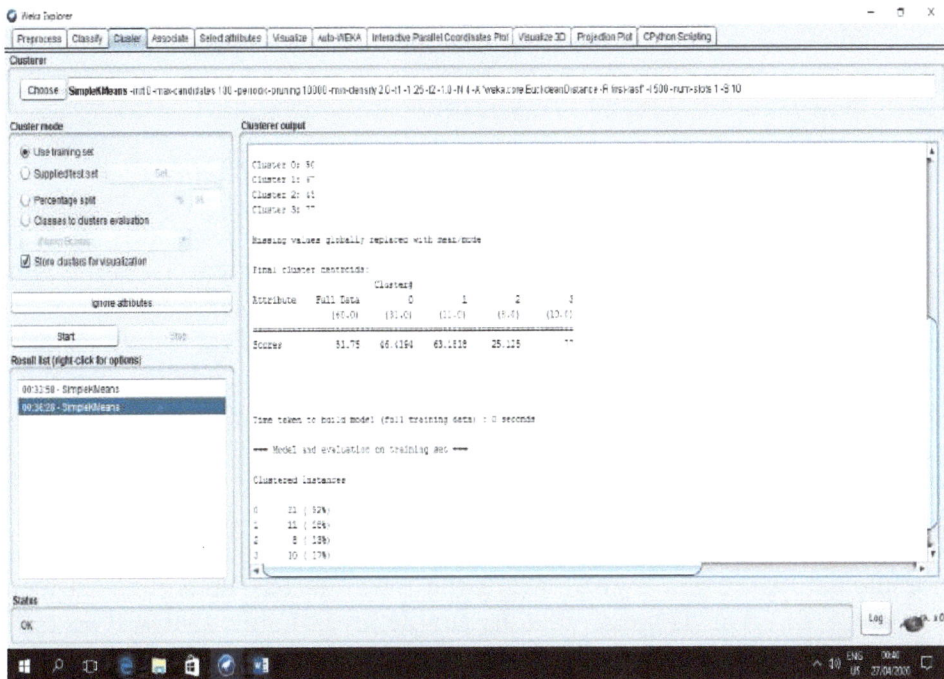

Fig. (19). Result of weka k-means clustering.

5.2. Data Visualization

One of the problems that unsupervised machine learning algorithms solve is visualization of dataset. Data visualization can be defined as the process of representing data as visual graphic image for the purpose of gaining more insight into the data. It has been said that a picture or graphic image is better than one thousand words. Therefore, data visualization helps us to easily understand the structure or pattern of a particular data [1, 2].

Furthermore, another problem that unsupervised machine learning algorithms solve is density extraction, which is the process of summarizing the distribution of data. Though there are different methods of performing density extraction, however, the use of probability distribution function can be used to show the probability distribution of data for a defined random variable of a particular dataset.

There are different techniques that can be used to visualize dataset. These various techniques can be classified as follows: geometric, pixel oriented, icon-based, hierarchical and graph based techniques. In a geometric technique of data visualization, a two dimensional space is used to visualize the training data or dataset as point. The geometric technique includes the following: scatter plot, radviz, polyviz and gridviz. Visualization of the probability distribution of dataset can also help to gain more insight of the data.

5.2.1. Visualizing Two Dimensional Linear Dataset Using Scatter Plot

Though the simple linear regression algorithm predicts the class attribute, given the non-class attribute. This prediction occurs after the system has been trained using the training data. Training the system means to determine the various parameters of the simple linear model using the method of least square. However, the simple linear regression algorithm does not help in visualizing the graphic image that represents the dataset. This is because the simple linear regression algorithm is a supervised machine learning algorithm, not an unsupervised machine learning algorithm. In order to visualize the graphic image that represents the training data, which is the straight line, the parameters of the determined linear model can be used to draw the straight line. Example, suppose, the parameters of the linear model that the machine has determined after the training are A and B. This means that the simple linear model that will be used to visualize the straight line, which represent the training data is $Y = A + BX$. Suppose a particular two dimensional dataset has this simple linear model after the training: $Y = 0.8862X + 5.7368$. It means that the intercept along the Y axis is 5.7368 and the slope is 0.8862. These two parameters of the simple linear model can be used to visualize the graphic image (straight line) that the training dataset represents.

Python programming language can be used to visualize the dataset that represents the above linear model as shown in Fig (**20**):

Y

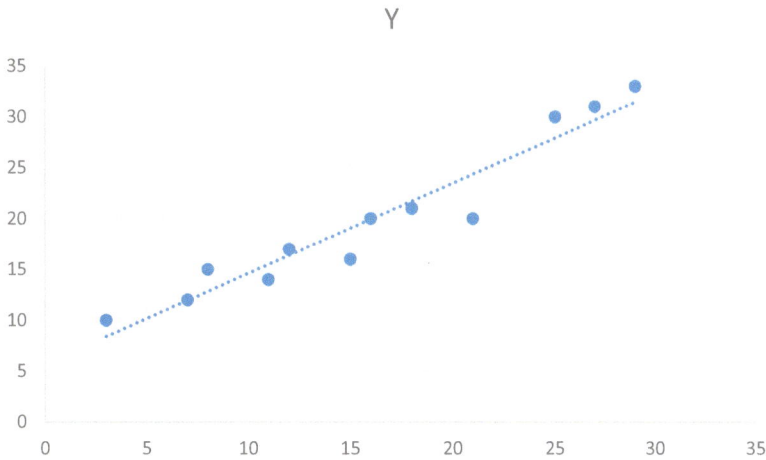

Fig. (20). Result of visualization of linear dataset model.

5.2.2. *Visualizing Probability Distribution of Dataset Using Scatter Plot*

Visualizing the probability distribution of a defined random variable of a dataset can provide insight into a dataset. There are different types of probability distribution functions, which can be classified as discrete or continuous probability distribution function. In a discrete probability distribution function, the random variable assumes distinct values, while in a continuous probability distribution function, the random variable assumes a range of value. Examples of discrete probability distribution functions are Poisson, Binomial, Bernoulli, *etc.* Examples of continuous probability distribution functions are Exponential, Normal probability distribution functions. Each probability distribution function has its own parameter(s) and mathematical model, and it is used for a specific defined random variable. Each of these probability distribution function will be considered in detail by identifying its defined random variable, mathematical model, Python codes that can be used to generate the random variable and for displaying its distribution for the purpose of visualization.

5.2.2.1. Binomial Probability Distribution Function

The Binomial probability distribution function is a discrete probability distribution function, which is used for a random variable that its value can have only two possible values (HEAD or TAIL, UP or DOWN, LEFT or RIGHT, 0 or 1, SUCCESS or FAILURE). The random experiment from which a binomial random variable is defined will be repeated n different number times, each repetition will have a known probability p, of one of the two possible outcome occurring. The mathematical function for the Binomial probability distribution function is given in Equation 14, as:

$$P(X = x) = \begin{cases} {}^{n}C_{x}p^{x}(1-p)^{n-x}, x = 0,1,2,3,4...n \\ 0, \quad otherwise \end{cases} \tag{14}$$

The following example will illustrate how a binomial random variable can be defined from a dataset and all the parameters of the binomial random variable obtained from the dataset. The dataset in Table **44**, below shows the scores of sixty students in an examination.

Table 44. Sample dataset of scores of sixty students.

77	62	46	53	78	67	71	37	65	60
45	81	46	62	53	50	72	62	75	77
46	52	23	42	51	42	29	34	52	38
50	61	54	50	47	68	50	43	46	45
72	85	47	70	62	46	40	56	46	82
16	45	27	50	39	48	19	23	30	40

Suppose a random variable X is defined as the number of students that passed the examination, where pass mark is defined as a score that is more than or equal to 45.

The random variable X is a binomial distribution random variable because each examination score can be regarded as a random experiment, whose outcome can either be success or failure. Since there are sixty scores, it means that there are n different trials of the random experiment. From the dataset, the probability p of success is 44/60 = 11/15. Therefore, the parameters of the binomial distribution random variable, X are n = 60 and p = 11/15.

Python programming language can be used to define the binomial random variable and generate the various probabilities of the random variable, X and plot the probability distribution of the random variable.

Table **45** and Fig. (**21**) show the distribution of probabilities for the various values of the random variable:

Table 45. Binomial distribution of the dataset in Table 4.

X	P(X)
0	3.62E-35
1	5.96E-33
2	4.84E-31
3	2.57E-29
4	1.01E-27
5	3.11E-26
6	7.83E-25
7	1.66E-23
8	3.03E-22
9	4.81E-21
10	6.74E-20
11	8.43E-19
12	9.46E-18
13	9.61E-17
14	8.87E-16
15	7.48E-15
16	5.79E-14
17	4.12E-13
18	2.71E-12
19	1.64E-11
20	9.27E-11
21	4.86E-10
22	2.37E-09
23	1.08E-08
24	4.56E-08
25	1.81E-07
26	6.69E-07
27	2.32E-06
28	7.50E-06
29	2.28E-05
30	6.47E-05
31	0.000172207
32	0.000429173

(Table 45) cont.....

X	P(X)
33	0.001001404
34	0.002186889
35	0.004467502
36	0.008531688
37	0.015218686
38	0.025331102
38	0.025331102
40	0.056733144
41	0.076105437
42	0.094678788
43	0.108990698
44	0.115802617
45	0.113229225
46	0.101537077
47	0.083173989
48	0.061947294
49	0.041719606
50	0.025240362
51	0.013609999
52	0.006477836
53	0.002688913
54	0.000958548
55	0.000287564
56	7.06E-05
57	1.36E-05
58	1.94E-06
59	1.81E-07
60	8.28E-09

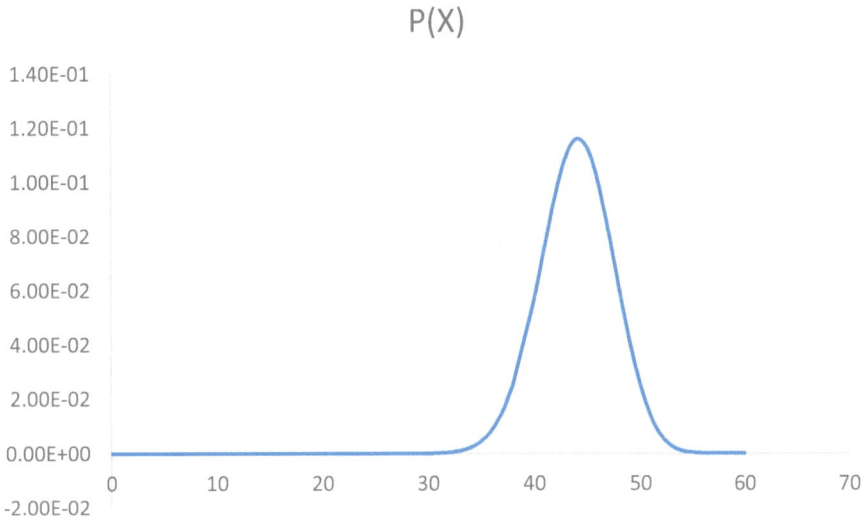

Fig. (21). Binomial probability distribution of the dataset in table 45.

5.2.2.2. Poisson Probability Distribution Function

Poisson probability distribution function is another discrete probability distribution function, which is used to represents a random variable that is defined as the number of items that occurred within a given period of time. The parameter of Poisson probability distribution function is, which is the rate of occurrence of event (*e.g.* arrival rate). The Poisson probability distribution function is given in Equation 15, as:

$$P(X = x) = \begin{cases} \dfrac{\lambda^x e^{-\lambda}}{x!}, & x = 0,1,2,3,4,5,6,7,... \\ 0, & otherwise \end{cases} \tag{15}$$

The following example will illustrate the use of Poisson probability distribution function in data analysis.

Suppose the arrival rates of students per minute into a lecture hall were randomly recorded for sixty days as shown in Table **46**, below:

Table 46. Sample dataset of arrival rates of students.

77	62	46	53	78	67	71	37	65	60
45	81	46	62	53	50	72	62	75	77
46	52	23	42	51	42	29	34	52	38
50	61	54	50	47	68	50	43	46	45
72	85	47	70	62	46	40	56	46	82
16	45	27	50	39	48	19	23	30	40

You are required to use appropriate probability distribution function analyze the dataset with the aim of obtaining useful information from the sample.

Since the dataset is about arrival rate, you can define a random variable X to be the number of arrivals per minute. You can use the sample data set to obtain the average arrival rate, which is 51.75.

Table **47** and Fig. (**22**) show the Poisson probability distribution of the various values of the random variable:

Table 47. Poisson probability distribution of the dataset in Table 46.

X	Poisson
0	3.35E-23
1	1.73E-21
2	4.49E-20
3	7.74E-19
4	1.00E-17
5	1.04E-16
6	8.94E-16
7	6.61E-15
8	4.28E-14
9	2.46E-13
10	1.27E-12
11	5.99E-12
12	2.58E-11
13	1.03E-10
14	3.80E-10
15	1.31E-09

(Table 47) cont.....

X	Poisson
16	4.24E-09
17	1.29E-08
18	3.71E-08
19	1.01E-07
20	2.61E-07
21	6.44E-07
22	1.52E-06
23	3.41E-06
24	7.35E-06
25	1.52E-05
26	3.03E-05
27	5.81E-05
28	0.000107302
29	0.000191479
30	0.000330302
31	0.000551391
32	0.000891703
33	0.001398352
34	0.002128374
35	0.003146953
36	0.004523745
37	0.00632713
38	0.008616553
38	0.008616553
40	0.014792094
41	0.018670509
42	0.023004734
43	0.02768593
44	0.032562429
45	0.037446794
46	0.042127643
47	0.046385224
48	0.050009069
49	0.052815701

(Table 47) cont.....

X	Poisson
50	0.05466425
51	0.055468136
52	0.055201462
53	0.053899541
54	0.051653727
55	0.048601461
56	0.044912958
57	0.040776238
58	0.036382247
59	0.031911547
60	0.027523709
61	0.023350032
62	0.019489744
63	0.016009433
64	0.012945127
65	0.010306313
66	0.008081086
67	0.006241735
68	0.004750144
69	0.003562608
70	0.002633785
71	0.001919695
72	0.001379781
73	0.000978132
74	0.000684032
75	0.000471982
76	0.000321382
77	0.000215994
78	0.000143304
79	9.39E-05
80	6.07E-05
81	3.88E-05
82	2.45E-05
83	1.53E-05

(Table 47) cont.....

X	Poisson
84	9.40E-06
85	5.73E-06
86	3.45E-06
87	2.05E-06
88	1.21E-06
89	7.01E-07
90	4.03E-07
91	2.29E-07
92	1.29E-07
93	7.17E-08
94	3.95E-08
95	2.15E-08
96	1.16E-08
97	6.19E-09
98	3.27E-09
99	1.71E-09
100	8.84E-10

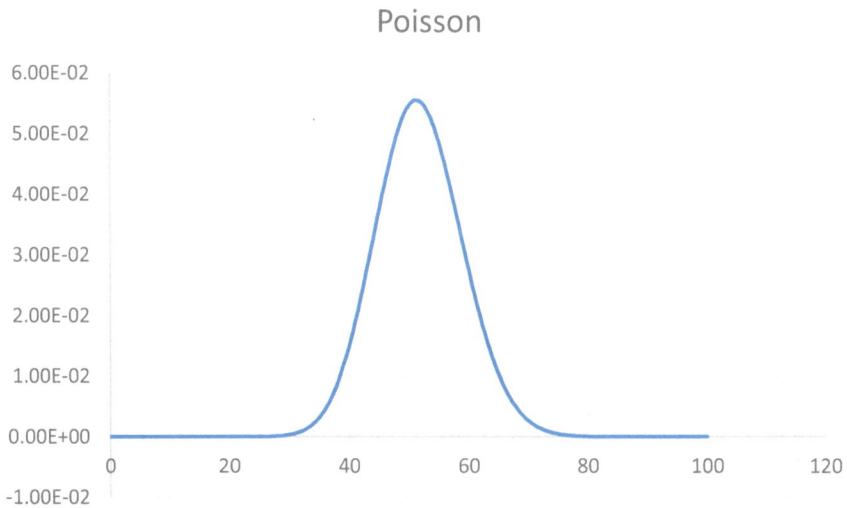

Fig. (22). Visualizing poisson probability distribution of the dataset in table 46.

5.2.2.3. Exponential Probability Distribution Function

The Exponential probability distribution function can be used to model a random variable that is defined as the time between occurrence of event, *e.g.* time between arrival of a customer into a facility. The parameter of the Exponential probability distribution function is, which is the rate of change of events (arrival rate). The mathematical formula for this distribution is given in Equation 16, as:

$$P(X = x) = \begin{cases} \lambda e^{-\lambda x}, & 0 \le x \le \inf inity, \\ 0, & otherwise \end{cases} \qquad (16)$$

The following example will illustrate the use of this probability distribution function in data analysis:

Suppose the arrival rates per minutes into the cafeteria were randomly recorded for sixty days as shown in Table **48**, below:

Table 48. Sample dataset of students arrival rates.

1.49	1.20	0.89	1.02	1.51	1.29	1.37	0.71	1.26	1.16
0.87	1.57	0.89	1.20	1.02	0.97	1.39	1.20	1.45	1.49
0.89	1.00	0.44	0.81	0.99	0.81	0.56	0.66	1.00	0.73
0.97	1.18	1.04	0.97	0.91	1.31	0.97	0.83	0.89	0.87
1.39	1.64	0.91	1.35	1.20	0.89	0.77	1.08	0.89	1.58
0.31	0.87	0.52	0.97	0.75	0.93	0.37	0.44	0.58	0.77

Based on past experience, suppose the rate of arrival per unit time is 51.75.

Table **49** and Fig. (**23**) show the distribution of probabilities for the various values of the random variable:

Table 49. Exponential probability distribution.

X	Exponential
0	1
1	0.367879441
2	0.135335283
3	0.049787068
4	0.018315639
5	0.006737947

(Table 49) cont.....

6	0.002478752
7	0.000911882
8	0.000335463
9	0.00012341
10	4.53999E-05

Exponential

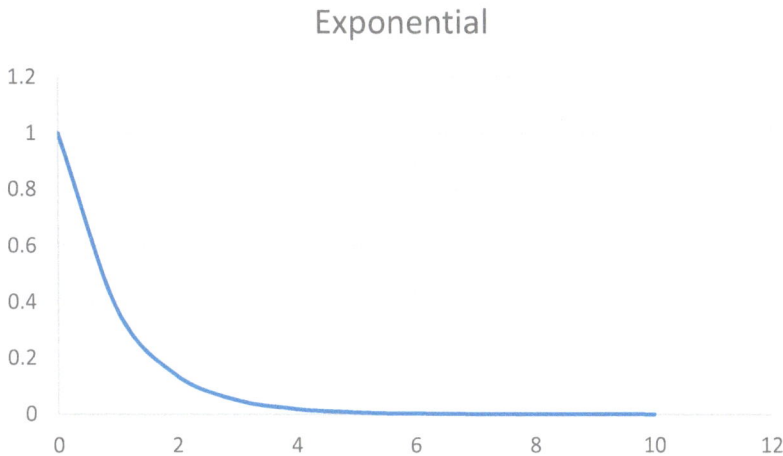

Fig. (23). Visualization of exponential probability distribution of the dataset in table 48.

5.2.2.4. Normal Probability Distribution Function

This is another example of continuous probability distribution function, which is regarded as the most important probability distribution function because many samples of dataset are normally distributed, *e.g.* height, weight, exams scores *etc.* The parameters of the normal probability distribution function are the mean, μ and the standard deviation, σ. The mathematical formula for the normal probability density function is given in Equation 17, as:

$$P(X = x) = \begin{cases} \dfrac{1}{\sigma\sqrt{2\Pi}} e^{-\frac{1}{2}\left(\frac{x-\mu}{\sigma}\right)^2}, & -\inf inity \leq x \leq \inf inity, \\ 0, & otherwise \end{cases} \tag{17}$$

The following example will illustrate the use of normal probability distribution function.

Suppose a random sample of sixty student scores were collected for analysis, as shown in Table **50**, below. You are required to define a random variable and use the normal probability distribution function to analyze the data.

Table 50. Sample dataset of students scores.

77	62	46	53	78	67	71	37	65	60
45	81	46	62	53	50	72	62	75	77
46	52	23	42	51	42	29	34	52	38
50	61	54	50	47	68	50	43	46	45
72	85	47	70	62	46	40	56	46	82
16	45	27	50	39	48	19	23	30	40

You will need to define a random variable X as the scores that the students obtained in the examination. This random variable is normally distributed with mean 51.75 and standard deviation, 16.27. The statistical formula for the standard deviation and mean are given in Equations 18 and Equation 19, as:

$$\varpi = \sqrt{\frac{\sum_{i=1}^{n} X_i^2 - \frac{\left(\sum_{i=1}^{n} X_i\right)^2}{n}}{n-1}} \qquad (18)$$

$$\mu = \frac{\sum_{i=1}^{n} X_i}{n} \qquad (19)$$

Next, you will use the formula for the normal probability distribution function to generate the various probabilities for all the possible values of the random variable.

Table **51** and Fig. (24), below show the Normal probability distribution for various values of the random variable X, using the dataset in Table **50**.

Table 51. Normal probability distribution of the dataset in Table 50.

X	Normal Distribution
1	0.00018909
2	0.000228618

(Table 51) cont.....

3	0.000275367
4	0.000330424
5	0.000394995
6	0.000470403
7	0.000558096
8	0.000659639
9	0.000776718
10	0.000911128
11	0.001064769
12	0.001239625
13	0.001437755
14	0.001661265
15	0.001912283
16	0.00219293
17	0.002505283
18	0.002851335
19	0.00323295
20	0.003651818
21	0.004109402
22	0.004606886
23	0.005145123
24	0.005724577
25	0.006345275
26	0.007006753
27	0.007708016
28	0.008447491
29	0.009223001
30	0.010031737
31	0.010870247
32	0.011734432
33	0.012619557
34	0.013520274
35	0.014430662
36	0.015344276
37	0.016254213

(Table 51) cont.....

38	0.017153188
39	0.018033628
40	0.018887773
41	0.019707784
42	0.02048586
43	0.021214362
44	0.021885936
45	0.022493635
46	0.02303104
47	0.02349237
48	0.023872587
49	0.024167488
50	0.024373782
51	0.02448915
52	0.024512288
53	0.024442937
54	0.024281879
55	0.02403093
56	0.023692901
57	0.023271548
58	0.022771502
59	0.022198185
60	0.02155771
61	0.020856775
62	0.020102546
63	0.019302535
64	0.018464477
65	0.017596207
66	0.016705538
67	0.015800152
68	0.014887488
69	0.013974651
70	0.013068323
71	0.012174697
72	0.011299412

(Table 51) cont.....

73	0.010447512
74	0.009623417
75	0.008830902
76	0.008073098
77	0.007352496
78	0.006670966
79	0.006029787
80	0.005429685
81	0.004870872
82	0.004353095
83	0.003875689
84	0.00343763
85	0.003037586
86	0.002673976
87	0.002345016
88	0.002048772
89	0.001783202
90	0.001546205
91	0.00133565
92	0.001149418
93	0.000985423
94	0.00084164
95	0.000716127
96	0.000607033
97	0.000512619
98	0.000431257
99	0.00036144
100	0.000301784

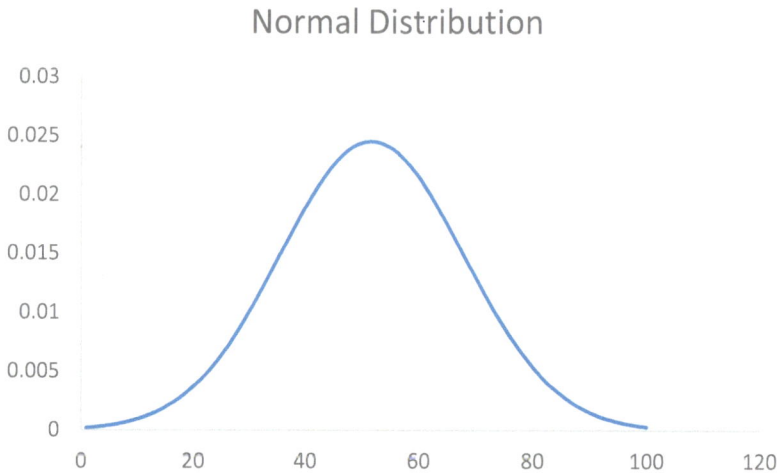

Fig. (24). Visualization of normal probability distribution of the dataset in table **50**.

5.3. Conclusion

Clustering and data visualization have been considered in this unit as two fundamental unsupervised machine learning problems. The clustering algorithm, which solves clustering problem has been considered with examples. On the other hand, the use of visualization in understanding dataset has been considered by using probability distribution function to visualize the distribution of datasets.

5.4. Summary

Unsupervised machine learning has been considered in this unit, together with the various unsupervised machine learning algorithm, like clustering algorithm. Waikato Environment for Knowledge Analysis WEKA is a machine learning tool that can be used to automate various supervised and unsupervised learning problems. This open source Java software will form the focus of the next unit.

6. WAIKATO ENVIRONMENT FOR KNOWLEDGE ANALYSIS, WEKA

WEKA, Waikato Environment for Knowledge Analysis is an open source machine learning software, which was developed in Java by the University of Waikato, New Zealand, Australia (Bouckaert, *et al.*, 2013). WEKA implemented most of the regression and classification based machine learning algorithms. This means that WEKA predicts and classifies test data using large datasets. WEKA requires that data must be converted into a structured format. This format is called

Attribute Relation File Format (ARFF).

6.1. Data Representation in WEKA

Machine learning algorithms are primarily designed to work with arrays of numbers. This is called tabular or structured data because it is how data looks in a spreadsheet. It consists different of rows and columns. However, WEKA requires that the dataset that it analyses must be converted to a data format, called Attribute Relation File Format, ARFF. WEKA uses the following terms to describe data in ARFF:

- **Instance**: An instance is a row of data.
- **Attribute**: An attribute is a column of data. Each attribute can have its own data type. **Real** is used for all numeric values like 1.2 and 5.
- **Nominal:** A nominal is a one-word data item to represent a symbol, text or string, *e.g.* "computer" and "radio".

Sometimes data can be represented in WEKA, using a format called Comma Separated Value, which means that each attribute data is separated by a comma. Any file that the data is in Comma Separated Value will have the extension, CSV. For example, the first few lines of the classic iris flowers dataset in CSV format looks as follows:

5.1,3.5,1.4,0.2,Iris-setosa

4.9,3.0,1.4,0.2,Iris-setosa

4.7,3.2,1.3,0.2,Iris-setosa

4.6,3.1,1.5,0.2,Iris-setosa

5.0,3.6,1.4,0.2,Iris-setosa

It means that there are five records, and each record contains five attributes. Each attribute of each row is separated by a comma.

When the above CSV file is converted to ARFF, the data will look as follows:

@RELATION iris

@ATTRIBUTE sepallength REAL

@ATTRIBUTE sepalwidth REAL

@ATTRIBUTE petallength REAL

@ATTRIBUTE petalwidth REAL

@ATTRIBUTE class {Iris-setosa,Iris-versicolor,Iris-virginica}

@DATA

5.1,3.5,1.4,0.2,Iris-setosa

4.9,3.0,1.4,0.2,Iris-setosa

4.7,3.2,1.3,0.2,Iris-setosa

4.6,3.1,1.5,0.2,Iris-setosa

5.0,3.6,1.4,0.2,Iris-setosa

It should be noted that the attributes of the data in CSV are not shown. However, the first line of the data in ARFF is @RELATION iris. The @RELATION declares the name of the file, iris. The next lines use @ATTRIBUTE to declare the various attributes of the file and the data type that each attribute belongs to. The @DATA shows the beginning of all data in the file. The data are listed like the CSV file.

Table **52** shows the rows and columns of a file called myfile. The class attribute of the dataset is age.

Table 52. Sample dataset.

Name	Gender	Age
Peter	Male	14
Mary	Female	20
Adamu	Male	35

You can be required to show the contents of the file in CSV and ARFF.

Contents of the file in CSV

peter,Male,14, age

mary,female,20, age

adamu,male,35. age

The contents of the file in ARFF

@RELATION myfile

@ATTRIBUTE name {peter,mary,adamu}

@ATTRIBUTE gender {male,female}

@ATTRIBUTE age REAL

@DATA

peter,Male,14, age

mary,female,20, age

adamu,male,35, age

6.2. Getting Started with WEKA

If your dataset is not in ARFF, but in CSV, it can easily be converted to ARFF before it can be used in WEKA as machine learning data set. WEKA provides a simple way of converting your data from CSV to ARFF. Follow the following steps [9,10]:

1. Run WEKA. The WEKA GUI Chooser will appear as shown in Fig. (**25**).
2. In WEKA GUI Chooser, click at Tools, and select "ARFF Viewer"
3. An empty ARFF-Viewer will be presented, as shown below in Fig. (**26**).
4. Click at "File" menu and select "Open". Navigate to your current working directory. Change the "Files of Type:" filter to "CSV data files (*.csv)". Select your CSV file and click the "Open" button as shown in Fig. (**27**).
5. You will see a sample of your CSV file loaded into the ARFF-Viewer.
6. Save your dataset in ARFF format by clicking the "File" menu and selecting "Save as...". Enter a filename with '.arff' extension and click the "Save" button. You can now load your saved .arff file directly into WEKA [9, 10].

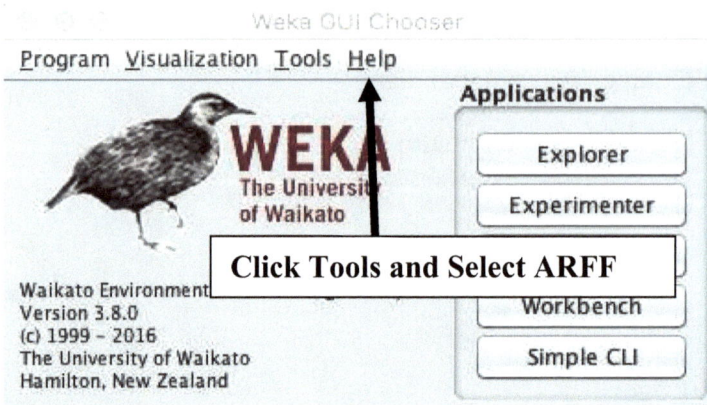

Fig. (25). Screen shot of the weka gui chooser.

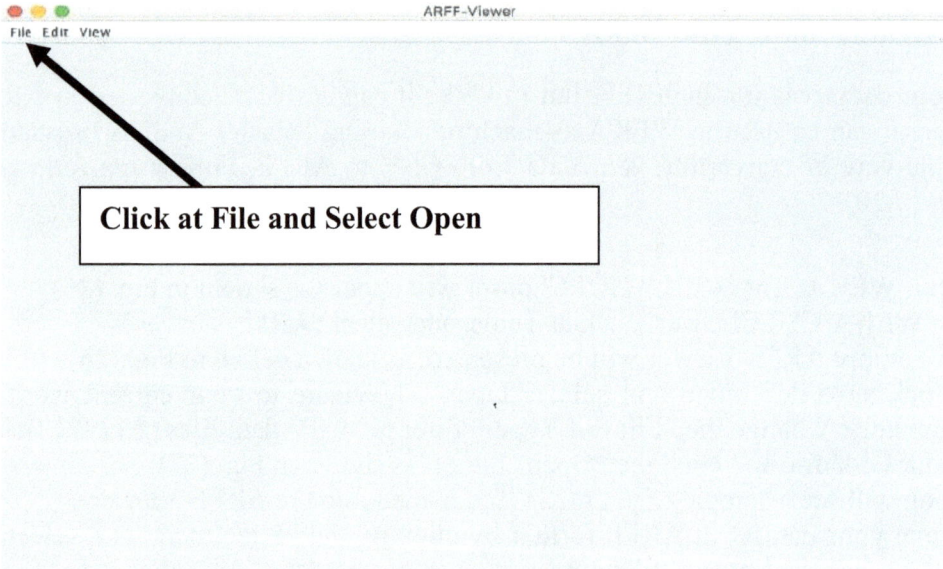

Fig. (26). WEKA ARFF viewer.

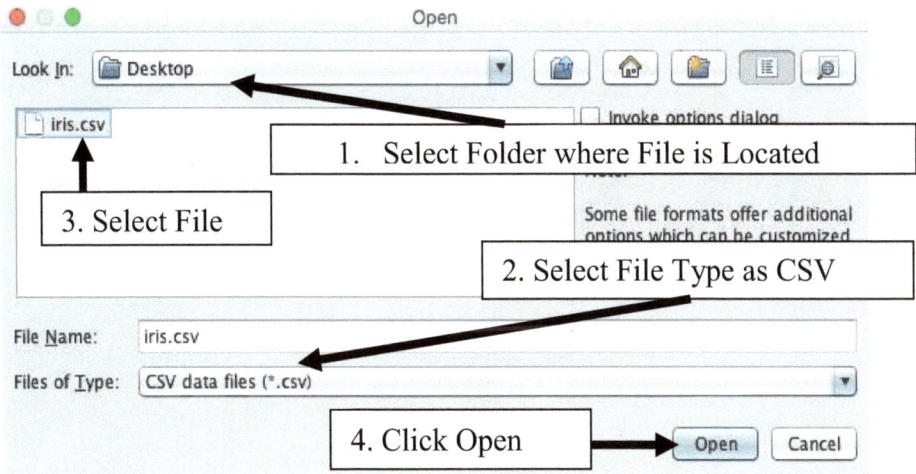

Fig. (27). Load CSV in ARFF viewer.

6.2.1. Loading CSV Files in the WEKA Explorer

Use the following steps if you want to open your CSV file directly in WEKA Explorer instead of converting it to ARFF before using it in WEKA:

1. Start WEKA, the WEKA GUI Chooser will appear.
2. Launch the WEKA Explorer by clicking the "Explorer" button.
3. Click the "Open file…" button as shown in Fig. (**28**).
4. Navigate to your current working directory. Change the "Files of Type" to "CSV data files (*.csv)". Select your file and click the "Open" button.

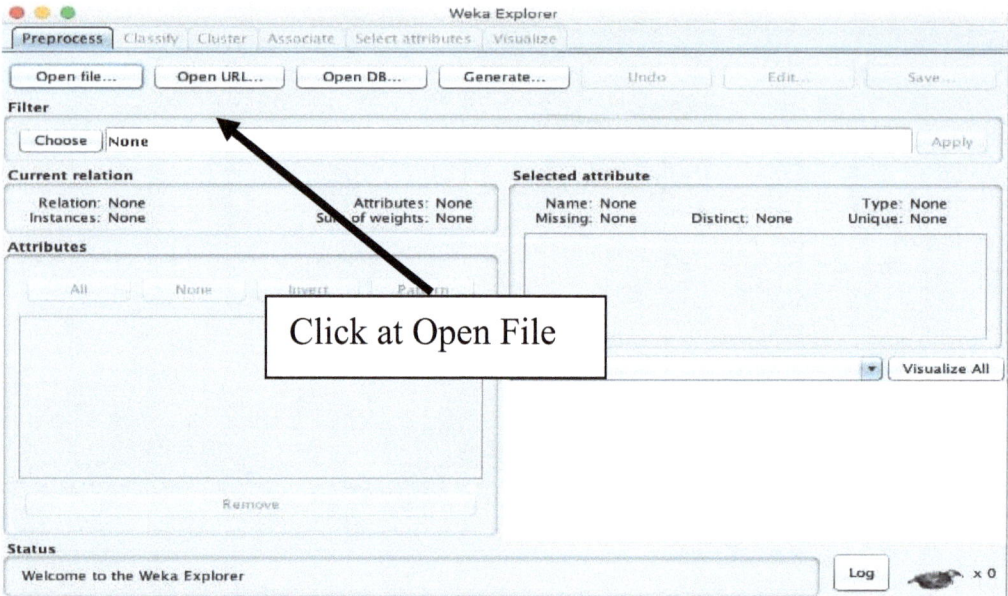

Fig. (28). Screen shot of the Weka Explorer.

You can work with the data directly. You can also save your dataset in ARFF format by clicking he "Save" button and typing a filename.

6.2. Using WEKA to Solve Machine Learning Problems

WEKA has many machine learning tools that can be used to mine data. In this section, a guide on how to use the various machine learning tools in WEKA will be presented. The machine learning tools that solve different problems are called Classifiers in WEKA. They include the following: Linear regression, Logistic regression, K-Means clustering, Naïve Bayes, and Support Vectors Machines among others. The following steps can be taken to use any of the classifiers in WEKA. Before using any of the classifiers, the data must be loaded or opened in WEKA. In order to load or open your data, click at the Explorer button after launching WEKA, then click at the Open File Tab, a dialogue window will appear for you to choose the file you want to load [9, 10].

1. Click at Classify Tab as shown in (Fig. **29**).
2. 'Classify' window comes up on the screen as shown in (Fig. **30**).
3. Use the Classify screen above to analyse your data by clicking at the Choose button as shown in (Fig. **31**). When you click at it, a pop up list will appear where you can choose the Classifier that you want to use.

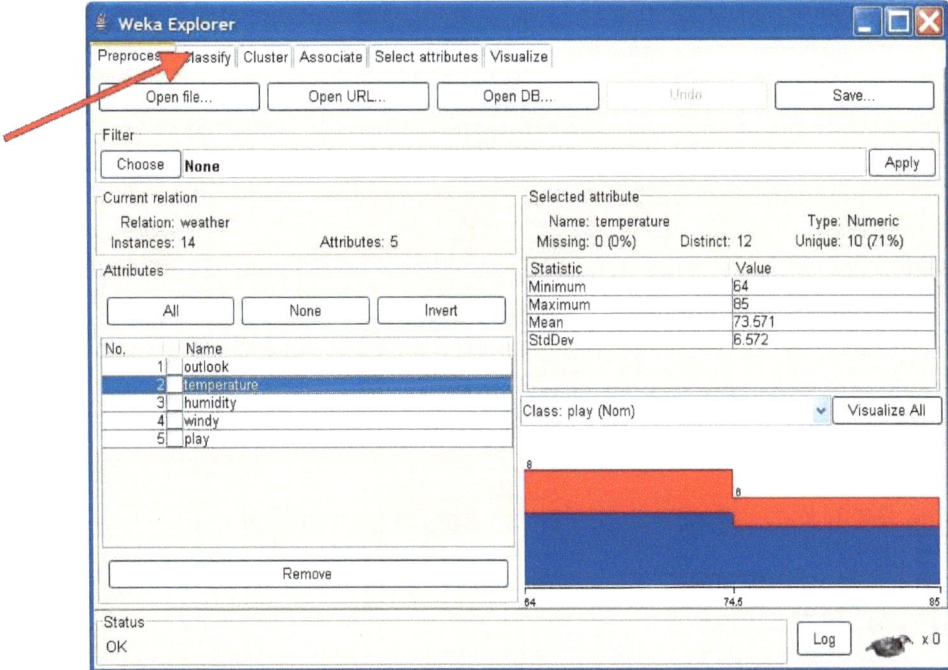

Fig. (29). WEKA explorer.

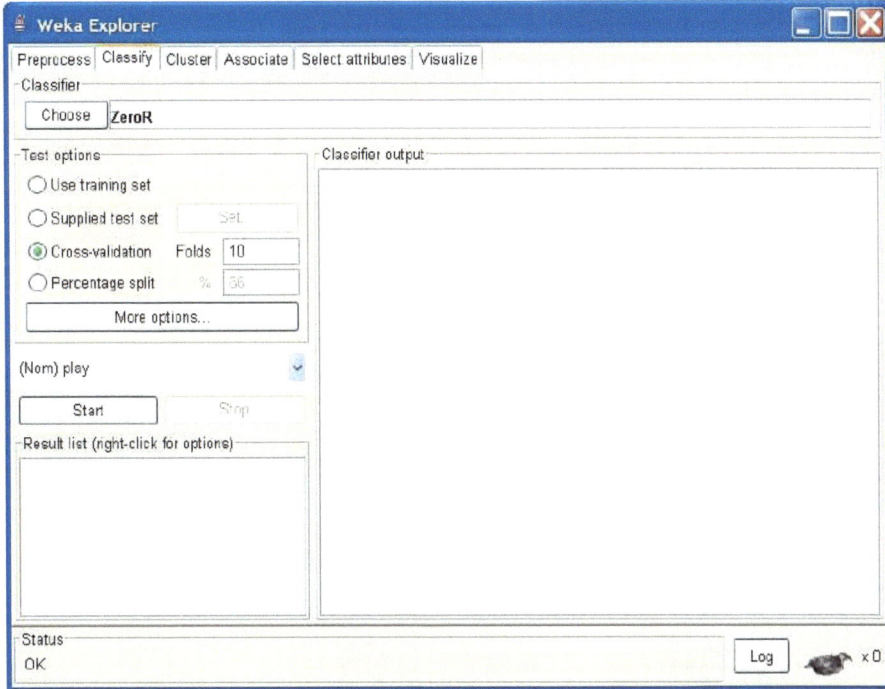

Fig. (30). Classify window.

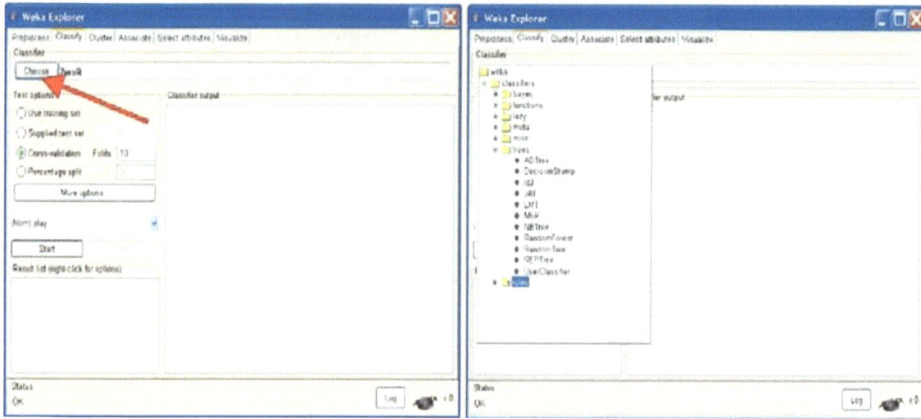

Fig. (31). Classify window with classify pop-up list.

6.4. Using WEKA to Solve Simple Linear Regression Problem

Linear regression is one of the classifiers that is available in WEKA. It determines the parameters of the linear regression equation, and uses it to make prediction. It also estimates the errors associated with using the model to make prediction. Assuming your data has been loaded in WEKA, as described earlier, you can use WEKA's linear regression classifier as follows:

1. After you have loaded your data, click at the classifier tab, as shown in Fig. **(32)**.
2. The Classify' window appears as shown below in Fig. **(33)**.
3. Choose Linear Regression classifier

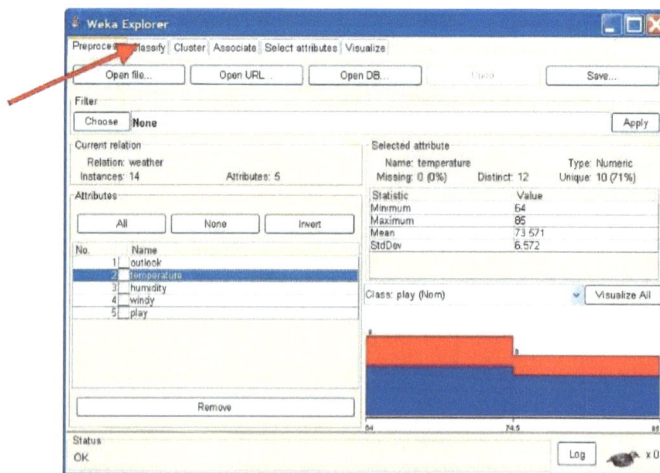

Fig. (32). WEKA explorer window.

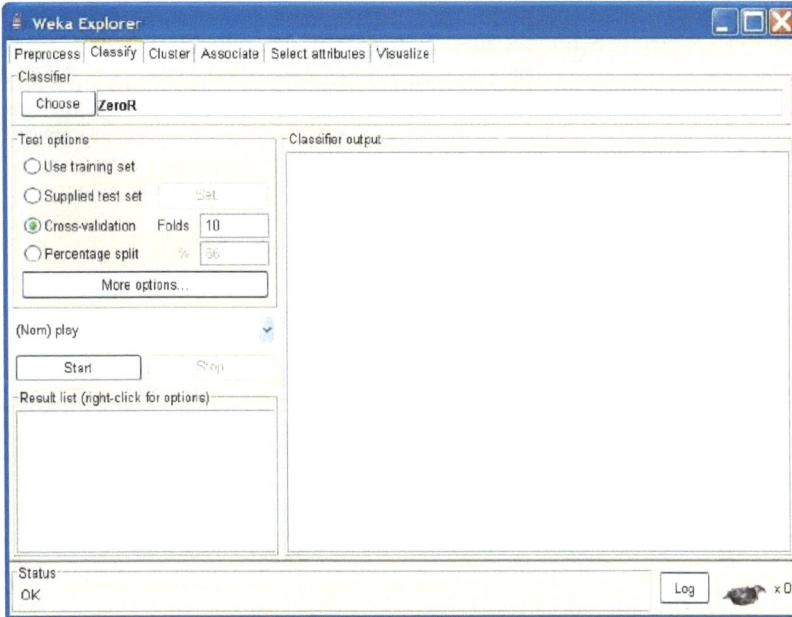

Fig. (33). Classify window.

A pop up list will appear, showing all the classifiers that you can choose from. Click at the Chooser button. Select "Linear Regression". You can also click at the name of the algorithm to review the algorithm configuration, as shown in Fig. (**34**). Click OK to close the configuration screen.

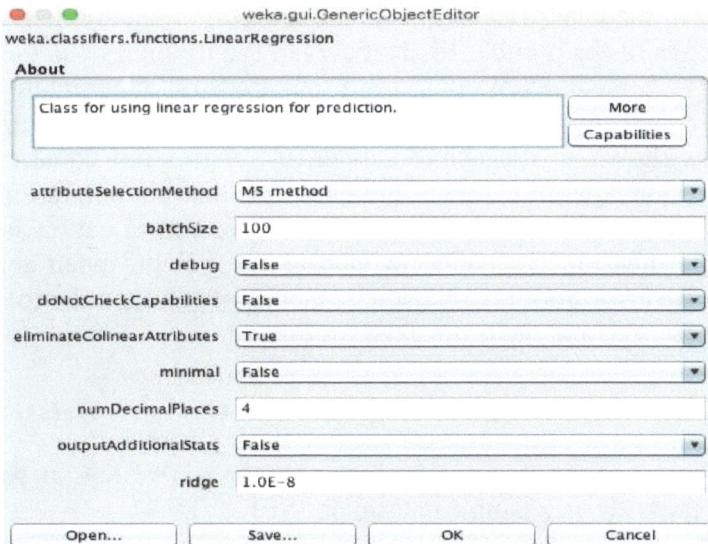

Fig. (34). WEKA configuration of linear regression.

4. To start the training, click "Start" in the WEKA Classifier screen. The training data will be used to train the computer by determining the parameters of the linear regression and the associated errors [9, 10], as shown in Fig. (35).

○ **Interpreting the Result of Linear Regression in WEKA**

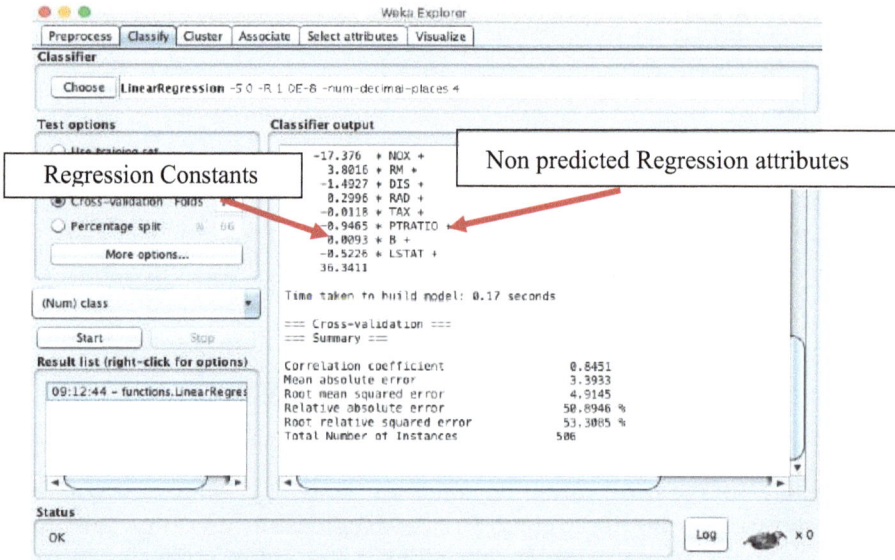

Fig. (35). Weka results for linear regression.

The first item in the Classifier output is the regression equation. The regression equation depends of the number of attributes in the training data. Generally, it is of the form, Y = A + BX + CW + DZ for a four 4 attribute regression equation. A, B, C and D are the constant that the Classifier determines after the training. After the training as shown in the above screen, the regression equation is a nine-attribute regression equation. Part of the measures that the output report displays are measures that determines how good the regression equation is, in making prediction. The measures include: correlation coefficient, mean absolute error, root mean square error, root relative square error, the total number of instances of the training data used, and the time taken for the training.

6.5. Using WEKA to Solve Linear Regression on CPU.arff Dataset

The screen shots in Figs. (36 - 38) show the use of WEKA in solving linear regression on the CPU.arff sample dataset on WEKA 3.9.4.

Fig. (36). CPU.ARFF sample dataset.

Fig. (37). WEKA explorer after opening sample dataset, CPU.ARFF.

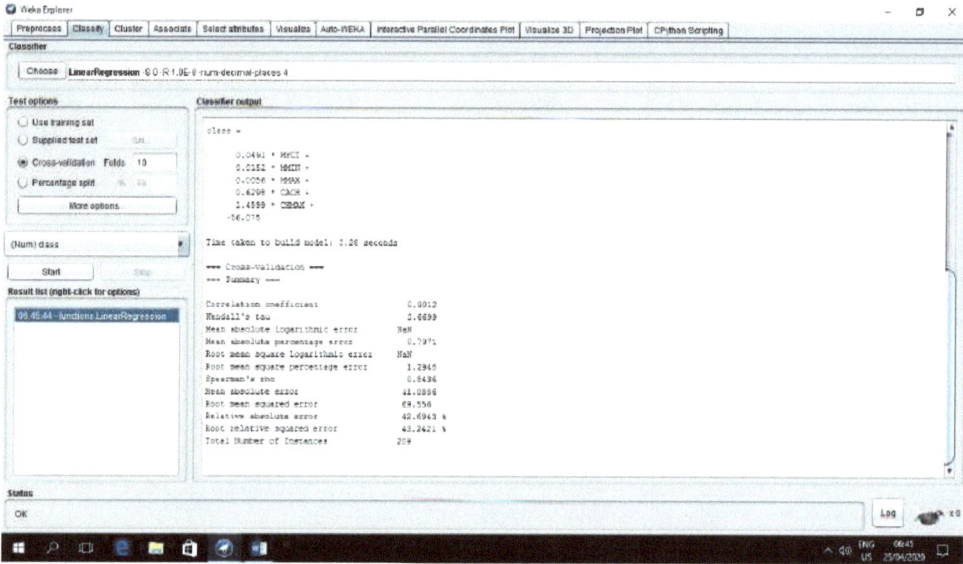

Fig. (38). Output of linear regression in WEKA (Regression Model and Correlation).

6.6. Using WEKA to do Naïve Bayes Classification on Norminal Weather.arff Dataset

The screen shots in Figs. (**39**, **40** and **41**) are WEKA screen shots on the use of Naïve Bayes classifier on the nominal weather data set.

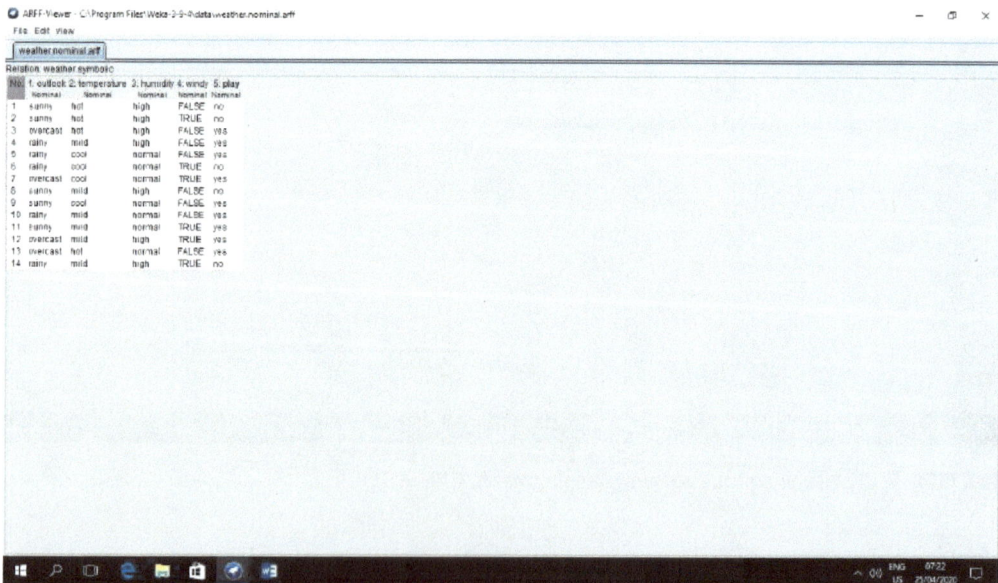

Fig. (39). Sample dataset in WEKA, Weather.ARFF.

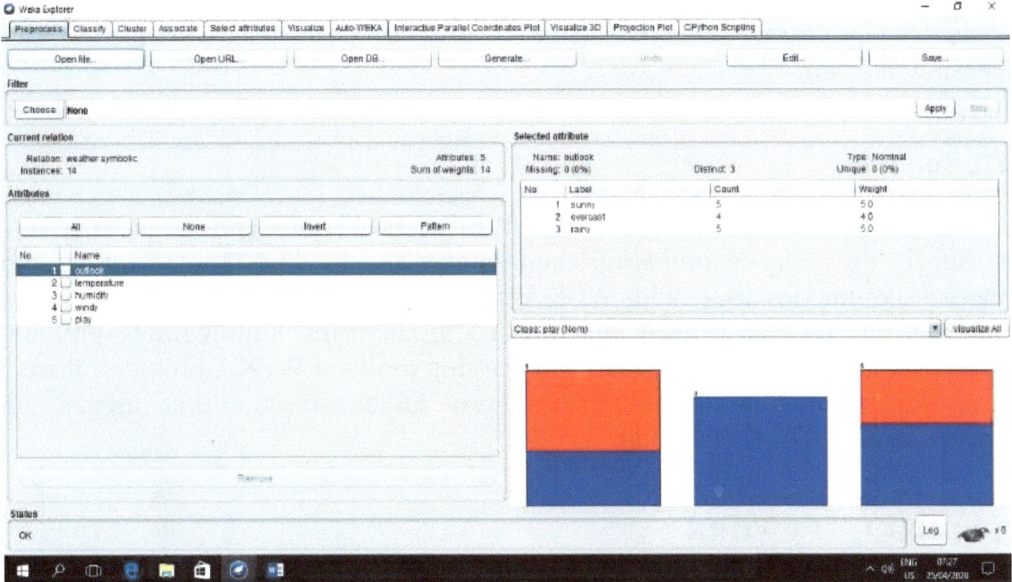

Fig. (40). WEKA explorer after opening sample dataset, Weather.ARFF.

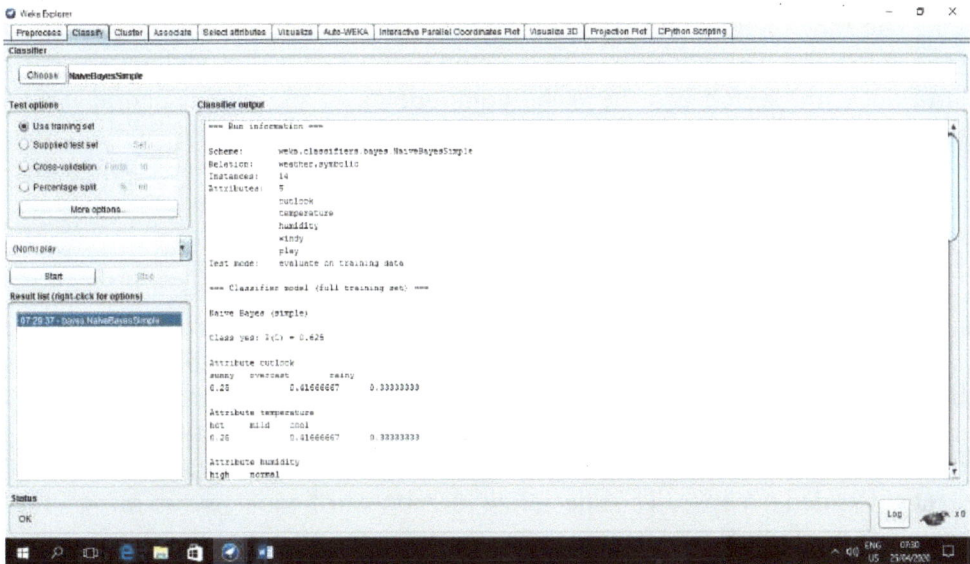

Fig. (41). Output from WEKA simple naive bayes using sample dataset, Weather.ARFF.

6.7. Conclusion

How to use WEKA to convert data from CSV file format to ARFF file format, using WEKA to load CSV file format to ARFF viewer and using WEKA to solve some machine learning problems (linear regression problems) are some of things learnt in this unit.

6.8. Summary

Using machine learning algorithms to solve problems with large dataset is extremely difficulty in preparing such dataset and loading it into your custom made program. However, with WEKA large data set that has been prepared can easily be accessed in WEKA and be used to solve machine learning problem. Before using any classifier or machine learning tool that WEKA provides, there is need to understand the machine learning tool. Other aspects of machine learning will be discussed in the next unit.

7. NEURAL NETWORK

Human brain consists of billions of biological cells, called neurons, which are connected together to form a network of neurons, called biological neural network. The main purpose of the neural network is that it enables human to learn. The fundamental and tiniest element of the neural network is neuron. The biological neural network is used to develop computational model called artificial neural network, which has the basic components of biological neural network. The artificial neural network uses different technologies and methodologies, which is used to make the computer to emulate the way the human brain learns.

7.1. Biological Neurons

Each neuron in the biological neural network has three main parts, which are links to another neuron, body of the cell and an extension from the body. The links to other neurons are called dentrites, while the body of the neuron contains the nucleus of the cell. The axon is the extension from the body of the neuron to the other side of the neuron. The point of connection between two dentrites of two neurons is called synapse. The specialize membrane of each neuron allows for the transmission of electrical signals within the neuron. The electrical signal is received from the dentrites at one end of the neuron and it is transmitted to another neuron at the other end of the neuron. This means that the signal moves in one direction within each neuron. It means that one side of the neuron receives the input signal, while the other side receives the output signal. The structure of an interconnected neuron is shown in Fig. (**42**) [11 - 14, 19, 20].

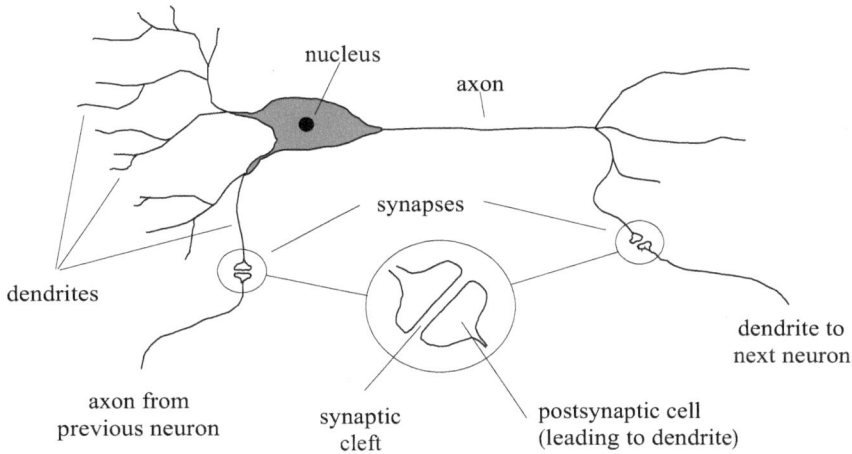

Fig. (42). Structure of neuron.

7.1.1. How the Biological Neuron Works

The transfer of Na$^+$ions along the axon to the synapse means that electrical pulses are transmitted along the axon to the synapse. Immediately the voltage pulse is received, it stimulates the release of neuro-transmitting chemicals across the synaptic cleft towards the post synaptic cell, which is the receiving part of the next neuron. The post synaptic cell then transfers the signal through the dentrite to the main cell body. All the inputs from all the dentrites are combined to form the output, which is transmitted along the axon. Electrical signal is produced at the axon if the inputs from all the dentrites is of sufficient strength to overcome a certain threshold value. The strength of the synaptic connection between neuron can be chemically altered by the brain when responding to favourable and unfavourable stimuli, while adapting to function optimally in the environment. Therefore, the synapse is the key to learning in biological neuron [15 - 20, 24].

7.2. Artificial Neural Network

Artificial Neural Network is a computational model, which represents the biological neural network. It consists of nodes, which represents the neurons. The connections between the nodes represent the various dentrites of the biological neural network. Just as the strength of synaptic connection between the neurons can be altered chemically by the brain, in the same way, the connections have adaptable parameters that modify the signal that pass between them. Artificial neural network can be used to model and solve different types of problem, which includes the following: memory modelling, pattern recognition, predicting the evolution of dynamic systems. Artificial neural network that models data can be classified as supervised artificial neural network and unsupervised artificial neural network. In a supervised artificial neural network, there is a distinction between class attribute and non-class attributes in the training data. The identity or class attributes of the various non-class attributes are known, and the problem is to predict a certain class attributes, given a non-class attributes as the test data. On the other hand, in an unsupervised artificial neural network, there is no distinction between the class attribute and non-class attribute. This means that the identify or class attribute of the training data is not known. The problem that it solves include: clustering problem.

7.2.1. Feedforward Multi-Layer Perceptron

This is one of the most important supervised neural network. The term perceptron is used to describe the function that each of the nodes that Artificial Neural Network performs. The term feedforward refers to definite input and output and data flow in one direction. Therefore, a feedforward multi-layer perceptron is an artificial neural network with input layer, output layer and multi-layers that are hidden. Fig. (**43**) shows a feedforward multi-layer neural network. The are two hidden layers, together with the input and output layers. Each input, output, hidden layer has a set of nodes. Each of the input nodes is connected to each of the nodes in the first hidden layer. Each node in the first hidden layer is connected to every node in the second hidden layer. Finally, each node in the second hidden layer is connected to every node in the output layer. Each of these connections has a weight that is associated with it. Each node in the inner layer forms a weighted sum of all its inputs, which it passes through a nonlinear transfer function.

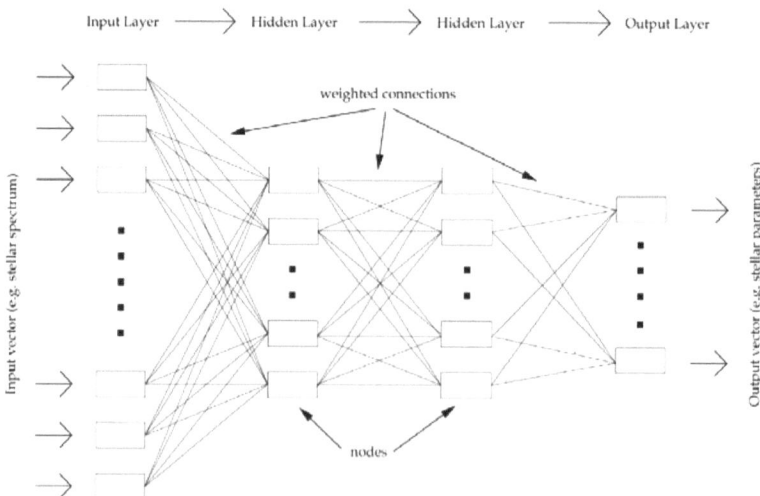

Fig. (43). Feedforward multi-layer perceptrons.

Inputs into a node is the weighted sum of all the inputs into that node. Illustrating with the following example, suppose there are five inputs into a node, which is represented as (1, 1, 1, 0, 0) and the weight for each of the inputs are (0.5, 1, -1, -0.5, 1.2). Therefore, the activation at the node will be obtained by the sum of the product of the inputs and the weights, which is given as:

$$\alpha = 1*0.5+1*1+1*1(-1)+0*(0.5)+0*1.2=0.5$$

Since the output y, which a node will transmit either 1 or 0, therefore, in order to determine the signal that the node will transit, the value of is compared with a certain threshold. If is greater than, 1 will be transmitted by the node, otherwise, 0 will be transmitted. This is called step function and it can be represented as follows in Equation 20.

$$y = \begin{cases} 1, & \alpha > \theta \\ 0, & otherwise \end{cases} \tag{20}$$

In the example that we have considered above, suppose the threshold, since therefore, the output that the node will transmit is 1. This type of artificial neuron is called Threshold Logic Unit (TLU) and its structure is shown in Fig. (**44**).

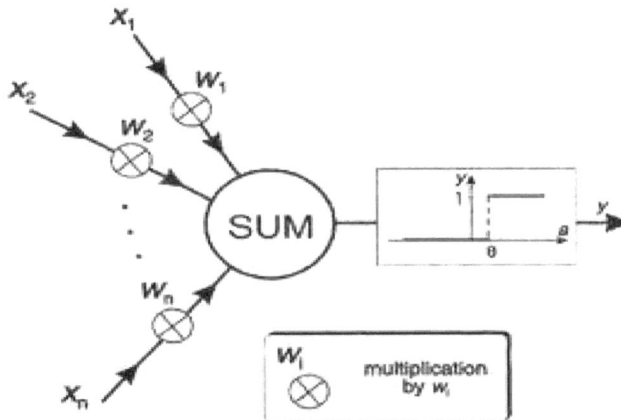

Fig. (44). The threshold logic unit.

7.2.2. Effect of Noise and Hardware Failure on the Artificial Neuron

Hardware failure of the artificial neuron (TLU) can affect weights of the input signal of the artificial neuron. Similarly, noise can also affect the input signals of the artificial neuron (node). The effect of noise and hardware failure on the output signal of the artificial neuron will be investigated by assuming a two input signal artificial neuron (TLU). Suppose the weights of the artificial neuron (TLU) are 0 and 1, *i.e.* (0, 1), and the value of the threshold The Table **53**, below shows all the possible inputs and outputs of the Artificial neuron (TLU), together with the various activations [11 - 13, 19, 20].

Table 53. TLU with weights (0,1) and threshold 0.5.

x_1	x_2	Activation	Output
0	0	0	0
0	1	1	1
1	0	0	0
1	1	1	1

Suppose due to the effect of hardware failure, the weights of the artificial neuron are 0.2 and 0.8. Table **54**, below shows all the possible inputs and outputs, together with all the Activations.

Table 54. TLU with weights (0.2,0.8) and threshold 0.5.

x_1	x_2	Activation	Output
0	0	0	0
0	1	0.8	1
1	0	0.2	0
1	1	1	1

It can be observed that the output signals remain the same for all the possible input signals, though the activations have changed. This illustrates the characteristic feature of a non-linear system, which is changes in the inputs do not produce corresponding change in the output. It also shows that the artificial neuron (ITLU) is very robust. However, if the effect of hardware failure on the Activation lead to large degree of change in the activation, the output signal will start producing wrong output.

Furthermore, suppose due to the effect of noise, all the possible inputs to the Artificial neuron were altered as shown in the Table **55**.

Table 55. TLU with degraded signal input.

x_1	x_2	Activation	Output
0.2	0.2	0.2	0

(Table 55) cont.....

x₁	x₂	Activation	Output
0.2	0.8	0.8	1
0.8	0.2	0.2	0
0.8	0.8	0.8	1

It can also be observed that though the various activations changed, the possible output signal did not change. Thus illustrating the same characteristic feature of a non-linear system. It also shows that the artificial neuron (TLU) is very robust. However, if the effect of noise on the artificial neuron leads to large degree of change in the input signal, the output signal will begin to yield wrong output. Therefore, the artificial neuron (TLU) is a non-linear system and very robust. In large artificial neural network, with large number of nodes, as the degree of noise and hardware degradation increases, the number of artificial neurons (TLU) that yield wrong output begins to increase gradually. This is called graceful degradation.

7.2.3. Continuous Input and Output Signals of Artificial Neuron

The inputs and outputs of the artificial neurom have been assumed so far to have only two possible values, 0 and 1. The reason for this assumption is based on the action-potential spiking voltage of the biological neuron. However, the action-potential voltage of biological neuron uses patterns of action-potential firing voltage. The pattens take a continuos form rather than discrete form. Therefore, there is the need to allow the inputs and outputs of Artificial neuron to assume continuous values. Continuous input signals have been demostrated to be possible in artificial neuron, when the effect of hardware failure and noise on the output signal were considered. However, encoding of continuous output signal on the artificial neuron (TLU) will be considered in this sub-section.

Doing this requires redefining the step function, so that instead of returning only two possible discrete values, it can return infinite continuous values. This will be done by softening the graph of the step function. The graph of the step function is shown in Fig. (45).

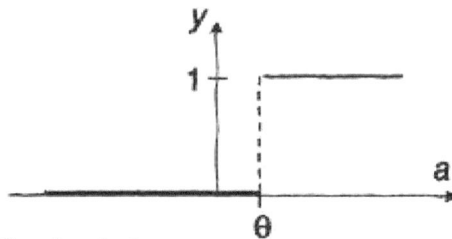

Fig. (45). Step function with discrete output.

When this graph of the step function is soften, the graph will be symmtric at y = 0.5. As the value of increases, the value of the output signal approaches to 1, and as the value of decreascs, the value of the output signal decreases to 0. The graph of the softened step function is shown in the Fig. (**46**).

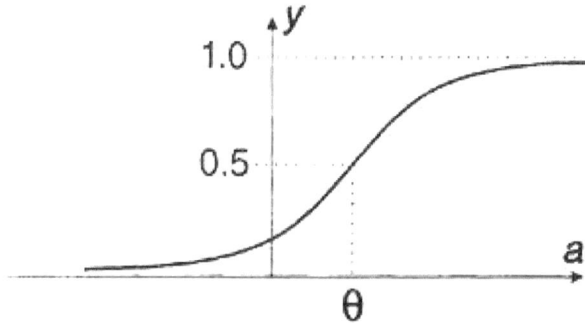

Fig. (46). Soften step function (sigmoid).

The softened step function is called Sigmoid, which is expressed as a mathematical function, shown in Equation 21.

$$y = \sigma(a) \equiv \frac{1}{1 + e^{\frac{(a-\theta)}{\rho}}} \tag{21}$$

α is the activation for the artificial neuron is shown below as:

$$a = \sum_{i=1}^{n} x_i w_i \tag{22}$$

w_i is the weight for the ith input signal of the artificial neuron, and x_i is the ith input signal of the artificial neuron (TLU). ρ is a constant that determines the shape of the curve and θ is the threshold parameter. If the value of ρ is large, it makes the shape of the sigmoid to be flat. If the value of ρ is small, it makes the shape of the sigmoid to be steep. Some literature omit ρ, which is the case when it is 1. However, making the value of ρ to be small makes the sigmoid to look like the hard-limiter used in TLU.

A semi-linear artificial neuron is one that uses the sigmoid function to determine its output. It is so called because the sigmoid function can be approximated as a continuous piece wise linear function, as shown in the Fig. (**47**).

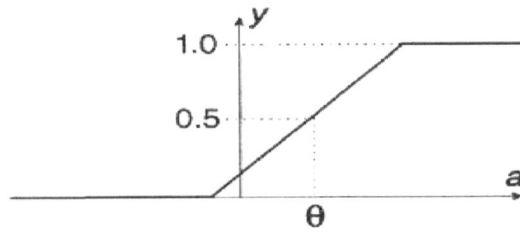

Fig. (47). Approximation of sigmoid function.

Fig. (**48**) illustrates what happens at each perceptron. How the perceptron computes the activation, and the activation function is applied to the activation in order to produce the output, which is sent to other neurons or nodes.

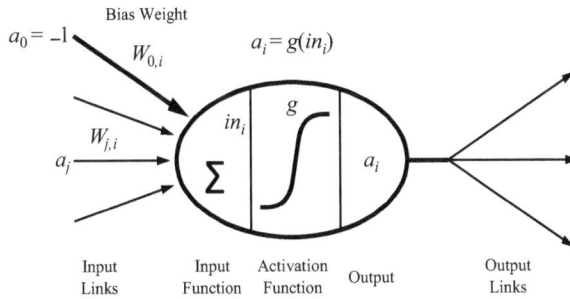

Fig. (48). Function of each perceptron.

7.2.4. Probabilistic Output Signal of Artificial Neuron

The probabilistic approach to determining continuous output signal is similar to the sigmoid function, but instead of using the sigmoid function to determine the output signal, it uses the probability of obtaining a '1' signal as the output signal. Any artificial neuron that determines its output signal in this way is called stochastic semi-linear artificial neuron. The output signal obtained using this approach is similar to the output of the biological neuron [19, 20].

7.2.5. Training the Artificial Neural Network

Since the artificial neural network is modelled after the learning process of the biological neural network. Training the artificial neural network is the process of using a set of training data to make each of the artificial neurons to identify the learning rule that will be used to predict or classify the output of each of the neuron based on its input. Each instance of the training data will consist of its output, which the artificial neural network will use to identify the learner rule that it will use to predict the class of output given any input test data. Therefore, the artificial neural network is a type of supervised machine learning. The process of training the network involves altering the weights and activation of each of the threshold logic unit so that the desired output will be obtained for each instance of the training data. This process will make the artificial neural network to know the learning rule, which will be used to determine the weights and activation value, for instance of the training data. This learner's rule will be used to predict or determine the output of any instance of the training data. In order to understand process of training an artificial neural network, it is important to consider how the threshold logic unit, which is one of the basic component of the artificial neural network, acts as a linear classifier.

7.2.5.1. Threshold Logic Unit as a Linear Classifier

The threshold logic unit can be regarded as a linear classifier, which uses a simple linear model to determine or predict the class of its output. Suppose the weight of a binary, two-input threshold logic unit are $(w_1, w_2) = (1, 1)$ and the threshold is 1.5. The TLU classifies each of the pattern of input data into any of the two classes, 0 or 1. Each input data has two components, which can be represented as a two dimensional table, x1, x2. The binary, two-input TLU determines the activation and output of each possible two-input data as shown in Fig. (49):

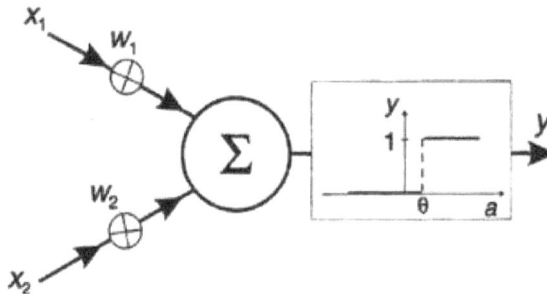

Fig. (49). A two-input TLU.

Table 56. Functionality of two-input tlu example.

x_1	x_2	Activation	Output
0	0	0	0
0	1	1	0
1	0	1	0
1	1	2	1

The critical condition for classification occurs when the activation is equal to the threshold θ,. Using the formula for activation, the following holds:

$$x_1 w_1 + x_2 w_2 = \theta$$

$$x_2 w_2 = \theta - x_1 w_1$$

$$x_2 w_2 = -x_1 w_1 + \theta$$

$$x_2 = -\left(\frac{w_1}{w_2}\right) x_1 + \frac{\theta}{w_2} \qquad (23)$$

Equation 23 is an equation of a straight line, which is a general form of $x_2 = ax_1 + b$, where a and b are constants, a is the slope of the straight line and b is the intercept along x_2 axis. When the values $(w_1, w_2) = (1, 1)$, $\theta = 1.15$ are substituted into the equation of a straight line, the straight line becomes: $x_2 = -x_1 + 1.5$. When the straight line is plotted in a two dimensional coordinate system, and all the points of the input data (x1, x2) identified in the coordinate system, Fig. (**50**), which is shown below will become obvious. Therefore, any point on the left hand side of the straight line will have a '0' output, while any point on the right hand side of the straight line will have a '1' output.

Therefore, the TLU can use the straight line as the decision rule to classify any binary two-digit input data. This concept can be generalized for any n dimensional input space [19, 20].

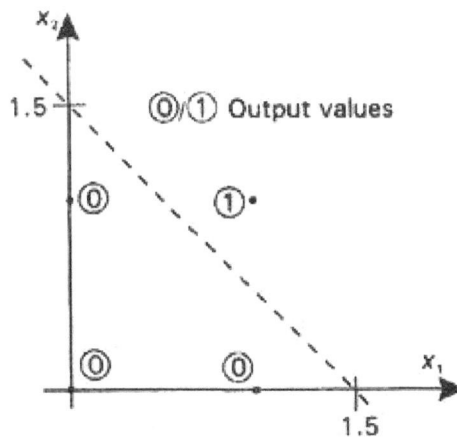

Fig. (50). Two dimensional coordinate system that determines output of two-input TLU.

7.2.5.2. Representing Logic Function/Gate Using Perceptron

Each of the following logic operators, AND, OR, NOT can be modelled as a perceptron with the following weights and threshold for its step function, as shown in Fig. (51).

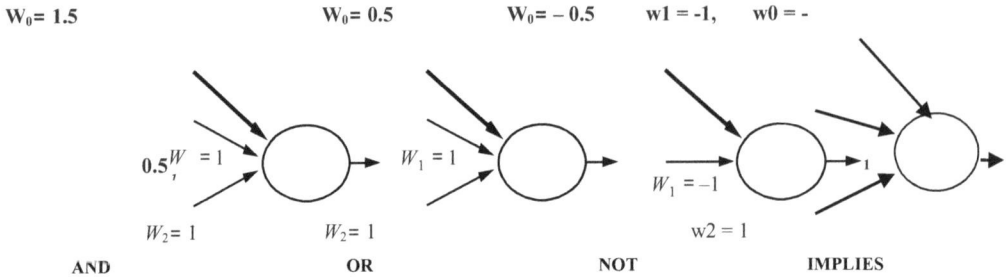

Fig. (51). Representing logic operator as perceptron.

$W_0 = 1.5$ $W_0 = 0.5$ $W_0 = -0.5$ w1 = -1, w0 = -0.51

$W_2 = 1$ $W_2 = 1$ w2 = 1

AND OR NOT IMPLIES

4.7.10 shows that for an 'AND' logic function or logic gate, the two inputs, x1 and x2 will have weights, w1 =1 and w2 = 1 and threshold of 1.5, while an 'OR' logic function or logic gate will have the following weights w1 = 1, w2 = 1 for its respective inputs, x1 and x2 and a threshold of 0.5. Finally, for a 'NOT' logic function or 'NOT' gate, the weight for its single input is -1, while the threshold is -0.5. This can be verified in Table **57** and Table **58** which are shown below.

Table 57. Output of logic operators using perceptron.

X1	X2	AND Activation	OR Activation	AND output	OR output
0	0	0	0	0	0
0	1	1	1	0	1
1	0	1	1	0	1
1	1	2	2	1	1

Table 58. Output of logic operators using perceptron.

X1	NOT Activation	NOT Output
0	0	1

(Table 58) cont.....

X1	NOT Activation	NOT Output
1	-1	0

It will be observed that the various outputs of the logic functions/gates are the same as the output, which will be obtained by evaluating the truth table of the logic function/gate. Therefore, from the above results, it means that any complex logic function, which consists of a combination of simple logic function/gate can be modelled as a combinations of different perceptron. This will be considered in detail under Deep Learning because it will be represented as a deep neural network.

Furthermore, the optimal weights for the implies logic function => are -1 and 1, while the threshold is -0.5. Therefore, the implies activation and activation step function can be used to evaluate the implies logic function, as shown in Table **59**, below.

Table 59. Output of implies logic operator using perceptron.

X1	X2	=> Activation	=> output
0	0	0	1
0	1	1	1
1	0	-1	0
1	1	0	1

7.2.5.3. Threshold Logic Unit as a Generalized Linear Classifier

The generalization of the TLU as a linear classifier for a binary two-input data to the TLU is to use a binary n dimensional input data to the TLU. Since the input data is n dimensional, therefore, the weights will be n dimensional, one weight for each of the input in the n-dimensional input space. In order to do this generalization, vectors will be used to represent the n-dimensional input space and the n-dimensional weight space. Therefore, basic knowledge of vector operators will be used and explained in this sub-section. Suppose the n-dimensional input space is represented as a vector, $\mathbf{x} = (x_1, x_2, x_3, x_4, \ldots, x_n)$, and the n-dimensional weight space is represented as a vector, $\mathbf{w} = (w_1, w_2, w_3, \ldots, w_n)$. Furthermore, suppose the threshold is θ, therefore, the critical condition for classification occurs when the activation is equal to the threshold, θ. Using the formula for activation and vector inner product, the following holds:

$\mathbf{x}.\mathbf{w} = \theta$

$$\sum_{i=1}^{n} x_i w_i = \theta$$

For an arbitrary x, the vector operation, projection of **x** onto **w** is given as:

$$x_w = \frac{x.w}{\| w \|} \quad \text{where the vector operation } \| w \| = \left(\sum_{i=1}^{n} w_i^2 \right)^{\frac{1}{2}}$$

$$x_w = \frac{\theta}{\| w \|}$$

Since w and θ are constant, therefore, the projection, must be a constant, and lie in a perpendicular straight line to the weight vector, w, as shown in Fig. (**52**).

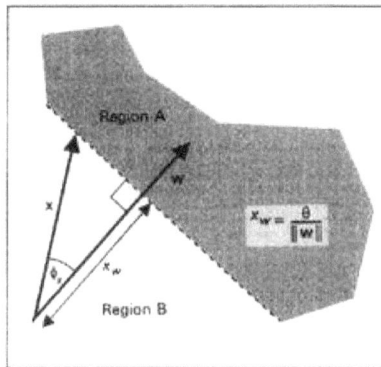

Fig. (52). Generalization of TLU as a Linear Classifier.

Therefore, the generalized condition for classification for n dimensional input space, represented by the vector **x**, and the weight vector **w**, with the threshold θ is given as **x.w** = θ. The relation defines an n-dimensional straight line. The generalized learners rule for the classifier, TLU is given in Equation 24, below.

$$y = \begin{cases} 1, & x.w > \theta \\ 0, & x.w < \theta \end{cases} \tag{24}$$

This generalized learners rule can be written in terms of the projection of **x** onto **w** as follows:

$$y = \begin{cases} 1, & x_w > \dfrac{\theta}{\|w\|} \\ \\ 0, & x_w < \dfrac{\theta}{\|w\|} \end{cases} \tag{25}$$

The value of the threshold θ, has been assumed to be positive, however, if the value of the threshold θ, is negative, the learners rule of the TLU classifier will be as follows:

$$y = \begin{cases} 1, & x.w > 0 \\ 0, & x.w < 0 \end{cases}$$

$$\tag{26}$$

$$y = \begin{cases} 1, & x_w > 0 \\ 0, & x_w < 0 \end{cases}$$

The reason for the change in the learners rule when the threshold θ is negative is

because $\|w\| = \left(\sum\limits_{i=1}^{n} w_i^2 \right)^{\frac{1}{2}}$ must always be positive.

7.2.5.4. Increasing the Dimension of the Input and Weight Vector by 1

From earlier discussion, training the Artificial neural network involves adjusting the weight and the threshold θ so that the TLU produces the expected output. In order to adjust these two parameters at the same time, the threshold can be included to part of the weight vector, **w**. Suppose x is the input vector and w is the weight vector and θ is the threshold. Since the condition for classification is given as:

x.w = θ

x.w-θ = 0

In order to make the negative sign explicit, we have the following:

x.w +(1) θ = 0

Therefore, the threshold can be regarded as a constant value of -1, which is tied to the input. This means that the input vector, $\mathbf{x} = (x_1, x_2, x_3, \ldots, x_n)$, with n-dimensional space can be regarded as an input vector $x = (x_1, x_2, x_3, \ldots, x_n, -1)$, with (n+1) dimensional space. The weight space will also be regarded as an (n+1) dimensional space, where the additional item is the threshold. This means that the vector, $w = (w_1, w_2, w_3, \ldots, w_n, \theta)$.

7.2.5.5. The Perceptron Learning Algorithm

Slight modification of the threshold logic unit gives rise to what is called Perceptron, which represents node of the artificial neural network. The Perceptron learning algorithm is an algorithm that can be used to train the Perceptron with the training it to learn the Perceptron rule that will be used to classify the output of an input. The process of training the Perceptron involves adjusting the (n+1) dimensional weight vector that includes the threshold as part of the components of the weight vector. The algorithm uses the (n+1) dimensional input vector, **v**, together with the output, t as the training data. With an initial (n+1) dimensional weight vector, **w**, the algorithm uses the same procedure that TLU uses to classify the output. If the classified output y is not the same as the training data output, t, the algorithm modifies the weight by a fraction of the input vector, **v**. Otherwise, if the classified output y is the same as the training data output, t, the algorithm does not modify. How to modify the weight vector when the classified output is not the same as the output from the training data is illustrated below.

Suppose the classified output y is 0, while the output in the training data, t = 1, with the current input vector, **v**. It means that the classification is wrong, therefore adjustment will be made to the weight vector, **w**. Since the classification is 0, it means that the activation is negative, which implies that the vector dot product, **v.w**< 0, In order to correct it, a fraction of the input vector, v will be added to the weight vector, **w** to produce a new weight vector **w'**, as follows:

$$w^1 = w + \alpha v \text{ where } 0 <= \alpha <= 1$$

However, suppose the classification was wrongly done, such that the classified output, y was 1, while the output from the training data t = 0. This means that adjustment will be done on the weight vector, **w** by subtracting a fraction of the input vector **v** from the weight vector, **w** in order to obtain a new weight vector, **v**. This can be expressed as follows:

$$w^1 = w - \alpha v \text{ where } 0 <= \alpha <= 1$$

Combining these two rules, in order to obtain the following rule:

$$w^1 = w + \alpha (t-y)v \text{ where } 0 <= \alpha <= 1$$

The change in the weight vector is given as: $\Delta w = w - w'$. This means that $\Delta w = \alpha(t-y)v$, For each component of the weight vector, change in weight is given as:

$\Delta w = \alpha(t-y)v_i$ where $1 <= i < n+1$, The parameter α, is called the learning rate because it determines how fast or how slow the learning takes place. The relations, w', Δw and Δw_i are called perceptron rule. This Perceptron algorithm can be formally stated as follows:

Repeat

For each training vector pair, (v, t)

Evaluate the output, y when v is the input to the

perceptron

IF y <> t then

Form new weight w' using $w^1 = w + \alpha \, (t-y)v$

ELSE

Do Nothing

END IF

END FOR

UNTIL y = t for all vectors, v

Illustrating the use of the Perceptron algorithm with the following example: Consider a binary, two-input perceptron, whose initial weights are 0, 4 and initial threshold is 0.3, the learning rate is 0.25. The above perceptron algorithm can be used to determine new weights and threshold after all the input data have been repeated. The preliminary computations can be presented in Table **60**.

Table 60. Training with the perceptron rule on two-input example.

w1	w2		x1	x2	A	Y	T				
0.0	0.4	0.3	0	0	0	0	0	0	0	0	0
0.0	0.4	0.3	0	1	0.4	1	0	-0.25	0	-0.25	0.25
0.0	0.15	0.55	1	0	0	0	0	0	0	0	0
0.0	0.15	0.55	1	1	0.15	0	1	0.25	0.25	0.25	-0.25

Since the y and t are not the same in the last training data, therefore the new weight vector will be obtained as follows:

$w = w + \alpha\ (t\text{-}y)\ v$

$\mathbf{w'} = (0.0, 0.15, 0.55) + 0.25.(1, 1, -1)$

$= (0.25, 0.4, 0.3)$

This means that $w_1 = 0.25$, w_2 0.4 and $= 0.3$

7.2.5.6. Gradient Descent Technique and Delta Rule

The problem with the perceptron rule in determining the new weight vectors using the training input pattern is that it cannot be generalized for any artificial neural network with n number of layers. The gradient descent technique allows this generalization, at the same time helps to minimize the error difference between the classified output, y and the target output, t. Since the classified output, y is a function of the activation, a, therefore, the activation parameter can be used to express the error. Using the gradient descent technique, the error for the pth pattern of the input data is stated below as:

$$e^p = \frac{1}{2}\left(t^p - a^p\right)^2 \qquad (27)$$

e^p is the error associated to the pth input pattern, t^p is the target output for the pth pattern of input while a^p is the activation for the pth input pattern. Expressing the activation for the pth pattern in terms of w_i and x_i, it can be shown that:

$$\frac{\partial e^p}{\partial w_i} = -\left(t^p - a^p\right)x_i^p \qquad (28)$$

Using the gradient descent technique, the following holds:

$$\Delta w_i = \alpha\left(t^p - a^p\right)x_i^p \qquad (29)$$

The above is called the delta rule, originally called Widrow-Hoff rule, is a constant of the artificial neural network, called the learning rate.

The training algorithm that uses the delta rule can be formally stated as follows:

REPEAT

For each training vector pair, **v,t**

Evaluate the activation, a, when v is the input

Adjust each of the weights using $\Delta w_i = a(t^p - a^p)x^p{}_i$

End for

Until rate of change of error is sufficiently small.

The delta rule as stated above can be generalized for any n layer ANN.

The following example will illustrate simple simulation of the delta rule.

Consider a binary, two-input TLU, whose initial weights are 0, 4 and initial threshold is 0.3, the learning rate is 0.25. The above algorithm that uses delta rule can be used to determine new weights and threshold after all the input data have been repeated. The preliminary computations can be presented in Table **61**, below.

Table 61. Training with the perceptron rule on two-input example.

w_1	w_2		x_1	x_2	A	t	$a\delta$	δw_1	δw_2	$\delta\theta$
0.0	0.4	0.3	0	0	-0.3	-1	-0.17	0	0	0.17
0.0	0.4	0.48	0	1	-0.08	-1	-0.23	0	-0.23	0.23
0.0	0.17	0.71	1	0	-0.71	-1	-0.07	-0.07	0	0.07
-0.07	0.17	0.78	1	1	-0.68	1	0.42	0.42	0.42	-0.42

Therefore the new weight vector, w can be obtained as **w'** = **w** + Δ**w**

w' = (-0.07, 0.17, 0.78) + (0,42, 0.42, -0.42) = (0.35, 0.59, 0.36).

This means that $w_1 = 0.35$, $w_2 = 0.59$ and $\theta = 0.36$

However, using the classified output instead of the activation for each of the pth pattern of input will require that the step function be smoothened. This means that the sigmoid will be required in the delta rule. Since the delta rule was obtained by taking derivative of the total error, therefore, the derivative of the sigmoid will be required in the delta rule. Recall that the sigmoid function as stated in Equation 30 is given as:

$$y = \sigma(a) \equiv \frac{1}{1 + e^{\frac{(a-\theta)}{\rho}}} \tag{30}$$

Therefore, the derivative of the sigmoid will be required in the delta rule that uses the classified output, y, as shown below:

$$\Delta w_i = \alpha \sigma'(\alpha)(t^p - y^p)x_i^p \tag{31}$$

The delta rule as stated above is for a single node, for a multi-layer artificial neural network with m nodes, the total error for the pth pattern of input data can be obtained by summing all the error for the pth pattern of input data, as stated below:

$$e^p = \frac{1}{2}\sum_{j=1}^{M}\left(t_j^{\ p} - \alpha_j^{\ p}\right)^2 \tag{32}$$

Since each node is independent, therefore the delta rule for the jth node can be stated below as:

$$\Delta w_{j_i} = \alpha \sigma'(\alpha_j)(t_j^{\ p} - y_j^{\ p})x_{ji}^{\ p} \tag{33}$$

7.3. Back Propagation Algorithm

Back propagation algorithm is an artificial neural network algorithm, which can be applied to a multi-layer artificial neural network. The multi-layer artificial neural network under consideration is a two-layer ANN. It consists of a set of input distribution points, two layers (the first layer is the hidden layer and the second layer is the output layer). The output layer is used to produce the output of the ANN, for a given input. The hidden layer consists of hidden nodes, they are so called because we do not have any direct access to their outputs during training, and they must generate their representations of the input. A two-layer Artificial neural network is shown below in Fig. (53) [19, 20].

The task is to compute the error gradient for each of the output nodes. The relation that computes this is the same as the delta rule for the jth output node, which can be stated as:

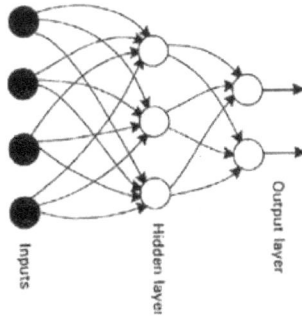

Fig. (53). Multi-layer artificial neural network.

$$\Delta w_{j_i} = \alpha \sigma'\left(\alpha_j\right)\left(t_j^{\ p} - y_j^{\ p}\right)x_{ji}^{\ p} \tag{34}$$

Furthermore, another problem is to compute the error gradient, $\partial e^p / \partial w_i k$ for each of the k node in the hidden layer. For each of the k hidden node, the errpr gradient can be computed using the relation:

$$\Delta w_{ki} = \alpha \sigma'\left(\alpha_k\right)\delta^k x_{ki}^{\ p}$$

$$\delta^k = \sum_{j \in I_k} \delta^j w_{jk}$$

In most literature, the slope of the sigmoid function is absorbed in the definition of 'd', in that case, for each hidden or output layer node, the error gradient can be expressed as:

$$\Delta w_{ki} = \alpha \sigma^k \delta^k x_{ki}^{\ p}$$

In particular, for each output node, the 'd' expression is:

$$\delta^k = \sigma'\left(\alpha_j\right)\left(t_j^{\ p} - y_j^{\ p}\right)$$

In particular, for each hidden layer node, the 'd' expression is:

$$\delta^k = \sigma'\left(\alpha_k\right)\sum_{j \in I_k} \delta^j w_{jk}$$

The back propagation algorithm can be formally stated as:

Initialize weights

REPEAT

FOR each input training pattern

Train on that input pattern

END for

UNTIL error is acceptably low

Each of the steps in the above back propagation algorithm will be explained further.

• Initialize the weight

This step allows you to initialize the weight by choosing small random values as initial values of the weights.

• Train on the input pattern

This main step is the body of a loop, which uses the input pattern and the current weight for the training. The steps of this main step are as follows:

1. Present the pattern at the input layer

2. Evaluation of the output by the hidden layer node using the input pattern.

3. Evaluation of the output by the output layer node using the outset of step 2.

4. Apply the target pattern to the output layer.

5. Compute the ds on the output nodes.

6. Train each output node using the gradient descent, $\Delta w_{ki} = \alpha \delta^k x_{ki}{}^p$

7. For each hidden node, compute the d, using $\delta_k = \sigma'(\alpha_k) \sum_{j \in I_k} \delta^j w_{jk}$

8. Use the d obtained in step 7 to train each of the hidden node, based on the gradient descent technique, $\Delta w_{ki} = \alpha \sigma^k(\alpha_k) \delta^k x_{ki}{}^p$

The first three steps are called forward pass because the input pattern is forwarded from the input layer nodes to the hidden layer nodes, then to the output layer nodes. On the other hand, steps 4 to 8 are called backward pass because the computation of the error gradient begins at the output layer node, which it passes backward to the hidden layer nodes. In particular, step 7 is the propagation step, which propagates the ds from the output nodes back to the hidden nodes. The backpropagation algorithm is sometimes called error backpropagation algorithm or back error propagation algorithm [19, 20].

7.4. Using WEKA to Solve Artificial Neural Network Problem

It may not possible to manually simulate the backpropagation algorithm using a set of training data, rather, there are machine learning simulation software that can be used to simulate various machine learning models, like the artificial neural network. The screen shot shown below in Fig. (54) is WEKA's simulation of the ANN on the cpu training data.

Fig. (54). WEKA's simulation of the ANN on the cpu.arff sample dataset.

7.5. Conclusion

In this unit, you have learnt the fundamentals of Artificial neural network, which includes: biological neuron, biological neural network, relationship between biological neural network and artificial neural network, together with some of the computational model of Artificial neural network.

7.6. Summary

Though Artificial Neural Network was modelled after the biological neural network, however, because the human brain contains billions of neurons, which makes it impossible to realise the accuracy of the biological neural network in artificial neural network. Because of this, the concept of artificial neural network is gradually giving way to the concept of deep learning.

8. DEEP LEARNING

Deep learning is another aspect of machine learning, which is similar to artificial neural network. It is the process of solving complex problems by using a hierarchy of other simpler concepts. When the graph of this hierarchy of concepts is drawn, it is deep. A large artificial neural network can be considered as deep learning. Deep learning allows the computer to build complex concept out of simpler concepts. Deep learning is very useful in solving software problems in the following area: computer vision, speech and audio processing, natural language processing, robotics, bioinformatics, chemistry, video games, online advertisement, finance *etc.* Though deep learning appears to be new, but it dates back to 1940s, and has been rebranded as different names, only recently, to be known as deep learning. The various rebranding names are: cybernetics, multi-layer artificial neural network, connectionism and deep learning. Deep learning is mainly used to engineer systems but it is inspired by the biological neural network. One of the reasons for the inspiration of biological neural network is the possibility of intelligent behaviour, which the biological neural network provides. Deep learning involves the use many layers, many nodes and many datasets that are more than the traditional artificial neural network [21, 22].

8.1. Deep Feedforward Network

The deep feedforward network is the same as the multi-layer feedforward neural network, which was considered in the previous unit. It is called deep because it has many layers [21, 22]. The depth or number of layers of the network is large. The depth of the network is measured by the number of layers of the artificial neural network. For a single layer ANN, the depth is 1, two-layer ANN has a depth of 2, while a three-layer ANN has a depth of 3 *etc.* Therefore, a deep feedforward network is an n-layer ANN, where n is very large. The backpropagation algorithm for minimizing the error gradient applies here. Figs. (**55 - 57**) illustrate the depth of feedforward network.

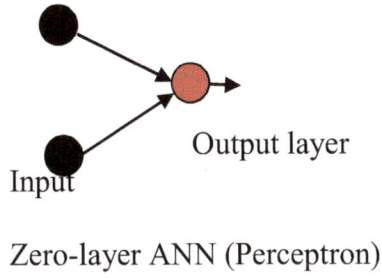

Output layer

Input

Zero-layer ANN (Perceptron)

Fig. (55). Hidden layer output layer.

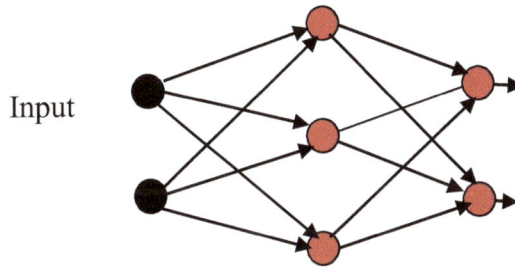

Input

Fig. (56). Zero and one-layer ANN.

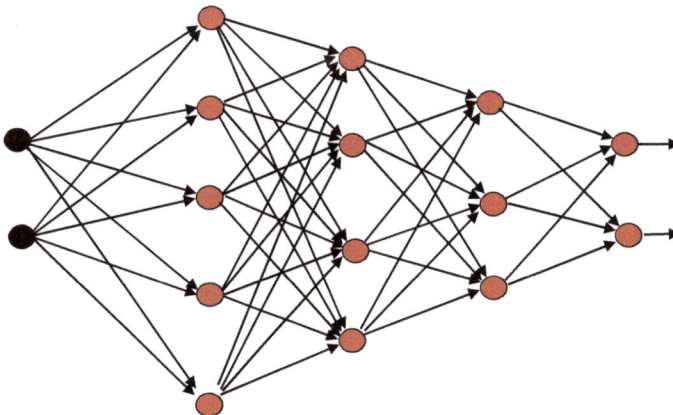

Fig. (57). Four-layer deep feedforward network.

If the depth or number of layers is greater than 2, it becomes a deep feedforward network.The input layer is not counted when determining the number of layers of a deep neural network, this is because the input layer nodes do not produce any output, What the input layer nodes produce is the input only.

8.2. Application of Deep Feedforward Network

The deep feedforward network as an aspect of machine learning can be used to solve both supervised and unsupervised machine learning problem in different area. In this section, detail illustration will be made to explain the use of deep feedforward network to model and determine the output of complex logic function. In the previous unit, the perceptron was used to determine the output of complex logic functions, like 'and' (.), 'or' (+), 'not' ('). In this section, deep feedforward network will be used to model and determine the output of complex logic function. A complex logic function is a logic function that uses combinations of different simple logic functions (., +. '). In this representation, each of the simple logic functions will be represented as the node of the deep feedforward network, while the various inputs and outputs will be represented by appropriate arrows. The weights and thresholds of the various simple logic function will be used to determine the output of a specific logic function. These examples will illustrate how the weights and thresholds are used to predict the output of any input. The following examples will illustrate further:

8.2.1. Application of Deep Learning to Logic Function Evaluation

The following examples illustrate the application of deep learning to the evaluation of logic functions:

Example 1:

Consider the following complex logic function, (X.Y) + (X+Y), the task is to represent the complex logic function using deep feedforward network, and use the optimal weights and thresholds to determine the various outputs of the complex logic function. The output of each node will help you to determine the simple logic function that the node represents, as shown in Fig. (**58**)

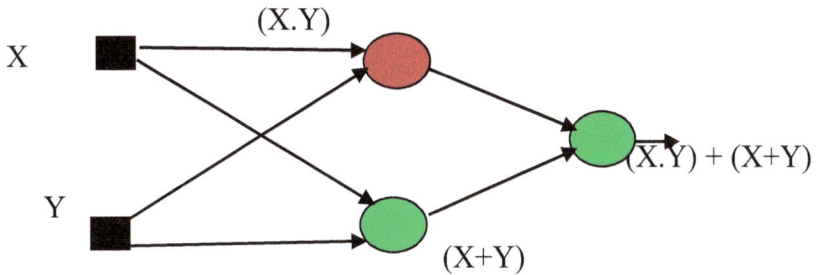

Fig. (58). Deep feed forward network for (X.Y) + (X+Y).

Using the weights and threshold for the logic functions, Table 4.8.1 will help to determine the output of the complex logic function represented in Table **62**.

Table 62. Output for the deep feedforward network in (Fig. 58).

X	Y	A(X.Y)	S(X,Y)	A(X+Y)	S(X+Y)	A((X.Y) + (X+Y))	S((X.Y) + (X+Y))
0	0	0	0	0	0	0	0
0	1	1	0	1	1	1	1
1	0	1	0	1	1	1	1
1	1	2	1	2	1	2	1

S((X.Y)+(X+Y)) is the result of the step function on the activation of (X.Y)+(X+Y). This is the output of the logic function, (X.Y)+(X+Y).

Example 2.

Consider the following complex logic function, (X.Y).(X+'Y), the task is to represent the complex logic function using deep feedforward network, and use the optimal weights and thresholds to determine the various outputs of the complex logic function. The output of each node as shown in Fig. **(59)** will help you to determine the simple logic function that each node represents.

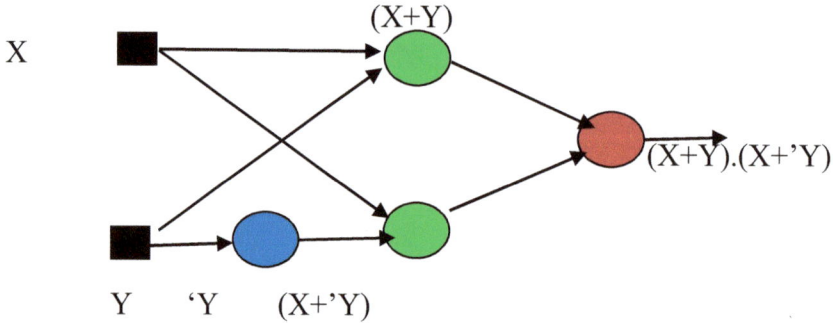

Fig. (59). Deep feedforward network for (X+Y).(X+'Y).

Using the weights and threshold for the logic operators, Table **63** shows the output of the complex logic function.

Table 63. Output for the deep feedforward network in (Fig. 59).

X	Y	A('Y)	S('Y)	A(X+'Y)	S(X+'Y)	A(X+Y)	S(X+Y)	A((X+'Y).(X+Y))	S((X+'Y).(X+Y))
0	0	0	1	1	1	0	0	1	0
0	1	-1	0	0	0	1	1	1	0
1	0	0	1	2	1	1	1	2	1
1	1	-1	0	1	1	2	1	2	1

$S((X+'Y).(X+Y))$ is the result of the step function on the activation of $(X+'Y).(X+Y)$. This is the output of the logic function, $(X+'Y).(X+Y)$.

Example 3

Consider the complex logic function, $(X+Y).('X+Z).(Y+Z)$, the task is to represent the logic function using deep feedforward network and use the defined weights of each of the simple logic operators and step function activation to determine the output of each of the possible inputs of the complex logic function. Since each of the simple logic functions have been defined with two binary inputs, therefore any complex logic functions that has more than two binary inputs will be split such that the maximum inputs in any node will be two, as shown in Fig. **(60)**.

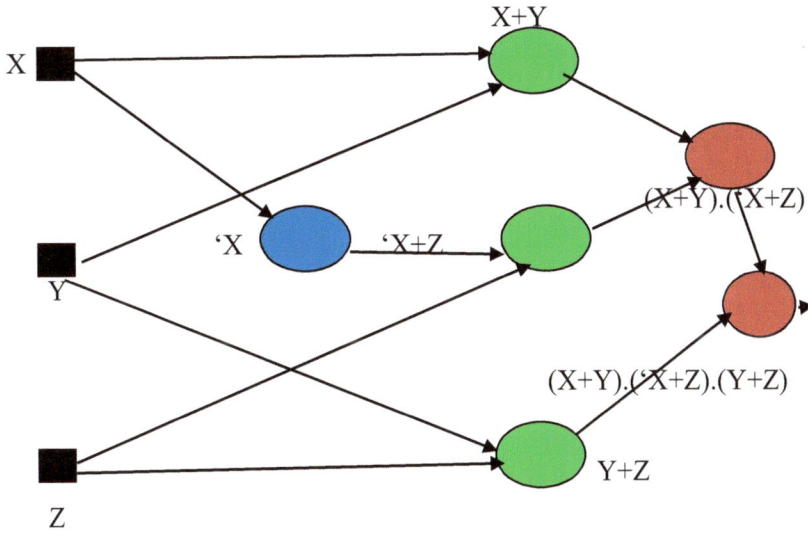

Fig. (60). Deep feedforward ntwork for (X+Y).('X+Z).(Y+Z).

Since there are three logic inputs, therefore, all the possible combinations of inputs will be eight. Table **64** illustrates the activations and outputs of each of the logic functions and their outputs.

Table 64. Output for the deep feedforward network in (Fig. 60).

X	Y	Z	A('X)	S('X)	A(X+Y)	S(X+Y)	A('X+Z)	S('X+Z)	A(Y+Z)
0	0	0	0	1	0	0	1	1	0
0	0	1	0	1	0	0	2	1	1
0	1	0	0	1	1	1	1	1	1
0	1	1	0	1	1	1	2	1	2
1	0	0	-1	0	1	1	0	0	0
1	0	1	-1	0	1	1	1	1	1
1	1	0	-1	0	2	1	0	0	1
1	1	1	-1	0	2	1	1	1	2

X	Y	Z	S(Y+Z)	A((X+Y).('X+Z))	S(W)=S((X+Y).('X+Z))	A(W.(Y+Z))
0	0	0	0	1	0	0
0	0	1	1	1	0	1
0	1	0	1	2	1	2
0	1	1	1	2	1	2
1	0	0	0	1	0	0

(Table 64) cont.....

X	Y	Z	S(Y+Z)	A((X+Y).('X+Z))	S(W)=S((X+Y).('X+Z))	A(W.(Y+Z))
1	0	1	1	2	1	2
1	1	0	1	1	0	1
1	1	1	1	2	1	2

X	Y	Z	S(W.(Y+Z))
0	0	0	0
0	0	1	0
0	1	0	1
0	1	1	1
1	0	0	0
1	0	1	1
1	1	0	0
1	1	1	1

Example 4

Consider the logic function The task is to represent the logic function using the deep feedforward network, and evaluate the logic function using activation and step function. The complex logic function can be represented as two simple logic functions as follows:

$X \Leftrightarrow Y = (X \Rightarrow Y).(Y \Rightarrow X)$. This can be represented using deep feedforward network as shown in Fig. (**61**).

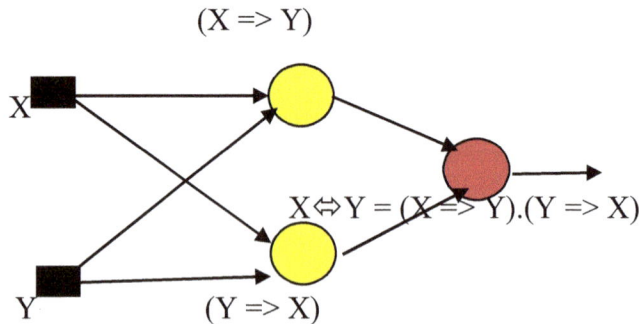

Fig. (61). Deep feedforward network for $X < = > Y$

The complex logic function can be evaluated using the following weights of the implies logic function, -1, 1, while the threshold for the implies logic function is -

0.5. Table **65** illustrates the activations and outputs of each of the logic functions and their outputs.

Table 65. Output for the deep feedforward network in Fig. (61).

X	Y	A(X=>Y)	S(X=>Y)	A(Y=>X)	S(Y=>X)	A((X=>Y).(X=>Y))	S((X=>Y).(X=>Y))
0	0	0	1	0	1	2	1
0	1	1	1	-1	0	1	0
1	0	-1	0	1	1	1	0
1	1	0	1	0	1	2	1

Example 5

Consider this complex logic function, $((X+Y).(X+'Y)).(X.Y.Z)$. Represent this complex logic function using deep feedforward network, and use appropriate weights and threshold for the simple logic function to determine the outputs of the logic function. Note that any node with more than two inputs will be split such that the maximum number of inputs in any node will be 2. This is shown in the deep feedforward network of Fig. (**62**).

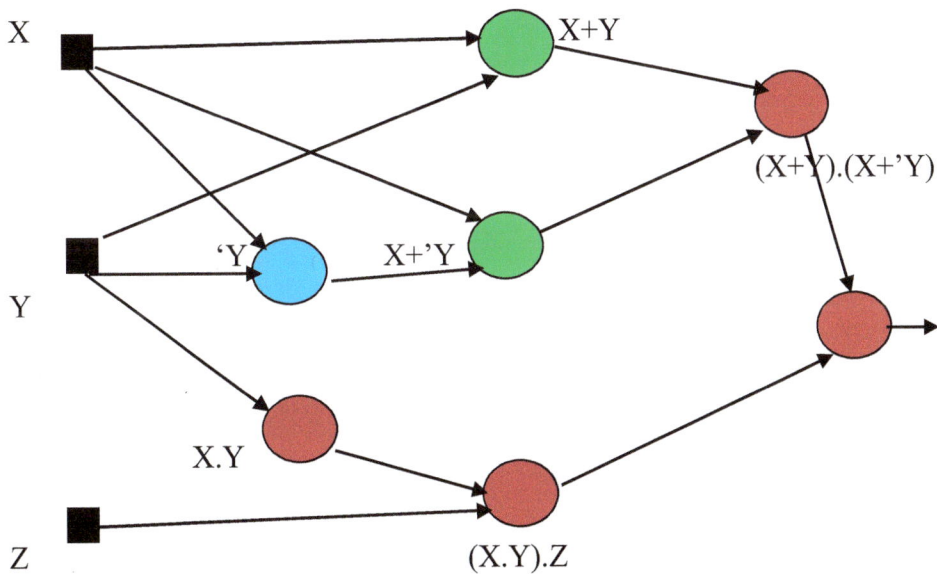

Fig. (62). Deep feedforward network for $((X+Y).(X+'Y)).(X.Y.Z)$.

The output of the logic function, using activations and step function is shown in Table **66**.

Table 66. Output for the deep feedforward network in Fig. (62).

X	Y	Z	A('Y)	S('Y)	A(X+Y)	S(X+Y)	A(X+'Y)	S(X+'Y)	A(X.Y)
0	0	0	0	1	0	0	1	1	0
0	0	1	0	1	0	0	1	1	0
0	1	0	-1	0	1	1	0	0	1
0	1	1	-1	0	1	1	0	0	1
1	0	0	0	1	1	1	2	1	1
1	0	1	0	1	1	1	2	1	1
1	1	0	-1	0	2	1	1	1	2
1	1	1	-1	0	2	1	1	1	2

X	Y	Z	S(X.Y)	A((X.Y).Z)	S((X.Y).Z)	A((X+Y).(X+'Y))	S((X+Y).(X+'Y))
0	0	0	0	0	0	1	0
0	0	1	0	1	0	1	0
0	1	0	0	0	0	1	0
0	1	1	0	1	0	1	0
1	0	0	0	0	0	2	1
1	0	1	0	1	0	2	1
1	1	0	1	1	0	2	1
1	1	1	1	2	1	2	1

X	Y	Z	A((X+Y).(X+'Y) ((X.Y).Z)))	S((X+Y).(X+'Y) ((X.Y).Z)))
0	0	0	0	0
0	0	1	0	0
0	1	0	0	0
0	1	1	0	0
1	0	0	1	0
1	0	1	1	0
1	1	0	1	0
1	1	1	2	1

8.3. Deep Convolutional Neural Network

Convolutional neural network is a type of neural network, which is used to process visual imagery. This means that the inputs of the convolutional neural network are images. Since the input is visual image, therefore the input layer will consist of different nodes, which will be fully connected to the various nodes of the hidden layers, but the output layer will have a single node as shown in the Fig. (**64**), below. When the convolutional neural network contains many layers, it can be regarded as Deep convolutional neural network [23].

8.3.1. Layers of Deep Convolutional Neural Network

Deep Convolutional neural network, ConvNet is made up of series of layers, which include the following: convolutional layer, pooling layer and fully connected layer. Each layer transforms its input using appropriate differentiable activation function.

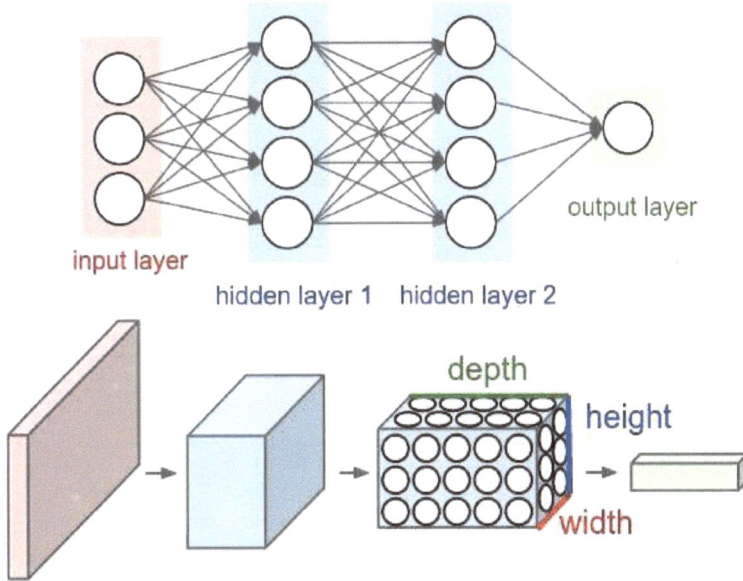

Fig. (64). Deep convolutional neural network.

<u>8.3.1.1. Convolutional Layer</u>

Convolutional layer is the core building block of a ConvNet, this is because it is the layer that does most of the computational tasks. It is positioned immediately after the input of the convolutional deep neural network. The parameters that the convolutional layer takes are a set of learnable filters. Each filter is small spatially, but it extends through the full height of the input volume. Fig. (**65**) below shows the interaction between the input and the convolutional layer in a convolutional deep neural network.

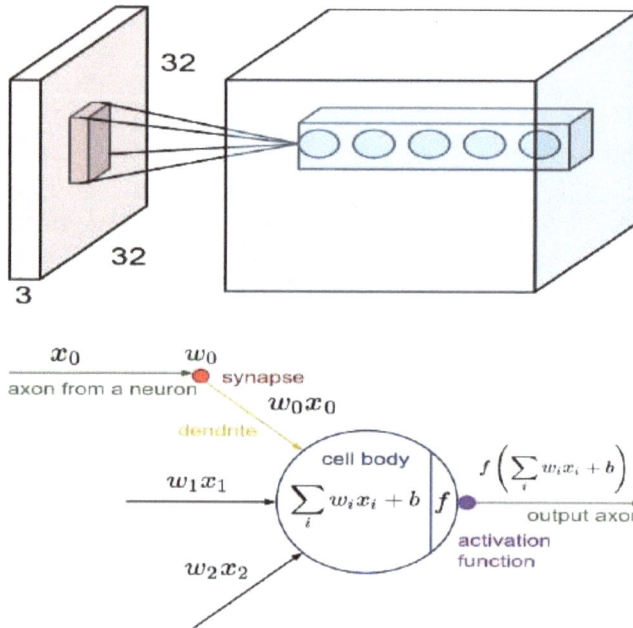

Fig. (65). Node in a convolutional layer.

8.3.1.2. Pooling Layer

The Pooling layer lies in-between successive convolutional layers of deep convolutional neural network. Its main function is to reduce the partial size of the parameters of the convolutional layer, thereby reducing the number of parameters and the amount of computations in the convolutional deep neural network. This process controls overfitting in the convolutional deep neural network. Fig. (66) illustrates further the function of the Pooling layer [25].

8.3.1.3. Full Connect Layer

The nodes of fully connected layer are connected to every other nodes of the previous layer.

8.4. Deep Recurrent Neural Network

A deep recurrent neural network is another class of multi-layer neural network, where the previous output of a neuron (node) can be combined with its present input to form the current output. This means that a node can have a directed edge or arc from itself, back to itself. The recurrent neural network has memory, which it uses to remember its previous output. The node or neuron of a recurrent neural network can be shown in Fig. (**67**).

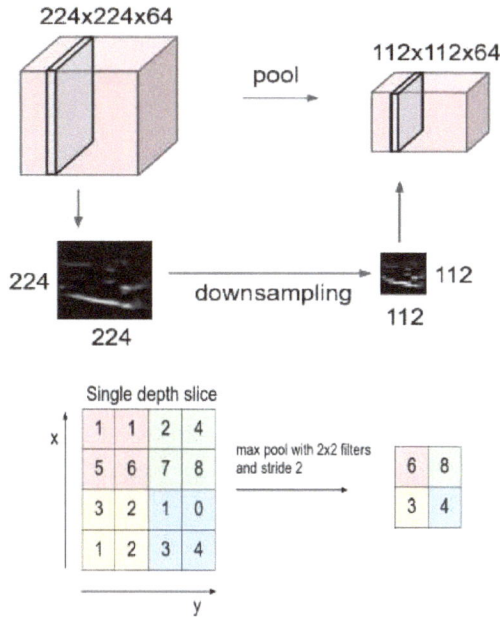

Fig. (66). Functions of poolingh layer.

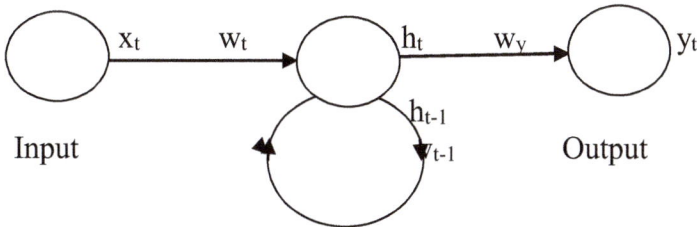

Fig. (67). Recurrent neural network.

Like in artificial neural network, recurrent neural network can have multi layers, to give rise to deep recurrent neural network. For a single neuron/node of a recurrent neural network as shown in Fig. (**67**), suppose h_t is the current state/output of the node at t, and x_t is the input to the node, $w_t$is weight of the node at time t, w_{t-1} is the weight at time t-1. Therefore, the formula for the output at time t, h_t will be a function of x_t and h_{t-1}, which can be written as:

$h_t = f(h_{t-1}, x_t)$

Suppose the activation function of the node is tanh, therefore the formula for the output at time t using the activation function is written as:

$h_t = \tanh(h_{t-1}w_{t-1} + x_t w_t)$

Furthermore, suppose the output of the output neuron/node is $y_t$and the weight of the output neuron/node is w_y, therefore the output function of the output node can be written as:

$y_t = h_t w_y$

8.5. Conclusion

In this unit, you have learnt the meaning and applications of the following types of deep learning: deep feedforward network, deep convolutional neural network, deep recurrent neural network. You have also learnt how to represent a complex logic function as a feedforward network, and use the activation and step function to determine the output of the complex logic function.

8.6. Summary

Deep learning, which is a variant of artificial neural network has been considered in detail. It helps us to devise policies and function that the neuron/node will use with the aim of accomplishing its goal. This leads to another aspect of machine learning, which is called reinforcement learning.

9. REINFORCEMENT LEARNING

In Unit 1 of Chapter 1, the rational agent model was used to explain what acting rationally means as part of the definition of Artificial Intelligence. It was stated that an agent is something that perceives and acts, in order to achieve its goal. Therefore, reinforcement learning is an aspect of machine learning, which is a process whereby an agent acts and interact with its environment with the aim of maximizing rewards. Whatever man does in life is done with the aim of getting the best out of it, this aspect of machine learning uses the same concept of maximizing rewards in the actions of agent, as it acts and interacts in its environment.

9.1. Introduction to Reinforcement Learning

Reinforcement learning is an aspect of machine learning that uses the learning theory of learning by interacting with our environment *i.e.* learning by trial and error. Babies, in general learn using this learning theory. Though reinforcement learning can be considered as unsupervised machine learning approach, because it does not require a teacher in the learning process, however, some authors considers it as the third approach to machine learning, alongside supervised and unsupervised machine learning. The reason is because the system learns by the rewards of its various action. Reinforcement learning involves the process of maximizing rewards by agent as its acts and interacts in its environment. It uses the Markov Decision Process of probability theory as illustrated in the Fig. (**68**).

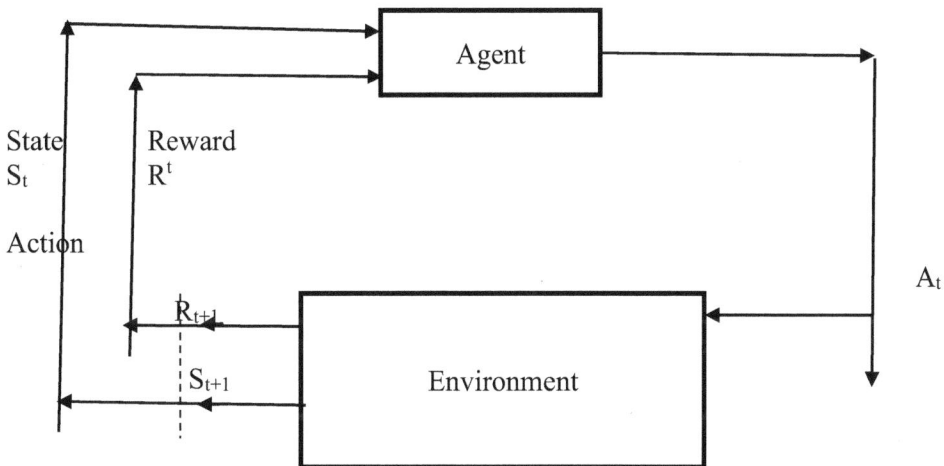

Fig. (68). Agent-environment interaction in a markov decision process.

As an agent interacts in its environment, it takes action, which makes it to be in a particular state and receives a particular reward based on its action. As it takes a new action in its environment, it assumes new state and receives new reward based on its new action. Based on the reward it receives in performing a particular action, it continues to learn the best action that will produce the best reward.

9.2. Features of Reinforcement Learning

Apart from the fact that reinforcement learning is another approach to machine learning, alongside supervised and unsupervised machine learning, it has other distinguishing features that make it different from other types of machine learning. These distinguishing features include the following:

9.2.1. Trade-off between Exploitation and Exploration

In reinforcement learning, there is a trade-off between exploitation and exploration. Exploitation is a concept where an agent takes an existing action that maximizes its reward, while Exploration is a concept where an agent tries new action with the aim of evaluating its reward. Reinforcement learning system does not use each of the concept exclusively. This is because in order to exploit, it must explore. Therefore, there must be a balance between exploitation and exploration. This trade-off is not present in other machine learning approaches, like supervised and unsupervised machine learning.

9.2.2. Holistic Approach to Problem Solving

Reinforcement machine learning considers the whole problem of an agent interacting in an uncertain environment with the aim of maximizing its reward, rather than considering in a sub-problem, without considering how it fits into the larger picture. This limitation of focusing on sub-problem has been used in both supervised and unsupervised machine learning approaches.

9.2.3. Goal of Agent is Central in Reinforcement Learning

All reinforcement learning problems have explicit goals, which the agent seeks to achieve, in most cases, the goal is to maximize a reward. In an uncertain environment, it is generally assumed that in the beginning, the agent has to operate in the uncertain environment. As it takes actions, it learns the new state of the environment and uses it to define its goal, which will maximize its rewards.

9.2.4. Fruitful Interaction with Other Discipline

Reinforce learning is part of a long trend within Artificial Intelligence towards successful integration with other engineering and scientific disciplines, like statistics, operation research, mathematics *etc.* Reinforcement learning has also interacted strongly with Psychology and Neuroscience.

9.2.5. Evaluative Feedbacks

This is another distinguishing features of Reinforcement learning, which makes it different from supervised learning. The training data of reinforcement learning are used to evaluate the actions in order to determine the rewards. Evaluative feedback determines how good the action taken is, not if the action taken is the best. This calls for the optimization methods, like dynamic programming method or evolutionary method, which helps to determine the best action to take at any time. In contrast to supervised learning, the training data are used to instruct the correct action to take.

9.3. Elements of Reinforcement Learning

The following are the various elements of reinforcement learning: policy, reward signal, value function and an optional model of the environment. Each of these elements will be discussed in detail.

9.3.1. Agent

The learner or decision maker is called the agent. From a system perspective, it is called system controller.

9.3.2. Environment

The thing that the agent interacts with, which consists of everything outside the agent is called the environment. From a system perspective, the environment is the controlled system.

9.3.3. Action

The agent interacts continually with the environment by performing action. Each action makes input to the environment. From system perspective, action of an agent in an environment can be regarded as signal that the controller sends to the controlled system.

9.3.4. Environment State

The action of the agent on the environment makes the environment to be in a particular condition, called state. From a system perspective, the state of the environment can be regarded as the condition of the controlled system as a result of the signal that the controller sends to the controlled system.

9.3.5. Policy

Policy is the way an agent act at any given time. It can be regarded as a mapping from the set of states that the environment can be in, to the set of actions to be taken when in those states. In Psychology, it is called stimulus-response rules or associations. Policy is a core element of reinforcement learning, because policy alone is sufficient to determine the behavior or action of agent. Policy can take different forms, which includes the following: simple function or lookup table, excessive computation and stochastic (mapping from states to probabilities of selecting each possible action).

9.3.6. Reward Signal

The goal of a reinforcement learning problem is called reward signal. At each time step, the reinforcement learning system sends to the reinforcement learning agent a reward in form of number. The goal of the agent is to maximize all the rewards over a long time. Reward signal can be regarded as what are good or bad signal. In a biological system, reward signals can be regarded as experience of pleasure or pain. Reward signals are determined by the action of the agent and the state of the environment. Reward signals can be altered by the agent through the action of the agent. This because the action of the agent has direct effect on the reward signal and indirect effect on the reward signal through changing the state of the environment. Reward signal can be a stochastic (probabilistic) function of the action of the agent and stochastic (probabilistic) function of the state of the environment.

9.3.7. Value Function

While the reward signal is what is good or bad at the moment, the value function show what is good or bad over a long period of time. The value of a state is the total amount of rewards that an agent is expected to accumulate over a future starting from that state.

9.3.8. Time Step

This is regarded as the arbitrary successive stages of decision making and acting.

9.3.9. Model of the Environment

The model of the environment is a representation of the environment that allows inferences to be made about how the environment will behave. This element of reinforcement learning is optional because some reinforcement learning methods do not require a model of the environment, while some require it.

9.4. History of Reinforcement Learning

The history of reinforcement learning can be traced back to two main research areas, which later merged into what is known today as modern reinforcement learning in the early 1980s. The first area of research is the trial and error, which started in the psychology of animal learning and continued through some of early researches in Artificial Intelligence, and led to the revival of Reinforcement learning in the early 1980s. The second early research area is the optimal control of dynamical system, which started in the late 1950. Its focus was on the design of controller that will minimize a measure of a dynamical system's behavior over time. One of the solutions to the optimal control of dynamical system was devised in the mid-1950s by Richard Bellman. Bellman's solution used the concepts of dynamical system state and value function (optimal return function) to define a functional equation called Bellman's Equation. Today, the class of methods for solving optimal control problems by solving the Bellman's equation is called dynamic programming. Bellman, in 1957 introduced the stochastic solution to the optimal control problem, which is known as Markovian Decision Processes (MDPs). However, in 1960, Ronald Howard devised the iterative policy method for MDPs.

The only feasible solution to the general stochastic optimal control problems remains dynamic programming. However, it suffers from what Bellman called 'curse of dimensionality.' This means that the computational requirement of dynamic programming grows as the number of state variables grow, but it is more efficient and more applicable than any other general solution. At that time, there was no connection between optimal control problems and dynamic programming with learning, and this could be due to the different goals of the disciplines involved. Paul Werbos, in 1977 was the first to connect optimal control problems and dynamic programming with learning. He devised an approximate solution to dynamic programming, which was called 'heuristic dynamic programming.' He also proposed a greater relationship between dynamic programming and optimal control in relation to neuroscience. However, the full inter-relationship between dynamic programming and learning was credited to Chris Watkins in 1989. Subsequent researches led to the formation of the term, 'neuro-dynamic programming, which is an integration of dynamic programming and neural network. Neuro-dynamic programming can also refer to integration between deep learning and reinforcement learning. This is because dynamic programming, which a solution to optimal control of the dynamic system is a solution of reinforcement learning problem, and deep learning refers to a neural network with many layers.

9.5. Conclusion

This unit has considered reinforcement learning as the third aspect of machine learning, alongside supervised and unsupervised machine learning. Its fundamental concept is learning by trial and error.

9.6. Summary

The features and elements of reinforcement learning have been considered in this unit.

CONCLUDING REMARKS

This chapter has focused on various aspects of machine learning, which include: supervised machine learning, unsupervised machine learning, reinforcement learning, neural network, deep learning, *etc.* However, these various aspects of machine learning are applied to solve different problems in various areas of life. This application will form the focus of the next chapter.

REFERENCES

[1]   C.M. Bishop, *Pattern Recognition and Machine Learning.* Springer, 2006.

[2]   I.H. Witten, and E. Frank, *Data Mining: Practical Machine Learning Tools and Techniques.* Elsevier, 2005.

[3]   D.J. Hand, H. Mannila, and P. Smyth, *Principles of Data Mining.* MIT Press: Cambridge, MA, 2001.

[4]   A. Smola, and S.V.N. Wishwanathan, *Introduction to Machine Learning.* Cambridge University Press, 2008.

[5]   T.M. Mitchell, *Machine Learning.* McGraw-Hill: New York, 1997.

[6]   S. Shalev-Shwartz, and S. Ben-David, *Understanding Machine Learning: From Theory to Algorithms.* Cambridge University Press, 2014.
       [http://dx.doi.org/10.1017/CBO9781107298019]

[7]   D. Pyle, *Data Preparation for Data Minning.* Morgan Kaufmann: San Francisco, 1999.

[8]   S.M. Weiss, and N. Indurkhya, *Predictive Data Mining: A Practical Guide.* Morgan Kaufmann: San Francisco, 1998.

[9]   S.S. Aksenova, *Machine Learning with WEKA.* School of Engineering and Computer Science, Department of Computer Science, California State University: Sacramento, California, 2004.

[10]   E. Frank, *Machine Learning with WEKA* University of Waikato: Newzealand.

[11]   A.L. Curyn, B. Jones, R. Gupta, and H.P. Singh, *An Introduction to Artificial Neural Network; In Automated Data Analysis* Narosa Publishing house: Mew Delhi, India, 2001.

[12]   C.M. Bishop, *Neural Networks for Pattern Recognition.* Oxford University Press: Oxford, 1995.

[13]   I. Hertz, A. Krogh, and R.G. Palmer, *Introduction to the Theory of Neural Computation.* Addison-Wesley Wokingham: England, 1991.

[14]   R. K. Singh, and Prajneshu, "Artificial neural network methodology for modelling and forecasting maize crop yield", *Agric. Econ. Res. Rev.,* vol. 21, pp. 5-10, 2008.

[15]   B. Cheng, and D.M. Titterington, "1994,"Neural Network: A Review from a Statistical Perspective", *Stat. Sci.,* vol. 9, pp. 2-54, 1994.
        [http://dx.doi.org/10.1214/ss/1177010638]

[16]   K. Gurney, *An Introduction to Neural Networks.* UCL Press: London, 1997.
        [http://dx.doi.org/10.4324/9780203451519]

[17]   K. Fukushima, "A Neural Network for Visual Pattern Recognition", *Computer,* vol. 21, pp. 65-75, 1989.
        [http://dx.doi.org/10.1109/2.32]

[18]   S. Haykin, *Neural Network: A Comprehensive Foundation.* Macmillan: New York, 1994.

[19]   A.L. Coryn, B. Jones, R. Gupta, and H.P. Singh, *An introduction to artificial neural networks.*
        https://cds.cern.ch/record/487162/files/0102224.pdf

[20]   K. Gurney, *An introduction to neural networks.* https://www.inf.ed.ac.uk/teaching/courses/nlu/assets/reading/Gurney_et_al.pdf

[21]   M. Deshpande, *Deep Learning for Human Beings: Understanding How Deep Neural Network Works.* Zenwa Pty Ltd., 2018.

[22]   B.X. Glorot, *Understanding the Difficulty of Training Deep Feedforward Neural Networks.* AISTATS, 2010.

[23]   M. Zeiler, and R. Fergus, *Visualizing and Understanding Convolutional Networks arXiv: 131.2901,* pp. 1-11, 2013.

[24]   D. Yu, and L. Deng, *Efficient and Effective Algorithms for Training Single-Hidden Neural Networks,* 2012.
        [http://dx.doi.org/10.1016/j.patrec.2011.12.002]

[25]   https://cs231n.github.io/convolutional-networks/

CHAPTER 5

Machine Learning Applications

Abstract: Most machine learning tools are applied to different areas to solve specific problems. This involves the use of a large dataset as training data. This chapter explores selected applications of machine learning algorithms to solve different problems using different datasets.

Keywords: COVID-19 dataset, Generalized least square, Polynomial regression, Terrorism dataset.

1. ANALYZING TERRORISM DATASET USING CLASSIFICATION BASED ALGORITHMS

The purpose of most machine learning datasets is to use machine learning algorithms in analyzing the dataset, with the aim of gaining insight into the dataset. This will be useful in making an informed decision that will be used to solve a particular problem. This paper uses a decision tree and naive bayes algorithm to analyze terrorism datasets for the purpose of gaining insight into the dataset, which will be used in decision making for the purpose of fighting against terrorism.

1.1. Introduction

There are more than one hundred definitions of terrorism in the literature [1], but in this study, we shall consider two of such definitions. Terrorism is defined in one of the studies [2] as the threatened or actual use of illegal force and violence by a non-state actor to attain a political, economic, religious, or social goal through fear, coercion, or intimidation. In a similar manner, terrorism is defined in another study [3] as the premeditated use or threat or use of violence by individuals or sub-national group to obtain a political or social objective through the intimidation of a large audience beyond that of an immediate victim.

Based on these definitions, it means that terrorist attacks cannot be perpetuated by the government but by an organized group or individual. It also means that every terrorist attack must be intentional; it cannot happen by accident. Furthermore, there must be some level of violence or immediate threat to violence. According to the definitions, the aim of every terrorist attack must be political, economic, religious, or social. In addition, there must be evidence of intention to coerce or intimidate. Globally, research on terrorism has increased in the wake of the September 11 terrorist attack on the United States of America [4]. Because of its effect on life and property, terrorism has become an important issue in international politics and, in particular, national politics [4]. Every government that is a victim of terrorism always strategizes on how to counter-terrorism. Counter-terrorism has been defined as the practices, tactics, strategies, and techniques that governments, militaries, police, and security agencies use to prevent or in response to terrorist threats [5].

Similarly, the issue of terrorism has captured the attention of the research community since the terrorist attack of September 11 on the USA [6]. This has led to an increase in the volume of publications, both books and journal publications. Research on terrorism has focused on terrorism tactics, which include the following aspects: research on suicidal terrorism and research on the use of chemical, biological, radiological, and nuclear weapons. Furthermore, because organized groups may claim responsibilities for most terrorist attacks, as reported in a study [6], therefore there has been increased terrorism research on the terrorist group. Most research on terrorism prior to 9/11 focused on a systematic review of terrorism. This does not provide any basis for helping in making a decision that will help to control terrorism. However, most terrorism research after 9/11 have used both descriptive and inference statistics to structure and organize the collection of terrorism data and analyze the terrorism data, with the aim of making an informed decision that can help to control terrorism.

However, there are promising Artificial Intelligence tools, like machine learning models, which can be used to analyze terrorism datasets, with the aim of aiding in decision making, thereby controlling terrorism. Most recent studies have used these machine learning tools to analyze the terrorism dataset of various countries, like Egypt, India, *etc.*, [1, 5, 7, 23, 24]. This is because machine learning models are best used in analyzing large datasets with the aim of discovering patterns in such datasets.

The terrorism dataset, as maintained by the Global Terrorism Dataset, contains several attributes. The dataset will not be useful except for machine learning algorithms that are used to obtain insight into the dataset. Therefore, this paper uses these two machine learning algorithms, decision tree and naive bayes algorithms, to analyze the global terrorism dataset for the purpose of obtaining insight that will be used in decision making while fighting against terrorism.

In this study, we tried to predict a chosen class attribute of any country using two different machine learning algorithms. The dataset is the Global Terrorism Database, between 1996 and 2018. The naive bayes algorithm and the decision tree algorithm are two supervised, classification-based machine learning algorithms that have been demonstrated to perform well in predicting any chosen class attribute of terrorism dataset [7, 1]. Specifically, we tried to:

- Identify relevant class-attribute and non-class attributes from the Global Terrorism Database for a particular country, for the purpose of predicting the class-attribute, given the non-class-attributes as test data.
- State and use the naive bayes machine learning algorithm to predict a chosen class-attribute of the Global Terrorism Database for a particular country.
- State and use the decision tree machine learning algorithm to predict a chosen class-attribute of the Global Terrorism Database for a particular country.
- Simulate the naive bayes and decision tree machine learning algorithms using WEKA as the simulation software and Global Terrorism Database for a particular country as the training data.

Machine Learning is an aspect of Artificial Intelligence that uses a large set of data to solve a particular problem [8]. One of the problems that Machine Learning solves is the classification problem, which identifies the category or class of a particular test data [8]. Classification based machine learning algorithms are supervised machine learning algorithms because the class or category of the training data is known [8]. Artificial Intelligence can be used as a tool for combating terrorism [9]. This can be demonstrated in the use of a big data analytic called SMACT. SMACT is an acronym for Social Media Analysis for Combating Terrorism [9]. It can be implemented using ApacheSpark, which is a machine learning tool. It involves a four-stage process involving data collection, data pre-processing, deep analysis, and detailed identity investigation. The data collection stage involves the collection of data from different social media, like Facebook, Twitter, SMS, email, WhatsApp, *etc.*, using a web scraper tool, while the data pre-processing stage involves cleaning the data using data cleaning tools, like SampleClean. The deep analysis consists of two stages. The first stage uses the lexicon text mining and semantic analyzer to filter the pre-processed data by extracting the keywords and related terms, together with the weighting factor or frequency of each term. The second stage of the deep analysis clusters the extracted keywords/terms into various clusters. The last stage of the four-stage process of the Apache sparks applies a technique that is based on graph theory to the output of the deep analysis with the aim of detecting pattern, which will be used to investigate the suspected terrorist communication channels, associated phone numbers, financiers/supporters, *etc.*

Furthermore, data mining, text mining, sentiment analysis, machine learning systems, and predictive analytics are some of the Artificial Intelligence techniques that can be used to battle terrorism [6]. In particular, the machine learning tools, like decision tree, random forest, lazy classifier IBK linear NN, lazy classifier IBK, filtered neighbor search, lazy tree, IBK, ball tree, lazy classifier K-star, multilayer perception, multiclass classifier, and naive bayes have been demonstrated to be good in analyzing terrorism dataset [6]. However, since analysis is based on user needs, therefore the same tools can be used to analyze the same dataset but with a different class attribute to be predicted. This means that if a study focuses on classifying the class attribute, attack-responsibility, another study can focus on classifying terrorist-group, while another study can focus on classifying attack-location, *etc* [6]. Another data mining tool that can be used to fight terrorism is sentiment analytics [10]. It is an opinion mining process, which can be used to detect the opinions of various social media users, like Twitter. By detecting the opinion of social media users, it detects acts of terrorism. It is a fact that the number of Twitter accounts has increased; as a result, the number of tweets has greatly increased. Since these tweets are used to share both good and bad messages on politics, religion, sports, terrorism, *etc.*, therefore, with sentiments analytics, opinions in every area can be mined, including terrorism [10]. Machine learning, therefore, serves as a tool that can be used to predict and classify different things, including terrorism. Terrorist attacks can be scientifically predicted and validated using machine learning [11]. Since there are different machine learning tools that can be used to predict and classify different things, including terrorism, therefore, the best machine learning tool for predicting terrorism can be identified, and the most important attributes in the dataset can be identified [11]. In machine learning, classification algorithms aim at accurately predicting the class for each data, provided that sufficient number of the classes is available [1]. This can be applied to different research areas, like terrorism prediction, medical, finance, weather prediction, business intelligence and homeland security. However, classification algorithms can be probabilistic or non-probabilistic, binary or multi class. The various machine learning algorithms, including classification algorithms can be validated with the use of machine learning software called WEKA. This piece of software has been used to validate the terrorism dataset on Egypt as provided by GTD, using different classification algorithms [1]. One of the most important attributes that can be considered as a class attribute, which needs to be predicted is the terrorist-group attribute, which identifies the terrorist group that is responsible for a particular terrorist attack [5]. This is because the first step in fighting against terrorism is to search for the group name that is involved in a terrorist attack, afterwards, strategy will be adopted to catch them [5].

Classification based machine learning algorithms will be helpful in this regard. Several studies have analyzed terrorism dataset from Global Terrorism Database with the aim of predicting the terrorist group responsible for a terrorist attack [12]. is one of such study, which used different machine learning algorithms, and compared the performances of the various outputs. Therefore, the trend in counter terrorism is the use of Artificial Intelligence and Big Data Analytics [13]. However, one of the challenges in the design of counter-terrorism policy is the uncertain nature of terrorism [14]. Therefore, both government and security agency need to understand the pattern that terrorist use to launch attacks. This pattern can be understood through the use of intelligence gathering and analysis of such dataset. Such intelligence will involve the use of pattern and network analysis *i.e.* relation [14]. Though different machine learning techniques have been used in literature to understand terrorism patterns, thereby predicting and preventing it from occurring, such machine learning techniques can be strengthened when it is combined with network analysis, which shows the interactions between the various terrorist attacks [14].

1.2. Methodology for Collection and Analysis of Terrorism Dataset

The terrorism dataset that this study predicts a chosen class attribute is the Global Terrorism Database, which is maintained by the National Consortium for the Study of Terrorism and Responses to Terrorism (START), University of Maryland, USA. It is a comprehensive, robust and methodical dataset on incidents of both domestic and international terrorism across the globe. Its main purpose is to enable researchers to increase their understanding on terrorism. The database contains about 120 separate attributes for each incidents of terrorist attack, spanning between 1996 and 2018. It is updated at the end of every year, so this study uses the technique used in both social and computational sciences. Before using the machine learning algorithms on the terrorism dataset, the method of data selection was used to choose part of the dataset that will be analyzed This was done by filtering the terrorism dataset for those data that the country_txt attribute is for a particular country. The method of pre-processing was used to convert the dataset into an appropriate format. The dataset is in Excel format, which needs to be converted to Attribute Relation File Format, ARFF. This is the format that WEKA, a machine learning software requires all datasets that it analyzes to be converted into. Feature engineering was also used to select the most useful and appropriate attributes from the dataset. After preparing the dataset, a machine learning software, called Waikato Environment for Knowledge Analysis (WEKA) was used to simulate the two machine learning algorithms on the terrorism dataset for Nigeria. During feature engineering, we carefully selected the following attributes for the purpose of the analysis, which are as follows: iyear, provstate, attacktype1, success, weapontype1, targtype1, gname, claimed, nkill. The codebook for the Global Terrorism Database has defined each of the selected attributes as follows: iyear is the attribute that indicate the year that the incident of terrorism occurred, while provstate is the attribute that indicate the Province/Administrative Area/State where the attack occurred The attribute, attacktype1 indicate the type of terrorist attack, which can be any of the following: Assassination, Armed Assault, Bombing/Explosion, Hijacking, Hostage Taking (Barricade Incident), Hostage Taking (Kidnapping) *etc.* The success attribute is used to indicate if the attack was successful or not, while the attribute Weapontype1 attribute indicate the type of weapon that was used in the terrorist attack. The attribute targtype1 indicate the type of target or victim of the terrorist attack, while the attribute, gname indicate the terrorist group that claimed responsibility of the attack. The claimed attribute indicates if a terrorist group has claimed the responsibility of the attack or not, while nkill is an attribute that indicate the number of casualties in the attack. To the best of our knowledge, no study has used any of these two algorithms to analyze the GTD terrorism dataset, with the chosen non-class attributes and class-attributes used in this study.

1.3. Design of the Two Machine Learning Algorithms

The two machine learning algorithms that we have chosen for the purpose of this analysis are the naïve bayes and decision tree algorithms. Both of them are supervised machine learning algorithms because the class attribute of the dataset is known, and we wish to predict the class attribute of a test dataset. Since analysis of dataset is based on user needs, therefore, the class attribute that we have chosen for this analysis is provstate. This attribute indicates the state where a terrorist attack occurs. The reason for the choice of this attribute is that it will help the relevant government to know how to deploy her counter terrorism teams to the various states for the purpose of fighting terrorism in that country. Each of these classifiers or machine learning algorithms/models will be explained in detail.

1.4. Naïve Bayes Algorithm

The naïve bayes algorithm is a classification based machine learning algorithm. This is because it determines the class value of a test data, given the training data. It is based on the Bayes theorem of conditional probability. The naïve bayes algorithm can be formally stated as follows:

1. Identify the input non class attributes and the output class-attribute.
2. Categorize the training data, where necessary.

3. Compute the class probabilities.
4. Compute the conditional probabilities.
5. Use Baye's theorem to determine decision rule for each instance of the input test data.

1.5. The Decision Tree Algorithm

The decision tree algorithm is an important supervised machine learning algorithm, which splits a dataset based on certain conditions. The learner's output is to create a model in form of a rule that is represented as a tree that will predict the class of an input data. This decision rule is also in form of if then statement. A general algorithm for a decision tree can be described as follows:

1. Pick the best attribute/feature. The best attribute is one which best splits or separates the data. It is also the attribute that has the most information gain. The most information gain is a measure that shows the attribute that best splits the dataset.
2. Ask the relevant question.
3. Follow the answer path.
4. Go to step 1 until you arrive at the answer.

Mathematical formula can be used to determine the information gain of each of the attributes. The attribute with the highest information gain is regarded as the most information gain attribute. Such attribute will best split the dataset. The mathematical formula that computes the information gain of an attribute is given as:

$$IG = Entropy(parent) - Weighted(Entropy(Children)) \tag{1}$$

$$Entropy(attribute) = \sum_{i=1}^{k} - p_i \log_2 p_i \tag{2}$$

p_i is the proportion of attribute class with ith category value in the dataset. Children are the various values of the attribute (sub-node), while parent is the node that has a particular set of children, and the value k is number of classes of the class-attribute.

1.6. Simulation, Results and Discussion

The coded sample data in Table **1** was used to simulate the naïve bayes algorithm.

Table 1. Sample coded terrorism dataset from GTD.

Iyear	Provstate	Attacktype1	Success	Weapontype1	Targtype1	Gname	Nkill
1996	24	2	1	8	4	1	0
1996	24	1	0	6	4	1	0
1999	10	2	1	5	4	2	10
2000	10	6	1	5	1	1	0
2001	14	2	1	5	3	3	2
2003	10	2	1	5	14	1	6
2003	38	6	1	5	1	4	1
2006	32	2	1	5	1	1	9
2007	38	7	1	11	21	5	0
2010	32	3	1	6	21	6	0

Table **2** shows the conditional probabilities, it will be used to determine the class attribute of given input attributes.

Table 2. Conditional probabilities of the various values of input attributes given values of class attribute, Provstate.

Other Input Attributes	Categories of Class Attribute, Provstate
Iyear	Provstate 24 10 14 38 32 1996 1 0 0 0 0 1999 0 0.3333 0 0 0 2000 0 0.3333 0 0 0 2001 0 0 1 0 0 2003 0 0.3333 0 0.5 0 2006 0 0 0 0 0.5 2007 0 0 0 0.5 0 2010 0 0 0 0 0.5
Attacktype1	Provstate 24 10 14 38 32 1 0.5 0 0 0 0 2 0.5 0.6667 1 0 0.5 3 0 0 0 0 0.5 6 0 0.3333 0 0.5 0 7 0 0 0 0.5 0
Success	Provstate 24 10 14 38 32 0 0.5 0 0 0 0 1 0.5 1 1 1 1

(Table 2) cont.....

Other Input Attributes	Categories of Class Attribute, Provstate
Weapontype1	Provstate 24 10 14 38 32 5 0 1 1 0.5 0.5 6 0.5 0 0 0 0.5 8 0.5 0 0 0 0 11 0 0 0 0.5 0
Targtype1	Provstate 24 10 14 38 32 1 0 0.3333 0 0.5 0.5 3 0 0 1 0 0 4 1 0.3333 0 0 0 14 1 0.3333 0 0 0 21 1 0 0 0.5 0.5
Gname	Provstate 24 10 14 38 32 1 1 0.6667 0 0 0.5 2 0 0.3333 0 0 0 3 0 0 1 0 0 4 0 0 0 0.5 0 5 0 0 0 0.5 0 6 0 0 0 0 0.5
Nkill	Provstate 24 10 14 38 32 0 1 0.3333 0 0.5 0.5 1 0 0 0 0.5 0 2 0 0 1 0 0 6 0 0.3333 0 0 0 9 0 0 0 0 0.5

Furthermore, using the coded sample data from the GTD, in Table **3**, for the decision tree algorithm, we obtain the decision tree shown in Fig. (**1**). With the decision tree in Fig. (**1**), we can determine the class attribute, provstate for a specific type of incident of terrorism that occurred in a particular year.

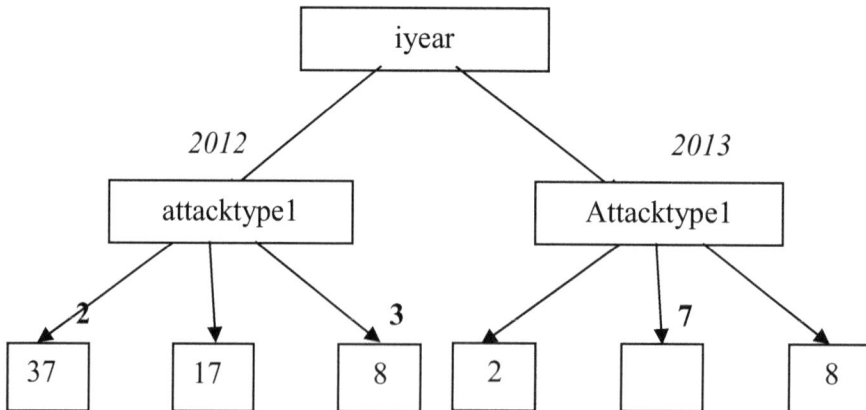

Fig. (1). Decision tree of the sample coded dataset from GTD for the decision tree algorithm.

Table 3. Sample coded terrorism dataset from GTD.

Iyear	Provstate	attacktype1
2012	37	2
2012	8	7
2012	19	3
2012	35	3
2012	19	3
2012	8	2
2013	8	2
2013	8	7
2013	20	2
2013	31	2

1.7. Simulation, Results and Discussion

In this paper, we have been able to use two different machine learning algorithms to analyze the terrorism dataset. The analysis involves the prediction of province/state where a particular terrorist attack had occurred. This will help the government to know the type of terrorist attacks that can occur in any state/province of a country. As a result, government will be able to make decision to know how to deploy anti-terrorism team to the various state/province.

2. ANALYZING TERRORISM DATASET USING PROBABILITY DISTRIBUTION FUNCTIONS

Probability distribution functions, like Poisson, Exponential, Binomial, Normal probability distribution functions are excellent tools that can be used to visualize the probability distributions of random variables defined from machine learning datasets. However, these probability distribution functions have not been widely used as machine learning tools for visualizing the probability distribution of terrorism dataset, thereby limiting the usefulness of these probability distribution functions in visualizing the probability distribution of machine learning dataset, like terrorism dataset.

This study aims at using various probability distribution functions to visualize the probability distribution of terrorism dataset. In carrying out the study, we:

- Defined appropriate random variables, based on the terrorism dataset.
- Identified the probability distribution function for a defined random variable.

• Simulated the identified probability distribution function for a defined random variable on the computer.
• Visualized the results of the simulated probability distribution function using the terrorism dataset.

One of the effects of September 11, 2002 terrorist attack on the United States of America is that the volume of research on terrorism has increased all over the world [4]. Terrorism has become an important issue in both international and national politics, all over the world, because of its effect on life and property [4]. The government of any country that is a victim of terrorism always strategizes, with the aim of discovering new approaches to counter terrorism. Counter terrorism is the various tactics, practices and strategies that various militaries, police and security agencies adopt in fighting terrorism through the prevention of terrorist attack or through response to terrorist threats [5].

Furthermore, since the September 11 terrorist attack on the United States of America, the attention of research community has focused on terrorism. This is evident based on the increase in the volume of publications on terrorism [6]. Recent researches on terrorism have focused on the use of machine learning tools for analyzing terrorism dataset, which will help in making informed decisions that will be used to fight against terrorism. This has been done for terrorism datasets for Egypt, India *etc.* [1, 5, 7]. Machine learning tools have the capability for analyzing large dataset, called training data, with the aim of discovering regularities or patterns in such dataset.

Data visualization has been defined as visual representation of data, which involves mapping data into numerical form and translating the numerical data into graphical representation [19]. Data visualization has been identified as an important tool for discovering complex structures and patterns in exploratory data analysis [15]. Though different methods of projecting multi-dimensional dataset exits, which includes: linear discriminant analysis, LDA [16], and projection pursuit [17]. This study projects two dimensional dataset from multi-dimensional terrorism dataset by defining appropriate random variables from the GTD and using relevant probability distribution function to compute the various probabilities of the random variables and visualizing the probability distribution as a two dimensional scatter plot.

In a similar manner, there are different techniques that can be used to visualize multi-dimensional dataset, like the terrorism dataset. These techniques can be classified into five different classes, which includes the following: geometric, pixel oriented, icon-based, hierarchical and graph based techniques [18]. In a geometric visualization technique, which this study uses, the training data are visualized as points in a two dimensional space. Examples of geometric visualization technique are scatter plot, radviz, polyviz and gridviz [19].

Different machine learning tools/algorithms, like support vector machine, regression, clustering *etc.* have visualization features, which enables one to understand the result of the algorithm [20 - 22].

2.1. Methodology for Collection and Visualization of Terrorism Dataset

The terrorism dataset that this study analyzes is the Global Terrorism dataset, which is maintained by the National Consortium for the Study of Terrorism and Response to Terrorism (START) at the University of Maryland, USA. The dataset contains incidents of domestic and international terrorism in all the countries of the world. The aim of maintaining the dataset is to enable researchers and analysts to increase their understanding on terrorism. There are about 120 separate attributes in the dataset, for each incident of terrorism, spanning between 1996 and 2018. The dataset is updated at the end of each year, so this study uses the 2018 edition of the database. It is designed to be amendable to the quantitative analytic technique used in both social and computational science. Therefore, it can filter incidents of domestic and international terrorism for a particular country.

Though different probability distribution functions will be used as machine learning tools to visualize the terrorism dataset for a particular country, we shall define appropriate random variables and use appropriate probability distribution function to visualize the terrorism dataset.

2.2. Theory of the Probability Distribution Functions

The following probability distribution functions were used as machine learning tools in analyzing the terrorism dataset for any country in the global terrorism database.

2.2.1. Binomial Probability Distribution Function

The binomial probability distribution function models a situation where any event has only two possible outcomes, with many of such events happening. In the terrorism dataset, one of the attributes for each of the terrorism incidents is success, which stored 1 if the terrorism incident was successful, otherwise, 0. Since there are several number of incidents of terrorism, therefore, we define a random variable, X as the number of successful terrorism incidents in Nigeria. The binomial probability distribution function is given in Equation **3**, as:

$$P(X=x) = \begin{cases} {}^{n}C_{x}p^{x}(1-p)^{n-x}, & x = 0,1,2,3,4...n \\ 0, & otherwise \end{cases} \tag{3}$$

In Equation (3), n is the total number of terrorism incidents, p is the probability that an incident of terrorism was successful. This probability distribution function can help us to visualize the probability of different number of successful incidents of terrorism in any or all the countries. It can also be useful in predicting the probability that a certain number of terrorism incidents will be successful or in determining the number of incidents of terrorism with the maximum probability of being successful.

2.2.2. Poisson Probability Distribution Function

The Poisson probability distribution function is used to model the number of events occurring within a given period of time. Since the terrorism dataset contains an attribute that indicate the date of occurrence of each incident of terrorism, therefore, we can obtain a parameter, as the rate of occurrence of terrorism. The random variable, X was defined as the number of incidents of terrorism per unit time. The Poisson probability distribution function is given in Equation **4**, as:

$$P(X=x) = \begin{cases} \dfrac{\lambda^{x}e^{-\lambda}}{x!}, & x = 0,1,2,3,4,5,6,7,... \\ 0, & otherwise \end{cases} \tag{4}$$

This probability distribution function is very useful in visualizing the distribution of probability that a particular number of incidents of events occurred per unit time. It can also be used to predict the number of incidents of terrorism per unit time, which has the highest probability of occurring.

2.2.3. Exponential Probability Distribution Function

The Exponential probability distribution function is used to model inter occurrence time of events. The terrorism dataset contains the date of occurrence of incidents of terrorism, therefore, we can obtain the rate of occurrence of incidents of terrorism from the terrorism dataset. We can define a random variable, X as the inter occurrence time of incidents of terrorism. The Exponential probability distribution function can be used to obtain the distribution of probabilities for all the values of the random variable, X. The Exponential probability distribution function is given in Equation **5**, as:

$$P(X = x) = \begin{cases} \lambda e^{-\lambda x}, & 0 \le x \le \inf inity, \\ 0, & otherwise \end{cases} \tag{5}$$

λ is the rate of occurrence of incidents of terrorism, whic can be obtained from the terrorism dataset.

2.2.4. Normal Probability Distribution Function

This is regarded as the most important probability distribution function because many samples of dataset are normally distributed. Examples of attributes of dataset that are normally distributed are: height, weight, exam score *etc.* The terrorism dataset contains an attribute, called nkill, which shows the number of people that are killed in each incident of terrorism. Therefore, a random variable X can be defined as the number of people killed in each incident of terrorism. This random variable is distributed to be normal, and we can use the Normal probability distribution function to obtain the probabilities for all the possible values of the random variable. The Normal probability distribution function is given in Equation **6**, as:

$$P(X = x) = \begin{cases} \dfrac{1}{\sigma\sqrt{2\Pi}} e^{-\frac{1}{2}\left(\frac{x-\mu}{\sigma}\right)^2}, & -\inf inity \le x \le \inf inity, \\ 0, & otherwise \end{cases} \tag{6}$$

2.3. Simulations, Results and Discussion

Java programming language was used to simulate each of the probability distribution functions. Each of the parameters of the various probability distribution functions was obtained from the terrorism dataset. Different experimental run of each of the simulated models of the probability distribution functions produced appropriate probabilities as results. These results were tabulated and Excel spreadsheet was used to visualize the results as two dimensional scatter plots.

2.3.1. Result of Simulated Models for Binomial Probability Distribution Function

A random sample of 100 incidents of terrorism was selected from the terrorism dataset, and a random variable X was defined as the number of successful incidents of terrorism. The random variable X is distributed to be binomial. From the ransom sample, the parameter, p of binomial probability distribution function was computed. Based on 2018 terrorism codebook, successful incidents of terrorism are those incidents of terrorism that their missions were accomplished. Fig. (1) shows the probability distribution of the random variable X, which represents the number of successful incidents of terrorism.

The result of Fig. (2) shows that between 75% and 95% of incidents of terrorism have high probability of being successful terrorist attacks. This means that most of incidents of terrorism were successful. Therefore, security personnel that fight against terrorism should intensify efforts in their fight against terrorism.

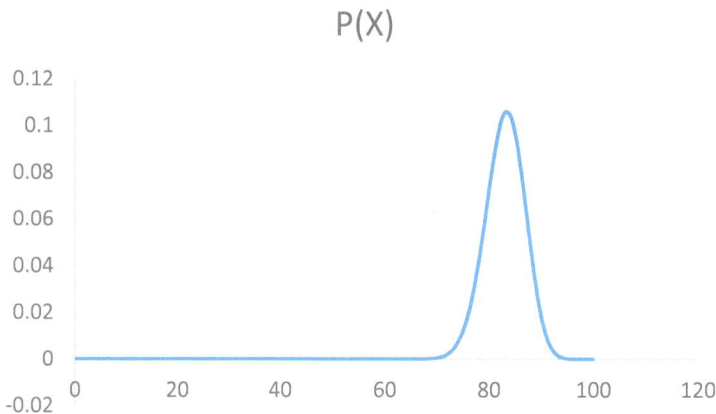

Fig. (2). Binomial probability distribution of the number of successful incidents of terrorism.

In a similar manner, a random sample of 100 incidents of terrorism was selected from the terrorism dataset and a random variable, X was defined as the number of incidents of terrorism that occurred in a particular region/state. The random variable X is distributed to be Binomial probability distribution function, the parameter p was computed from the random sample of 100 incidents of terrorism and Fig. (3) shows the probability distribution of number of incidents of terrorism that occurred in that region/state.

P(X)

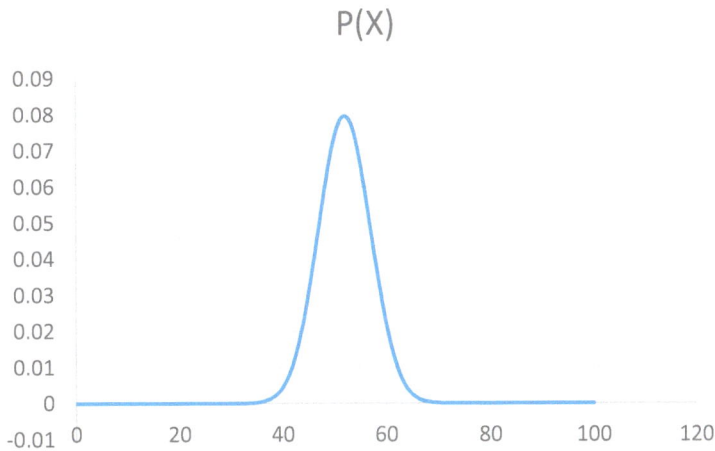

Fig. (3). Binomial probability distribution of the number of incidents of terrorism that occurred in a particular region/state.

The result in Fig. (**3**) shows that between 40% and 65% of incidents of terrorism have high probability of occurring in the chosen region/state. Therefore government and security agents that fight against terrorism should intensify efforts in that region/state,

2.3.2. Result of Simulated Models for Poisson Probability Distribution Function

With a random sample of 100 incidents of terrorism from the terrorism dataset, which occurred within an interval of 3 months. The average rate of occurrence of terrorism was computed to be approximately 33 incidents of terrorism every month *i.e.* $\lambda = 33$. Therefore, we define a random variable X to be the number of incidents of terrorism that occurred every month, it means that X is distributed to be Poission probability distribution function. The probability distribution of the number of incidents of terrorism every month is shown in Fig. (**4**).

The result of Fig. (**4**) shows that between 20 and 40 incidents of terrorism per month has high probability of occuring.

2.3.3. Result of Simulated Models for Normal Probability Distribution Function

Finally, with a random sample of 100 incidents of terrorism, from the terrorism dataset, we define a random variable X to be the number of people killed in the various incidents of terrorism in the collected sample. X is distributed to be Normal probability distribution function. The paramaters of Normal probability distribution function, which are mean and standard deviation were obtained from the random sample, as 10 and 17.7 respectively.

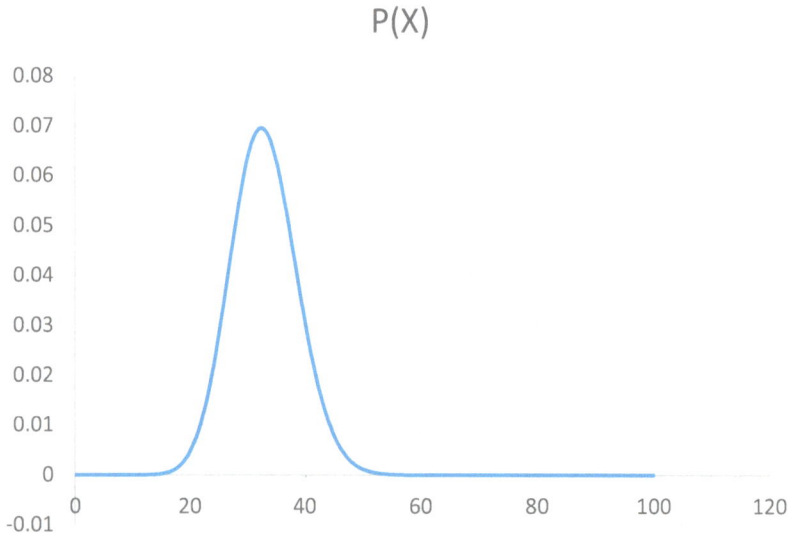

Fig. (4). Poisson probability distribution of the number of incidents of terrorism per month.

The result of Fig. (**5**) shows that at least an average of 60 people has high probability of being killed in every incidents of terrorism in the chosen country.

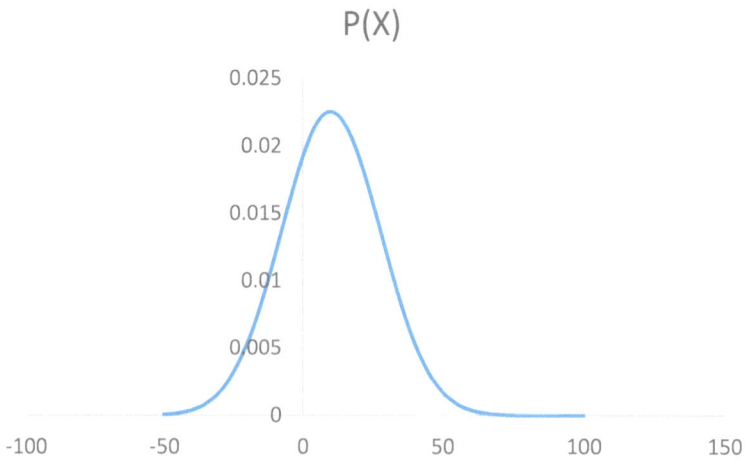

Fig. (5). Normal probability distribution of the number of people killed in every incidents of terrorism in a chosen country.

2.4. Conclusion

In this paper, we have shown that the various probability distribution functions can be used to visualize the probability distribution of terrorism dataset. Such visualization of terrorism dataset will help the government to make informed decision on how to fight terrorism in any country.

3. POLYNOMIAL REGRESSION ALGORITHM FOR ANALYSING COVID-19 DATASET

Polynomial regression is a type of regression where the relationship between the prediction attribute and non-prediction attribute shows a rising and falling pattern, which is called polynomial. This type of classification based machine learning algorithm is ideal for COVID-19 dataset, where the number of incidents of COVID-19 exhibits a falling and rising pattern. Polynomial regression algorithm can be used to predict yhe number of incidents of COVID-19 in any particular day. This prediction can be very useful for health workers and government health agencies to know how to apply COVID-19 restrictions. This unit uses the method of generalized least square to develop polynomial regression algorithm.

3.1. Generalized Ordinary Least Square Method

The generalized ordinary least square method splits the dataset into different partitions. Each of the partitions will be regarded as a linear dataset, whose parameters of the linear model will be determined by using the method of least square. Therefore, for a polynomial of degree n, there will be n different ordinary linear models. This is necessary because a polynomial of degree n can be regarded as n different linear models. One of the important assumption of this approach is that a polynomial of degree n will have n different roots, which means that each of the linear models must intersect the x-axis. Therefore, in order to determine the roots of the polynomial, each of the linear model will be equated to zero. Solving for x, means determining the roots of the polynomial. Having determined the roots of the polynomial, the polynomial can be obtained by expressing it as products of linear factors, using the roots. Illustrating with the following examples, suppose the linear models were obtained as $Y = A_i X + B_i$. In order to obtain the various roots of all the linear model of the polynomial, equate the linear model to zero and solve for x. This means that $root_i = -B_i/A_i$. Therefore, the polynomial can be expressed as the product of the various linear factors, using the roots. Using the above example, the prediction rule of the polynomial dataset can be expressed as: $\prod_{i=1}^{n}(X - root_i)$.

3.2. Literature Review

Polynomials have been defined as mathematical expressions that are frequently used in solving problems in science and engineering. On the other hand, curve fitting has been defined as the process of finding an equation that can be used to model data [28]. Curve fitting, therefore is a statistical term, which aims at determining the machine learning rule, in form of the prediction polynomial equation that can be used to make prediction from the data set. The importance of polynomial model cannot be overemphasised ; polynomial models have been shown to be an alternative to neural network [25], which means that neural network problems can be solved using polynomial model. This alternative shows that at each layer of neural network, there is a rough correspondence to some fitted parametric polynomial regression model. This also means that in many applications, one can fit polynomial model, thereby bypassing neural network.

Furthermore, empirical investigation on the possible use of polynomial regression in other areas of neural network has been done in [26]. Theoretical relationship between neural networks and polynomials has been reported in [27]. Six different degrees of polynomial equations were used to analyse COVID-19 dataset for India [29]. The author computed the root mean square of the sixth degree of polynomial, and found that it was lower than the root mean square of the lower degree polynomial. With the current spread of corona virus, like wide fire, the author proposed the use of polynomial regression based machine learning analysis for analysing COVID-19 dataset in the next seven days, for Indian doctors, with its implementation, using MATLAB [29]. Though no country in the world has approved pharmaceutical solution to COVID-19 [30], however, the best that can be done in order to reduce the effect of corona virus is to develop machine learning algorithms that data scientists can use to analyse COVID-19 dataset, with the aim of making informed decision that will lower the peak of corona virus pandemic. Furthermore, regression polynomial has been used to analyse COVID-19 dataset of twenty different countries [31, 32], though the analysis was done using MS Excel spreadsheet. While using the polynomial regression model, the class attribute, Y will be the number of incidents of COVID-19, while the non-class attribute will be the various days. The relationship between X and Y represent polynomial relationship, based on the dynamics of COVID-19. The dynamics of COVID-19 shows that initializing incidences of the virus will increase until it reaches its peak before it starts to fall. After some time, if there is violation of the rules for its containment, the incidence of the virus will spike and it will continue to increase again, thereby representing polynomial relationship.

Though standard software exist, like MATLAB and Excel, which have been used to analysis COVID-19 dataset, it make be necessary to develop customized software, this justifies the need for this paper.

3.3. Development of the Polynomial Regression Algorithm

The principle of mathematical deduction will be used to develop the supervised machine learning algorithm for polynomial dataset. Since the degree of polynomial ranges from degree 2 to degree n, therefore, we start with when n = 2, the prediction rule will be polynomial, of degree 2.

3.3.1. Polynomial of Degree 2 with Minimum Point

The following algorithm can be used to determine prediction rule of polynomial, of degree 2, with minimum point.

1 Read Data

1.1 Read n

1.2 Read x0

2 Determine y0

2.1 count = 0

2.2 count = count + 1

2.3 Read x1, y1, x2, y2

2.4 sumx1 = sumx1 + x1

2.5 sumy1 = sumy1 + y1

2.6 sumx1y1 = sumx1y1 + (x1 * y1)

2.7 sumsqx1 = sumsqx1 + (x1 * x1)

2.8 sumx2 = sumx2 + x2

2.9 sumy2 = sumy2 + y2

2.10 sumx2y2 = sumx2y2 + (x2 * y2)

2.11 sumsqx2 = sumsqx2 + (x2 * x2)

2.12 Repeat 2.2, 2.3, 2.4, 2.5, 2.6, 2.7, 2.8, 2.9, 2.10, 2.11 until count = n

2.13 beta1 = (sumx1y1 – sumx1 * sumy1/n)/(sumsqx1 – sumx1 * sumx1/n)

2.14 alpha1 = sumy1/n – beta1 * sumx1/n

2.15 beta2 = (sumx2y2 – sumx2 * sumy2/n)/(sumsqx2 – sumx2 * sumx2/n)

2.16 alpha2 = sumy2/n – beta2 * sumx2/n

2.17 root1 = -alpha1/beta1

2.18 root2 = -alpha2/beta2

2.19 y0 = (x0 – root1) * (x0 – root2)

3 Display y0

3.3.2. Polynomial of Degree 2 with Maximum Point

The following algorithm can be used to determine prediction rule of polynomial, of degree 2, with maximum point.

1 Read Data

1.1 Read n

1.2 Read x0

2 Determine y0

2.1 count = 0

2.2 count = count + 1

2.3 Read x1, y1, x2, y2

2.4 sumx1 = sumx1 + x1

2.5 sumy1 = sumy1 + y1

2.6 sumx1y1 = sumx1y1 + (x1 * y1)

2.7 sumsqx1 = sumsqx1 + (x1 * x1)

2.8 sumx2 = sumx2 + x2

2.9 sumy2 = sumy2 + y2

2.10 sumx2y2 = sumx2y2 + (x2 * y2)

2.11 sumsqx2 = sumsqx2 + (x2 * x2)

2.12 Repeat 2.2, 2.3, 2.4, 2.5, 2.6, 2.7, 2.8, 2.9, 2.10, 2.11 until count = n

2.13 beta1 = (sumx1y1 – sumx1 * sumy1/n)/(sumsqx1 – sumx1 * sumx1/n)

2.14 alpha1 = sumy1/n – beta1 * sumx1/n

2.15 beta2 = (sumx2y2 – sumx2 * sumy2/n)/(sumsqx2 – sumx2 * sumx2/n)

2.16 alpha2 = sumy2/n – beta2 * sumx2/n

2.17 root1 = -alpha1/beta1

2.18 root2 = -alpha2/beta2

2.19 y0 = -(x0 – root1) * (x0 – root2)

3 Display y0

3.3.3. Polynomial Dataset, of Degree 3 with Minimum Point on the Right

The following algorithm can be used to determine prediction rule of polynomial, of degree 3, with minimum point on the right.

1 Read Data

1.1 Read n

1.2 Read x0

2 Determine y0

2.1 count = 0

2.2 count = count + 1

2.3 Read x1, y1, x2, y2, x3, y3

2.4 sumx1 = sumx1 + x1

2.5 sumy1 = sumy1 + y1

2.6 sumx1y1 = sumx1y1 + (x1 * y1)

2.7 sumsqx1 = sumsqx1 + (x1 * x1)

2.8 sumx2 = sumx2 + x2

2.9 sumy2 = sumy2 + y2

2.10 sumx2y2 = sumx2y2 + (x2 * y2)

2.11 sumsqx2 = sumsqx2 + (x2 * x2)

2.12 sumx2 = sumx2 + x2

2.13 sumy2 = sumy2 + y2

2.14 sumx2y2 = sumx2y2 + (x2 * y2)

2.15 sumsqx2 = sumsqx2 + (x2 * x2)

2.16 Repeat 2.2, 2.3, 2.4, 2.5, 2.6, 2.7, 2.8, 2.9, 2.10, 2.11, 2.12, 2.13, 2.14, 2.15 until count = n

2.17 beta1 = (sumx1y1 – sumx1 * sumy1/n)/(sumsqx1 – sumx1 * sumx1/n)

2.18 alpha1 = sumy1/n – beta1 * sumx1/n

2.19 beta2 = (sumx2y2 – sumx2 * sumy2/n)/(sumsqx2 – sumx2 * sumx2/n)

2.20 alpha2 = sumy2/n – beta2 * sumx2/n

2.21 beta3 = (sumx3y3 – sumx3 * sumy3/n)/(sumsqx3 – sumx3 * sumx3/n)

2.22 alpha3 = sumy3/n – beta3 * sumx3/n

2.23 root1 = -alpha1/beta1

2.24 root2 = -alpha2/beta2

2.25 root3 = -alpha3/beta3

2.25 y0 = (x0 – root1) * (x0 – root2) * (x0 – root3)

3 Display y0

3.3.4. Polynomial Dataset, of Degree 3 with Maximum Point on the Right

The following algorithm can be used to determine prediction rule of polynomial, of degree 3, with maximum point on the right.

1. Read Data

1.1 Read n

1.2 Read x0

2. Determine y0

2.1 count = 0

2.2 count = count + 1

2.3 Read x1, y1, x2, y2, x3, y3

2.4 sumx1 = sumx1 + x1

2.5 sumy1 = sumy1 + y1

2.6 sumx1y1 = sumx1y1 + (x1 * y1)

2.7 sumsqx1 = sumsqx1 + (x1 * x1)

2.8 sumx2 = sumx2 + x2

2.9 sumy2 = sumy2 + y2

2.10 sumx2y2 = sumx2y2 + (x2 * y2)

2.11 sumsqx2 = sumsqx2 + (x2 * x2)

2.12 sumx2 = sumx2 + x2

2.13 sumy2 = sumy2 + y2

2.14 sumx2y2 = sumx2y2 + (x2 * y2)

2.15 sumsqx2 = sumsqx2 + (x2 * x2)

2.16 Repeat 2.2, 2.3, 2.4, 2.5, 2.6, 2.7, 2.8, 2.9, 2.10, 2.11, 2.12, 2.13, 2.14, 2.15 until count = n

2.17 beta1 = (sumx1y1 – sumx1 * sumy1/n)/(sumsqx1 – sumx1 * sumx1/n)

2.18 alpha1 = sumy1/n – beta1 * sumx1/n

2.19 beta2 = (sumx2y2 – sumx2 * sumy2/n)/(sumsqx2 – sumx2 * sumx2/n)

2.20 alpha2 = sumy2/n – beta2 * sumx2/n

2.21 beta3 = (sumx3y3 – sumx3 * sumy3/n)/(sumsqx3 – sumx3 * sumx3/n)

2.22 alpha3 = sumy3/n – beta3 * sumx3/n

2.23 root1 = -alpha1/beta1

2.24 root2 = -alpha2/beta2

2.25 root3 = -alpha3/beta3

2.25 y0 = (x0 – root1) * (x0 – root2) * (x0 – root3)

3. Display y0

3.3.5. Polynomial Dataset, of Degree n with Minimum Point on the Right

The following algorithm is the generalized algorithm for determining the prediction rule of polynomial, of degree n, with minimum point on the right.

1 Read Data

1.1 Read n

1.2 Read x0

2 Determine y0

2.1 count = 0

2.2 count = count + 1

2.3 Read x1, y1, x2, y2, x3, y3, …, xn, yn

2.4 sumx1 = sumx1 + x1

2.5 sumy1 = sumy1 + y1

2.6 sumx1y1 = sumx1y1 + (x1 * y1)

2.7 sumsqx1 = sumsqx1 + (x1 * x1)

2.8 sumx2 = sumx2 + x2

2.9 sumy2 = sumy2 + y2

2.10 sumx2y2 = sumx2y2 + (x2 * y2)

2.11 sumsqx2 = sumsqx2 + (x2 * x2)

2.12 sumx2 = sumx2 + x2

2.13 sumy2 = sumy2 + y2

2.14 sumx2y2 = sumx2y2 + (x2 * y2)

2.15 sumsqx2 = sumsqx2 + (x2 * x2)

…

2.n sumxn = sumxn + xn

2.n +1 sumyn = sumyn + yn

2.n +2 sumxnyn = sumxnyn + (xn * yn)

2.n +3 sumsqxn = sumsqxn + (xn * xn)

2.n+4 Repeat 2.2, 2.3, 2.4, 2.5, 2.6, 2.7, 2.8, 2.9, 2.10, 2.11, 2.12, 2.13, 2.14, 2.15, …, 2.n, 2.n+1, 2.n+2, 2.n+3 until count = n

2.n+5 beta1 = (sumx1y1 – sumx1 * sumy1/n)/(sumsqx1 – sumx1 * sumx1/n)

2.n+6 alpha1 = sumy1/n – beta1 * sumx1/n

2.n+7 beta2 = (sumx2y2 – sumx2 * sumy2/n)/(sumsqx2 – sumx2 * sumx2/n)

2.n+8 alpha2 = sumy2/n – beta2 * sumx2/n

2.n+9 beta3 = (sumx3y3 – sumx3 * sumy3/n)/(sumsqx3 – sumx3 * sumx3/n)

2.n+10 alpha3 = sumy3/n – beta3 * sumx3/n

…

2.n+k betan = (sumxnyn – sumxn * sumyn/n)/(sumsqxn – sumxn * sumxn/n)

2.n+k+1 alphan = sumyn/n – betan * sumxn/n

2.n+k+2 root1 = -alpha1/beta1

2.n+k+3 root2 = -alpha2/beta2

2.n+k+4 root3 = -alpha3/beta3

…

2.n+k+j rootn = -alphan/betan

2.n+k+5 y0 = (x0 – root1) * (x0 – root2) * (x0 – root3) * … * (x0 – rootn)

3 Display y0

3.3.6. Polynomial Dataset, of Degree n with Maximum Point on the Right

The following algorithm is the generalized algorithm for determining the prediction rule of polynomial, of degree n, with maximum point on the right.

1 Read Data

1.1 Read n

1.2 Read x0

2 Determine y0

2.1 count = 0

2.2 count = count + 1

2.3 Read x1, y1, x2, y2, x3, y3, …, xn, yn

2.4 sumx1 = sumx1 + x1

2.5 sumy1 = sumy1 + y1

2.6 sumx1y1 = sumx1y1 + (x1 * y1)

2.7 sumsqx1 = sumsqx1 + (x1 * x1)

2.8 sumx2 = sumx2 + x2

2.9 sumy2 = sumy2 + y2

2.10 sumx2y2 = sumx2y2 + (x2 * y2)

2.11 sumsqx2 = sumsqx2 + (x2 * x2)

2.12 sumx2 = sumx2 + x2

2.13 sumy2 = sumy2 + y2

2.14 sumx2y2 = sumx2y2 + (x2 * y2)

2.15 sumsqx2 = sumsqx2 + (x2 * x2)

…

2.n sumxn = sumxn + xn

2.n +1 sumyn = sumyn + yn

2.n +2 sumxnyn = sumxnyn + (xn * yn)

2.n +3 sumsqxn = sumsqxn + (xn * xn)

2.n+4 Repeat 2.2, 2.3, 2.4, 2.5, 2.6, 2.7, 2.8, 2.9, 2.10, 2.11, 2.12, 2.13, 2.14, 2.15, …, 2.n, 2.n+1, 2.n+2, 2.n+3 until count = n

2.n+5 beta1 = (sumx1y1 – sumx1 * sumy1/n)/(sumsqx1 – sumx1 * sumx1/n)

2.n+6 alpha1 = sumy1/n – beta1 * sumx1/n

2.n+7 beta2 = (sumx2y2 – sumx2 * sumy2/n)/(sumsqx2 – sumx2 * sumx2/n)

2.n+8 alpha2 = sumy2/n – beta2 * sumx2/n

2.n+9 beta3 = (sumx3y3 – sumx3 * sumy3/n)/(sumsqx3 – sumx3 * sumx3/n)

2.n+10 alpha3 = sumy3/n – beta3 * sumx3/n

…

2.n+k betan = (sumxnyn – sumxn * sumyn/n)/(sumsqxn – sumxn * sumxn/n)

2.n+k+1 alphan = sumyn/n – betan * sumxn/n

2.n+k+2 root1 = -alpha1/beta1

2.n+k+3 root2 = -alpha2/beta2

2.n+k+4 root3 = -alpha3/beta3

...

2.n+k+j rootn = -alphan/betan

2.n+k+5 y0 = -(x0 – root1) * (x0 – root2) * (x0 – root3) * ... * (x0 – rootn)

3 Display y0

3.4. Simulation and Discussion of Results

Java programming language was used to simulate the above algorithms. Suppose the two-attribute dataset below represents a polynomial of degree 4, with minimum point on the right. An appropriate algorithm was used on a polynomial dataset, which visualized in Fig. (**6**).

After splitting the dataset into four partitions, the first partition represents this linear model, which is shown below in Fig. (**7**).

From Fig. (**7**), the values of the parameters, A_1 and B_1 for the linear model of the first partition are -241891 and -2E+06, respectively. Therefore, the value of $root_1$ is -8.268.

Furthermore, the second partition represents this linear model, which is shown in Fig. (**8**) below.

From Fig. (**8**), the values of the parameters, A_2 and B_2 for the linear model of the second partition are 63651 and -2E+06, respectively. Therefore, the value of $root_2$ is -31.42.

In a similar manner, the third partition represents this linear model, which is shown in Fig. (**9**) below. From Fig. (**9**), the values of the parameters, A_3 and B_3 for the linear model of the third partition are -63713 and 4E+06, respectively. Therefore, the value of $root_3$ is 62.78.

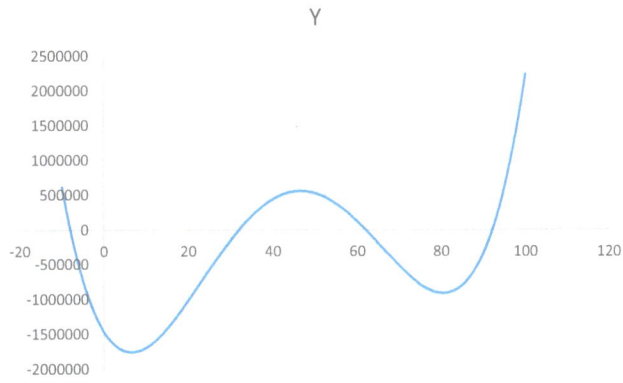

Fig. (6). Visualization of the polynomial dataset.

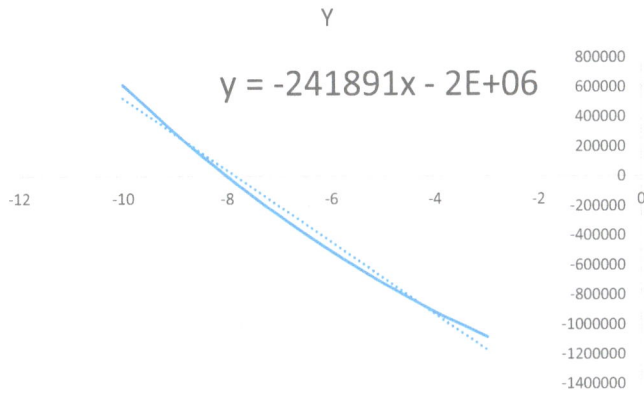

Fig. (7). Visualization of the first partition of the dataset.

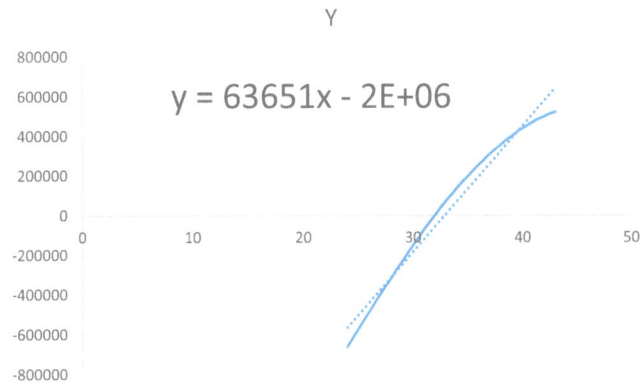

Fig. (8). Visualization of the second partition of the dataset.

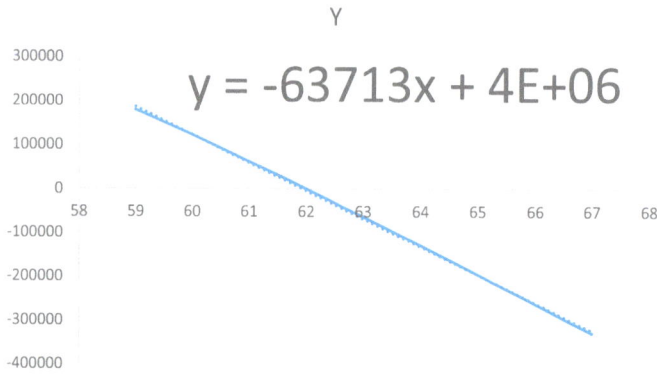

Fig. (9). Visualization of the third partition of the dataset.

From Fig. (**9**), the values of the parameters, A_3 and B3 for the linear model of the third partition are -63713 and 4E+06, respectively. Therefore, the value of $root_3$ is 62.78.

Finally, the fourth partition represents this linear model, which is shown in Fig. (**10**) below.

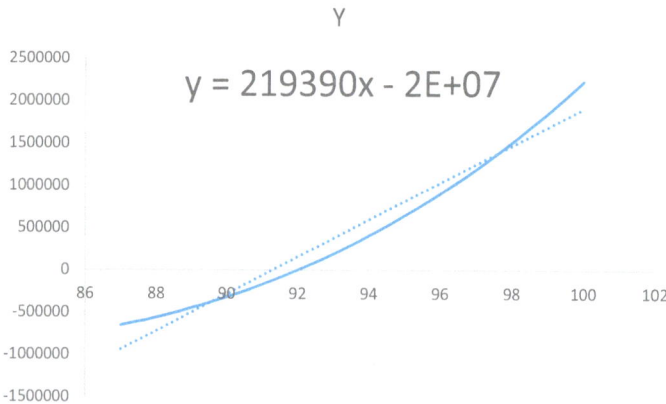

Fig. (10). Visualization of the fourth partition of the dataset.

From Fig. (**10**), the values of the parameters A_4 and B_4 for the linear model of the fourth partition are 219390 and -2E+07, respectively. Therefore, the value of $root_4$ is 91.16.

Having obtained all the roots of the polynomial, therefore, the prediction rule, which has been obtained from the polynomial dataset, is:

y0 = (x0 + 8.268) * (x0 – 31.42) * (x0 – 62.78) *(x0 – 91.16)

However, the actual polynomial equation for the dataset is given as:

y0 = (x0 + 8) * (x0 – 32) * (x0 – 62) *(x0 – 92)

The insignificant variation can be attributed to the regression error. Therefore, the prediction rule, which has been obtained from the dataset using the novel machine learning algorithm, can be used to accurately predict the value of the target attribute when given the value of the non-target attribute. The accuracy of the prediction rule would depend on how the training data was partitioned.

3.5. Conclusion

This paper has shown that the novel supervised machine learning algorithm accurately predicts the value of target attribute when given the value of non-attribute, using a two-attribute polynomial dataset. The developed algorithm can be used to analyse datasets that represent polynomial relationships, such as the COVID-19 dataset.

CONCLUDING REMARKS

This chapter has focused on the applications of machine learning, which includes the analysis of terrorism datasets using various machine learning tools and the development of algorithms that can be used to analyse the COVID-19 dataset.

REFERENCES

[1]   M.T. Ghada, and S.S Omar, "Experimental study of classification algorithms for terrorism prediction", *International Journal of Knowledge Engineering,* vol. 1, no. 2, pp. 107-113, 2015. [http://dx.doi.org/10.7763/IJKE.2015.V1.18]

[2]   National consortium for the study of terrorism and responses to terrorism (START), *Global Terrorism Database Codebook.,* 2018. https://www.start.umd.edu/gtd

[3]   T. Sandler, *Walter Enders: Economic Consequence of Terrorism in Developed and Developing Countries: An Overview in Terrorism, Economic Development and Political Openness.,* P. Keefer, N. Loayza, Eds., Cambridge University Press, 2008, pp. 17-47.

[4]   Andrew Silke, *Andrew silke: research on terrorism: a review of the impact of 9/11 and the global war on terrorism.,* 2008.

[5]   Adhishek Sachem and Devshi Roy, "TGPM: terrorist group prediction model of counter terrorism", *Int. J. Comput. Appl.,* vol. 44, no. 10, pp. 49-53, 2012.

[6]   Vivek Kumar, Manuel Mazzare, and Maj Gen, " (Rtd) Angelo messina, joo yound: a conjoint application of data mining techniques for analysis of global terrorist attack: prevention and prediction for combating terrorism",

[7]   M. Naur Eldeen, *Khalifa, Mohamed Hamed N. Taha, Sarah Hamed N. Taha, and Aboul Ella Hassanien: Statistical Insight and Association Mining for Terrorist Attacks in Egypt.,* A.E. Hassarien, Ed., , 2020, pp. 291-300.

[8]   J. Stuart, *Peter Norvig: Artificial Intelligence: A modern Approach.* Prentice Hall: Eaglewood Cliffs, 1995.

[9]   T. Kolajo, and O. Daramola, "Leveraging big data to combat terrorism in deveoping countries", *Conference on Information Communication Technology and Society,* 2017

[10]   S.A. Azizan, and I.A. Aziz, "Terrorism detection based on sentiment analysis using machine learning", *J. Eng. Appl. Sci. (Asian Res. Publ. Netw.),* vol. 12, no. 3, pp. 691-698, 2017.

[11]   T. James, " Predicting terrorism, a machine learning approach",

[12]   *Mohammed ALfaith, Chunlin Li and Naila Elhagsaadala: Prediction of Groups Responsible for Terrorism Attack Using Tree Based Model,* 2019.

[13]   B. Ganor, "Artificial or human: a new era of counter terrorism intelligence prediction", *Stud. Conflict Terrorism,* 2019.
        [http://dx.doi.org/10.1080/1057610X.2019.1568815]

[14]   Salih Tutun, "New framework that uses pattern and relation to understand terrorist behaviour", *Expert System with Applications,* vol. 78, pp. 358-375, 2017.

[15]   G. Leban, B. Zupan, G. Vidmar, and I. Bratko, "VizRank: data visualization guided by machine learning", *Data Min. Knowl. Discov.,* vol. 13, pp. 119-136, 2006.
        [http://dx.doi.org/10.1007/s10618-005-0031-5]

[16]   R.D. Cook, and X. Yin, "Dimension reduction and visualization in discriminant analysis", *Aust. N. Z. J. Stat.,* vol. 43, no. 2, pp. 147-199, 2001.
        [http://dx.doi.org/10.1111/1467-842X.00164]

[17]   P. Huber, "Projection Pursuit (with discussion)", *Ann. Stat.,* p. 13, 1985.

[18]   D.M. Keim, and H. Kriegel, "Visualization technique for mining large databases: a comparison. transactions on knowledge and data engineering", *Special Issue on Data Mining,* vol. 8, no. 6, pp. 923-938, 1996.

[19]   G. Grinstein, M. Trutschi, and U. Cvek, "High-dimensional visualizations", *Proceedings of the Visual Data Mining Workshop, KDD,* 2001.

[20]   L. Hamel, *Visualization of Support Vector Machine with Unsupervised Learning.* IEEE, 2006.
        [http://dx.doi.org/10.1109/CIBCB.2006.330984]

[21]   Patrick Breheny, and Woodrow Burchett, *Visualization of Regression Models Using visreg.,* 2013.

[22]   Luis Rueda, and Yaunquan Zhang, *Geometric Visualization of Clusters Obtained from Fuzzy Clustering Algorithm, Stuart J. Russel, Peter Norvig: Artificial Intelligence: A modern Approach* Prentice Hall: Eaglewood Cliffs, 1995.

[23]   S.A. Azizan, and I.A. Aziz, "Terrorism detection based on sentiment analysis using machine learning", *J. Eng. Appl. Sci. (Asian Res. Publ. Netw.),* vol. 12, no. 3, pp. 691-698, 2017.

[24]   T. Hassan, I.S. Bajwar, and H. Shoaib, "Prediction of terrorist activities by using unsupervised learning techniques", *J. Appl. Emerg. Sci,* vol. 6, no. 2, 2016.

[25]   Xi Cheng, *Polynomial Regression as an Alternative to Neural Nets,* 2019.

[26]   O.H. Choon, "A functional approximation comparison between neural networks and polynomial regression", *WSEAS Trans. Math.,* vol. 7, no. 6, pp. 353-363, 2008.

[27]   K. Hornik, "Multilevel feedforward networks are universal approximations", *Neural Netw.,* vol. 2, no. 5, pp. 359-366, 1989.
        [http://dx.doi.org/10.1016/0893-6080(89)90020-8]

[28]   A. Gilat, *MATLAB: An Introduction with Applications.* 5th ed. Wiley, 2014. https://www.oreilly.com/ library/view/matlab-an-introduction/9781118629864/Chapter08.html

[29]   Ramjeet Singh Yadav, *Data analysis of COVID-2019 epidemic using machine learning methods: a case study of India, International Journal of Information Technology, Springer.,* 2020. https://www.oreilly.com/library/view/matlab-anintroduction/9781118629864/Chapter08.html

[30]   C. Wu, X. Chen, Y. Cai, X. Zhou, S. Xu, H. Huang, L. Zhang, X. Zhou, C. Du, Y. Zhang, and J. Song, *Risk factors associated with acute respiratory distress syndrome and death in patients with coronavirus disease 2019 pneumonia in Wuhan.,* 2020.www.googlescholar.com [http://dx.doi.org/10.1001/jamainternmed.2020.0994]

[31]   F. Armando, *Regression polynomial analysis of covid19 epidemics: progress report 1, research on artificial and natural intelligence (RANI),* 2020. https://www.researchgate.net/publication/341279745

[32]   Armando Freitas Rocha, *Regression polynomial analysis of covid19 epidemics: some initial findings, research on artificial and natural intelligence (RANI),* 2020.   https://www.researchgate.net/publ ication/340510867

CHAPTER 6

Sensory Perception

Abstract: One of the qualities of an intelligent system is perception ability. It refers to the ability that provides information to agents using sensors. Human beings have five main sensory organs, which include: sense organ of hearing, vision, tasting, feeling, and smelling. Therefore, to act like man, which means to possess the attributes of an intelligent system, the system must have the ability to perceive the outside world it inhabits using the five sensors, ear, eye, tongue, skin, and nose. The following sensors have been developed in artificial agents, which they share with human sense organs: vision, hearing, and touch. This chapter focuses on these three sensors of an artificial agent.

Keywords: Computational photography, Eye tracker, Face recognition, Gesture recognition, Image-based modelling, Image-based rendering, Image formation, Speech recognition.

1. COMPUTER VISION

The human eye is the sense organ in humans that is responsible for sight. In a similar manner, computer vision is the sensor in the computer that is responsible for sight. The human eye performs three basic and fundamental functions, which are formation and manipulation of images, recognition of images, and path navigation while a human is in motion. In the same way, computer vision performs the three basic and fundamental functions of the human eye. This means that computer vision enables the computer to form and manipulate images on the computer, recognize images, and finds paths while the computer (robots, autonomous vehicle) is in motion [1, 2].

1.1. Fundamentals of Computer Vision

The most useful sensor for dealing with the outside world is the vision sensor. This is due to its usefulness because it is used for object recognition, path navigation, and manipulation of objects. Object recognition is a useful skill for distinguishing between two different objects, while path navigation helps the agent to find clear paths, thereby avoiding obstacles and calculating one's current velocity and orientation. On the other hand, object manipulation helps in grasping and inserting objects, which require local shape information and feedback, *i.e.,* too close or too far. This is very useful for vehicle control and graphic design. The various use of computer vision has defined several areas of applications of computer vision in entertainment, industry, ducation, commerce, transportation, *etc.*

1.2. Applications of Computer Vision

The following are the various systems, which have defined the various applications of computer vision. The systems have been classified into various classes, as shown below [1, 2].

1.2.1. Vehicle Driver Assistance and Traffic Management

- **Image Sensing Systems:** Real time traffic management using roadside cameras and license plate recognition system.
- **Iteris:** Real time traffic management and signaling using video detection.
- **MobilEye:** Vision system that warns vehicle drivers of danger, provides adaptive cruise control and gives driver assistance such as active braking.
- **TrafficVision:** Real time traffic management using computer vision.

1.2.2. Eye and Head Tracker

- **Gazepoint:** Low-cost eye and head trackers for consumers and research applications
- **Mirametrix:** Free head eye-tracker.
- **Smart Eye:** System that tracks eye and gaze position. Part of its function includes detection of drowsiness or inattention of vehicle drivers.
- **SMI:** Eye and gaze tracking system.

1.2.3. File and Video for Sports Analysis

- **Hawkeye:** Refereeing and analysis system that uses high-speed camera to precisely track balls in tennis, cricket, and other sports.
- **Playful Vision:** Real time video analytic and statistics for team sports.
- **QuesTec:** Systems for tracking sports action to provide enhanced broadcasts.
- **Sportvision:** Vision systems to provide real-time graphics augmentation for sports broadcasts.
- **Vizrt**: Creates 3D graphics for television broadcasts. Includes Viz Libero computer vision product for 3D visualization of sporting events.

1.2.4. Film and Video for Sports Analysis

- **2d3:** Systems for tracking objects in video or film and solving a 3D motion to allow for precise augmentation with 3D computer graphics.
- **Image Metrics:** A markerless tracking system for the human face that can be used to map detailed motion and facial expressions to synthetic characters.
- **Imagineer Systems:** Computer vision software for the film and video industries.
- **MirriAd:** Uses computer vision methods to track consistent regions in video and insert virtual advertising.

1.2.5. Gesture Recognition

- **GestureTek:** Tracks human gestures for playing games or interacting with computers.
- **Microsoft Kinect:** Provides full-body motion sensing and gesture recognition for the Xbox gaming system and other applications.
- **PointGrab:** Gesture recognition for control of computers and other devices.

1.2.6. General-Purpose Vision System

- **Cognex:** This is one of the largest machine vision companies. It develops systems for inspection, assembly, localization tasks, and many other areas.
- **InfoDif:** Vision systems for a broad range of industries and applications.
- **MathWorks:** Matlab modules and components for computer vision applications.
- **Matrox Imaging:** Software and hardware for machine vision applications.
- **National Instruments:** Vision software and systems used for many applications, including inspection, biomedical, and security.
- **Neptec:** Laser-based 3D vision systems for use on the space shuttles and other applications.
- **Newton Research Labs:** Vision systems for precision inspection, non-contact measurement, and robotics.
- **Point Grey Research:** Real-time stereo vision systems, spherical vision systems, and imaging hardware.
- **RSIP Vision:** Customized vision systems for medical, industrial, and other applications.
- **Seeing Machines:** Systems for tracking faces and eye gaze direction for human-computer interaction.
- **Soliton:** Smart cameras for industrial inspection and other applications.
- **SpikeNet:** Trainable vision systems for performing recognition.
- **ViSSee:** Developing a low-cost real-time sensor for measuring speed using an

approach modeled on vision in the fruit fly.

- **VISIONx:** Vision systems for high accuracy measurement and other applications.
- **Vitronic:** Vision systems for inspection, manufacturing, logistics, traffic management, and other applications.

1.2.7. Industrial Automation and Inspection for Electronic Industry

- **KLA-Tencor:** Systems for inspection and process control in semiconductor manufacturing.
- **Orbotech:** Automated inspection systems for printed circuit boards and flat panel displays.

1.2.8. Industrial Automation and Inspection for Agriculture Industry

- **Montrose Technologies:** Vision systems for the baked goods industry. Systems monitor bake color, shape, and size of bread, cookies, tortillas, *etc.*
- **Ellips:** Vision systems for inspecting and grading fruits and vegetables.

1.3. History of Computer Vision

The history of computer vision will be presented in form of different research areas done in computer vision and the year each was done, together with the various computer vision algorithms that solve computer vision problems and the year that each of the algorithms was developed [1]. This will help us to understand the various research areas of computer vision and the various algorithms of computer vision without reference to who did what. Table **1** and Table **2** illustrate further.

Table 1. Computer Vision Researches and Year.

Year	Computer Vision Research Area
2000	Learning
	MRF inference algorithm
	Feature based recognition
	Computational photography
	Texture synthesis and impainting
	Image based modelling and rendering
	Subspace method
	Face recognition and detection
1990	Energy based segmentation
	Particle filtering
	Graph cuts
	Physics based vision
	Factorization
	Projective invariants
	3D range data processing
	Kalman filters
	Markov random fields
1980	Regularization
	Physically-based modelling
	Texture and focus
	Shapes from shading
	Scale-space processing
	Image pyramid
	Structure from motion
	Optical flow
1970	Intristic images
	Stereo correspondence
	Pictorial structures
	Generalized cylinder
	Blocks world link labelling
	Digital image processing

Table 2. Computer Vision Algorithms and Year Developed.

Period	Year	Computer Vision Algorithms
Early Algorithms	1993	Line labelling
	1973	Pictorial structures
	1982	Articulated body model
	1981	Intristic images
	1982	Stereo correspondence
	1986	Optical flow
Recent Algorithms	1996	Imaged-based rendering
	1996	Image-based modelling
	2006	Interactive tone mapping
	2001	Texture synthesis
	2007	Feature-based recognition
	2004	Region-based recognition

1.4. Image Formation

Image manipulation remains one of the main uses of computer vision. Before one understands how images are manipulated, the process that forms a particular image, given a set of lighting condition, scene geometry, surface properties and camera optics must first be understood. Image formation, therefore is the process of forming a particular image given a set of condition, scene geometry, surface properties and camera optics [1].

1.4.1. Geometry of Image

Images are usually formed on a two or three dimensional plane. Therefore, the geometry of the scene where images are formed can either be a two or three-dimension.

1.4.1.1. Two and Three-Dimensional Geometry

Images exist in real world in three dimensional space, *i.e.* space that has three levels of measurements, x, y and z. However, these images that exist in a three dimensional space need to be formed in a two dimensional plane (*i.e.* two-dimensional plane has two levels of measurement, x and y.

In a two dimensional coordinate geometric system, a point can be represented by a vector, $\mathbf{x} = (x, y)$, while in a three-dimensional coordinate geometric system, a point can be represented by a vector, $\mathbf{x} = (x, y, z)$. Suppose $\mathbf{l}$ is a constant vector, $\mathbf{l}$

= (a, b, c) and **x** is an augmented vector, x = (x, y, 1). Therefore, in a two dimensional coordinate geometric system, a line is represented as:

x.l = (a, b, c).(x, y, 1) = ax + by + c

Furthermore, in a three-dimensional coordinate geometric system, suppose **l** is a constant vector, **l** = (a, b, c, d) and **x** is an augmented vector, **x** = (x, y, z,1), A line is represented in a three-dimensional coordinate geometric system as:

x.l = (a, b, c, d).(x, y, z,1) = ax + by + cz + d

1.4.1.2. Two and Three-Dimensional Transformations

Transformation can be defined as the process of changing the coordinate of an image in two or three-dimensional coordinate geometric system. There are different types of transformation, but the general transformation which can be used to change the pixel coordinates of an image, which can also be used to define other types of transformation is called Affine transformation. For a two-dimensional coordinate system, suppose the constants of Affine transformation is given by the 2x3 matrix A and the augmented matrix is shown as a 3x1 matrix, which are shown below as:

$$A = \begin{bmatrix} a,c,e \\ b,d,f \end{bmatrix}, x = \begin{bmatrix} x \\ y \\ 1 \end{bmatrix}$$

Therefore, the general Affine transformation formula is shown below as:

$$\begin{bmatrix} a,c,e \\ b,d,f \end{bmatrix} \begin{bmatrix} x \\ y \\ 1 \end{bmatrix} = \begin{bmatrix} ax + cy + e, bx + dy + f \end{bmatrix}$$

For a three-dimensional coordinate system, suppose the constants of Affine transformation is given by the 3x4 matrix A and the augmented matrix is shown as a 4x1 matrix, which are shown below as:

$$A = \begin{bmatrix} a,d,g,j \\ b,e,h,k \\ c,f,i,l \end{bmatrix}, x = \begin{bmatrix} x \\ y \\ z \\ 1 \end{bmatrix}$$

Therefore, the general Affine transformation formula is shown below as:

$$\begin{bmatrix} a,d,g,j \\ b,e,h,k \\ c,f,i,l \end{bmatrix} \begin{bmatrix} x \\ y \\ z \\ 1 \end{bmatrix} = \begin{bmatrix} ax + dy + gz + j, hx + ey + hz + k, cx + fy + iz + l \end{bmatrix}$$

1.4.1.3. Types of Two and Three-Dimensional Transformations

There are different types of two and three-dimensional transformation. Each type changes the pixel position of the image. Each type has its own formula, which can be obtained from the general formula for two or three dimensional Affine transformations [1].

- **Translation**

Translation changes the position of the image by adding a certain value to the x coordinate, and another certain value to the y coordinate, and another certain value to the z coordinate.

For a two-dimensional coordinate system, the formula for the Translate transformation can be obtained by using the following constant values for the matrix, A as follows:

$$A = \begin{bmatrix} 1,0,e \\ 0,1,f \end{bmatrix}, x = \begin{bmatrix} x \\ y \\ 1 \end{bmatrix}$$

Therefore, the formula for a two-dimensional translation transformation will be given by:

$$\begin{bmatrix} 1,0,e \\ 0,1,f \end{bmatrix} \begin{bmatrix} x \\ y \\ 1 \end{bmatrix} = \begin{bmatrix} x+e, y+f \end{bmatrix}$$

This means that a certain constant value e is added to x and a certain constant value f is added to y.

Furthermore, for a three-dimensional coordinate geometry system, the formula for translate transformation can be obtained by using the following constant values for the matrix A, as follows:

$$A = \begin{bmatrix} 1,0,0,j \\ 0,1,0,k \\ 0,0,1,l \end{bmatrix}, x = \begin{bmatrix} x \\ y \\ z \\ 1 \end{bmatrix}$$

Therefore, the formula for a three-dimensional translate transformation will be given by:

$$\begin{bmatrix} 1,0,0,j \\ 0,1,0,k \\ 0,0,1,l \end{bmatrix} \begin{bmatrix} x \\ y \\ z \\ 1 \end{bmatrix} = \begin{bmatrix} x+j, y+k, z+l \end{bmatrix}$$

This means that the translation transformation adds a certain constant value j to the x coordinate, adds another constant value k to the y coordinate and adds another constant value l to the z coordinate [1].

• **Rotation**

Rotation is another type of affine transformation where every point of the graphic image is rotated about a point through the same angle. For a two-dimensional coordinate system, the formula for the rotate transformation can be obtained by using the following constant values for the matrix, A as follows:

$$A = \begin{bmatrix} \cos(r), -\sin(r), 0 \\ \sin(r), \cos(r), 0 \end{bmatrix}, x = \begin{bmatrix} x \\ y \\ 1 \end{bmatrix}$$

Therefore, the formula for a two-dimensional rotation transformation will be given by:

$$\begin{bmatrix} \cos(r), -\sin(r), 0 \\ \sin(r), \cos(r), 0 \end{bmatrix} \begin{bmatrix} x \\ y \\ 1 \end{bmatrix} = \left[\cos(r)x - \sin(r)y, \sin(r)x + \cos(r)y\right]$$

If the angle of rotation is given in degree, d, this has to be converted to radian, using the following, $r = 0.01745 * d$. This is because 1 degree is 0.01745 radians.

• Scaling

This transformation makes an image smaller or bigger. The transformed image will be similar to the original image. Scaling a two-dimensional image involves multiplying the x and y coordinate by a constant value. Using the general Affine transformation formula, a two-dimensional image can be scaled to a factor k, using this formula:

$$\begin{bmatrix} k, 0, 0 \\ 0, k, 0 \end{bmatrix} \begin{bmatrix} x \\ y \\ 1 \end{bmatrix} = \left[kx, ky\right]$$

The formula for scaling a three-dimensional image by a factor, k can be obtained, using the general Affine transformation as follows:

$$\begin{bmatrix} k, 0, 0, 0 \\ 0, k, 0, 0 \\ 0, 0, k, 0 \end{bmatrix} \begin{bmatrix} x \\ y \\ z \\ 1 \end{bmatrix} = \left[kx, ky, kz\right]$$

1.4.1.4. Combined Transformation

More than one transformation can be applied to an image at the same time, example, rotation and translation, scaled rotation.

• Rotation and Translation

First, rotation is performed, afterwards, translation is applied. For a two-dimensional image, the Affine general formula can be used to obtain the formula as follows:

$$\begin{bmatrix} \cos(r),-\sin(r),e \\ \sin(r),\cos(r),f \end{bmatrix} \begin{bmatrix} x \\ y \\ 1 \end{bmatrix} = \begin{bmatrix} \cos(r)x - \sin(r)y + e, \sin(r)x + \cos(r)y + f \end{bmatrix}$$

• Scaled Rotation

First, scaling is performed, afterwards rotation is performed. For a two-dimensional image, the general Affine formula can be used to obtain the formula for scaled rotation as follows:

$$\begin{bmatrix} k\cos(r),-k\sin(r),0 \\ k\sin(r),k\cos(r),0 \end{bmatrix} \begin{bmatrix} x \\ y \\ 1 \end{bmatrix} = \begin{bmatrix} \cos(r)kx - \sin(r)ky, \sin(r)kx + \cos(r)ky \end{bmatrix}$$

1.5. Image Recognition

While computer can accurately form three-dimensional shapes from images taken from different views, computers cannot easily and accurately name all the objects in a formed image of a scene. Image recognition can be defined as the process of detecting and recognizing a particular object or class of object in an image. It consists of the following parts of problem:

• Object detection: This involves scanning an image in order to detect where a match of a particular item that we are looking for occurs.
• Instance recognition: This involves searching for characteristic feature points of specific rigid objects that we are trying to recognize.
• Category (class) recognition: This involves recognizing instances of extremely different classes, such as animals or furniture.

The solutions to these different problems of image recognition use different techniques, which includes different machine learning techniques. Each of these different parts of image recognition problem and techniques that solve the problem will be considered in detail.

1.5.1. Object/Face Detection

This can be defined as the process of finding particular regions in an image where particular objects/human faces can be found [1]. Face detection can be used in digital camera to find faces for auto focusing. It can also be used in video camera for finding faces in video conferencing and focus on the speaker either manually or automatically. A wide range of face detection algorithms have been developed over the years, which can be classified as follows:

1.5.1.1. Features Based Face Detection Technique

This class of face detection algorithms aim at finding the locations of distinctive features of human face, like eyes, nose, mouth *etc.*

1.5.1.2. Appearance-Based Approach

This class of face detection algorithms scans over small overlapping rectangular patches, searching for likely occurrence of human faces [1].

All the face detection algorithms are machine learning algorithms, which use a collection of faces as training data. They include the following machine learning techniques, boosting, neural network and support vector machine. The training set of the face detection machine learning algorithms consist of collection of images with labelled patches of faces, together with images that do not contain human faces, but with patches. After the set of images are collected as training data, and optional pre-processing performed on them, the following machine learning techniques can be used to determine where human faces are likely to occur in the image.

1.5.1.3. Clustering and PCA.

The clustering technique involves clustering each of the dataset into six different clusters using K-means clustering technique. Afterwards, PCA will be fitted on each of the six clusters. At detection time, the two Mahalanobis metrics (DIFS and DFFS) will be computed for each of the clusters. The 24 Mahalanobis metrics will serve as input into a deep neural network, trained using backpropagation algorithm. The deep neural network determines where human face is located in the image.

1.5.1.4. Deep Neural Network

An alternative solution does not cluster or compute the Mahalanobis metrics, rather, it uses a deep neural network on the 20x20 pixel patches of gray-level intensities. The output of the deep neural network determines the likelihood of faces at the center of every overlapping patch in a multi-resolution pyramid.

1.5.1.5. Support Vector Machine

This is another machine learning technique that can be used to detect the locations of human faces in an images. It searches for a series of maximum margin separating planes in feature spaces separating different classes.

1.5.1.6. Boosting

The best known and most widely used human face detection algorithm uses the concept of boosting. It involves training a series of increasingly discriminating simple classifiers and then blending their outputs. The main focus in this area of recognition is on speed of detection and accuracy of the detection.

1.5.2. Pedestrian Detection

Like object/human face detection, pedestrian detection determines where pedestrians can be found in an images. Pedestrian and car detection have received attention in computer vision research. This is due to its importance, especially its importance in autonomous or self-driving vehicles. A well-known pedestrian detection algorithm, which was developed in 2005 used a series of histogram of oriented gradient, which was fed into a support vector machine [1].

1.5.3. Face Recognition

This can be defined as the process of recognizing or identifying a particular face. Face recognition can be used in the following applications: identity verifications, desktop login, Facebook photo tagging, *etc.* Face recognition requires that full frontal images of different people be stored in a database, which will be used to compare any real time or static photo of any individual [1, 11]. Early work on face recognition involves finding the locations of distinctive image features, like eyes, nose, mouth and measuring the distance between these feature locations. However, recent works on face recognition involves the use of eigenfaces and modelling shape and appearance variations. Eigenfaces is a concept, which uses an observation that a face x can be compressed and reconstructed using mean m and adding small number of scaled signed images. Faces can be hard to find and recognize, especially if the face is very small in the image or if the face is turned away from the camera. In that case face recognition can be combined with person detection and cloth recognition. Face recognition can also be combined with other context recognition, like location recognition and event/activity recognition.

1.5.4. Instance Recognition

In general, object recognition falls into two parts, which are instance recognition and class recognition. Instance recognition involves recognizing a known 2D or 3D object, while class recognition, which can be called category or generic object recognition involves recognizing an instance of a particular general class, such as "car", "cat", "bicycle" *etc.*

One of the early approaches to instance recognition involves extraction of lines, contours or 3D surfaces from images and matching them to known 3D object models. However, one of the recent approaches to instance recognition involves the use of viewport-invariant 2D features. One of applications of instance recognition is in the area of location recognition, which does not only identify the place where a particular image was taken, but also identify important landmarks in the image, like building names. However, category recognition remains a challenging problem, and most of its problem remain largely unsolved. One of the simplest approach to category or class recognition is based on bags-of-feature, which represents objects and images as unordered collection of feature descriptors. In the recent time, the use of machine learning in recognition algorithm has been widely used. This has led to the development of several recognition databases, which are available online as datasets.

1.6. Use of Computer Vision in Motion

Any device like robot or autonomous vehicle, which have the capability to move from one place to another, and equipped with vision sensor, need to know where the obstacles are, where free space corridors are available. Focusing on autonomous vehicle, the tasks before the vehicle are as follows: keep moving at a reasonable speed, ensures that the vehicle remains securely within its lane (lateral control), ensures that there is a safe distance between it and the vehicle in front of it (longitudinal distance), monitors vehicle in the neighboring lane and be prepared for appropriate maneuver, if one of them changes lane. In order for the autonomous vehicle to solve these problems, it is always equipped with sensors and mirrors, which it uses to monitor and maintain the lateral control, longitudinal control and maneuver. Therefore, these problems are typical problems that computer vision algorithms can be used to solve [3].

1.7. Conclusion

Computer vision is the sight sensor of the computer. Its main functions are image formation, image recognition and path navigation for image on motion. The various user-level applications and algorithms for these three main functions of computer vision have been the main focus of this unit.

1.8. Summary

Computer vision is just one of the perception sensors of the computer. It is responsible for the sight function. However, there are other perception sensors of the computer that are responsible for other functions. One of such perception sensors is the one that performs the function of hearing. Its main task is termed speech recognition. This will be discussed in detail in the next unit.

2. SPEECH RECOGNITION

Another sense organ in human is the sense organ of hearing, which is the ear. This allows human to communicate with one another using speech act. Speech act is the most dominant means of communicate between humans. In the same way, speech act promises to be the most dominant means of communication between human and computer and between computers. Therefore, computers need perception sensors that will enable it to recognize speech act. The process of recognizing speech act by computers is called speech recognition. It is regarded as the front end to most natural language processing components [4 - 7].

2.1. Basics of Speech Recognition

Technically, speech recognition is the process of mapping from digitally encoded acoustic signal to a string of words. Speech recognition is different from speech understanding. The latter is the process of deriving meaning from the digitally encoded acoustic signal [3, 8]. Technically, it is the process of mapping from the digitally encoded acoustic signal to an interpretation of the meaning of the speech act (utterance). Speech understanding cuts across two disciplines, which are computer audition/computer hearing and natural language processing. Whenever two people communicate using speech act (utterance), the following questions must be resolve: what speech sounds does the speaker utter? What words does the speaker intend to express with the speech sound ? What meaning does the speaker intends to express with the words. The first two questions are part of speech recognition, while all the three questions are part of speech understanding. Fig. (**1**) illustrates the process of speech recognition and speech understanding.

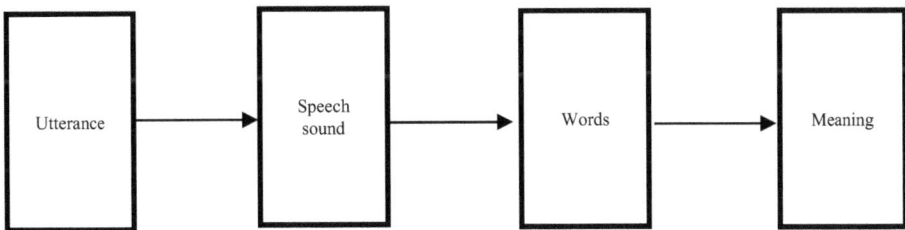

Fig. (1). Processes of speech recognition and speech understanding.

In order to determine the speech sound of an utterance, every human language has a collection of about 40 – 50 sounds, called phones. A phone is a sound that corresponds to every vowel or consonant, though some combinations of letters, each has its phone, and some letters have different phones under different context. Therefore, in order to determine the sound, the various phones can be characterized in terms of features that we can use to pick the acoustic signal, like frequency and amplitude of the sound wave of the utterance. In order to determine the words, a dictionary of different pronunciations can be looked up. Each pronunciation is a combination of one or more phones, with its words. Example, suppose we have a pronunciation, which is a collection of three phones, *[k]*, *[a]* and *[t]*. Looking up this pronunciation in the dictionary, it gives the word, 'cat'. Two problems need to solved with respect to word determination, which are the problems of homophone and segmentation. The problem of homophone is the problem of choosing a particular word in a situation where one pronunciation has two or more words in the dictionary, like two and too. The problem of segmentation is the problem of determining where a word ends. In order determine the meaning, the most likely sequence of words is passed to semantics analysis algorithm to determine the possible meaning of the sequence of words.

2.2. Basic Components of Speech Recognition System

Fig. (**2**), shows the basic components of a speech recognition system. The application components are the various systems that use speech recognition system [8]. The applications interact with the decoder, which produces the speech recognition results. The results may be used to adapt other components in the system. The language model is the system's knowledge of what constitute a possible word, what words are likely to co-occur, and in what sequence [8 - 10]. The language model provides the probability, P(Word) in the Bayes equation that the speech recognition system aims at maximizing.

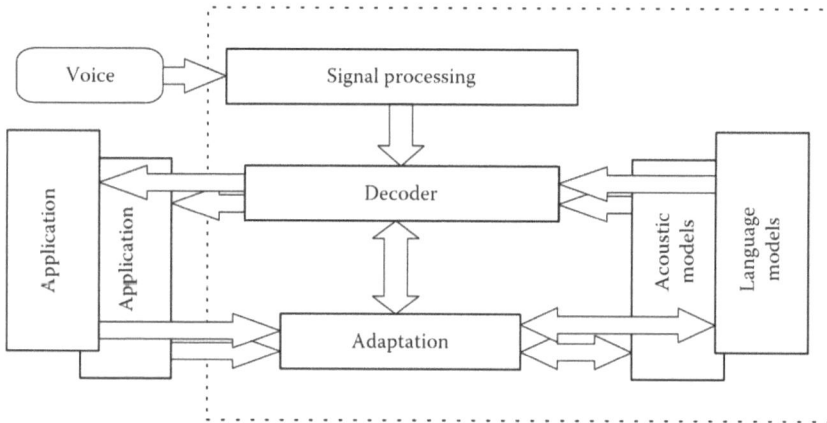

Fig. (2). Components of speech recognition system.

The acoustic model plays an important role in improving the accuracy of the speech recognition system. This is because there are many factors that determine the accuracy of speech recognition system. They include the following: context variations, speaker variations, and environment variations. Therefore, acoustic model represents knowledge about acoustic, phonetics, microphone and environment variables (gender, dialect differences among speakers) [8].

The signal-processing module processes the speech signal, first by converting it to acoustic digital signal, then extracting silent feature vector for the decoder. The decoder uses the acoustic and language models to generate the word sequence as the result of the speech recognition system. The word sequence, which is the result of speech processing has the maximum probability, given the input voice signal. The decoder also provides information necessary for the adaptation component will use to modify the acoustic model or language model.

2.3. Signal Processing

The sound that is produced as utterance is an analog signal, therefore it must be converted to digital signal. When the sound utterance strikes the microphone or mouthpiece of an electronic device, it is converted into electrical current, which is passed to the analog to digital converter to produce a stream of bits or digital signal representing the sound [8]. The digital sound wave needs a compact representation, at the same time, a representation of the digital sound wave that will encode features of the digital sound wave, which will be useful in word recognition will be necessary. Since the sound can be pronounced in different ways (loud or soft, fast or slow, high-pitched or low-pitched, noisy or silence background) and from different speakers with different assent, therefore enough important features of the digital sound wave need to be captured. This will also be useful in solving the problem of speaker identification, *i.e.* who the speaker of the sound utterance is.

2.4. Uncertainties in Speech Recognition

Since speech recognition uncovers the words that are used to produce a certain digital sound signal, therefore, there are many uncertainties that are involved. Example, there is uncertainty on how well the microphone and digitization hardware captures the actual sound. There is uncertainty on which phone produced the sound signal. There is uncertainty on which word is used to produce the phone. The uncertainty in speech recognition can be measured using the Bayes conditional probability, which is given in Equation **1**, below as [11]:

$$P(\text{Words}|\text{Signal}) = \frac{P(Words)P(Signal\,|\,Words)}{P(Signal)} \tag{1}$$

Speech recognition system aims at maximizing the above Bayes conditional probability. P(Signal) is called the normalizing constant), P(Signal|Words) is the acoustic model, it informs us that cat is more likely to be pronounced as *[kcet]*. Finally, as noted earlier, P(Words) is the language model, it is what informs us, when we are not sure of what we heard, that the chosen word is more likely.

2.5. Historical Development of Speech Recognition

One of the most significant development in speech recognition is the shift from non-statistical method to statistical method. This had led to stochastic processing, which was introduced in the acoustic model component of speech recognition system in 1970s, which is still actively used till date. Since the introduction of stochastic processing, a number of algorithms have been developed, which are: Expectation Maximum algorithm, EM and Forward–Backward or the Baum–Welch algorithm in 1972 and 1977 respectively. Furthermore, large speech corpora, which are large collection of speech datasets have been developed for speech training. These speech corpora were created, annotated, and distributed to research community by organizations, like National Institute of Standard and Technology (NIST), Linguistic Data Consortium (LDC) *etc*. Another historic advance in the development of speech recognition is in the area of speech knowledge representation. This include the development of perceptually motivated speech signal representations such as Mel-Frequency Cepstral Coefficients (MFCC), in 1980 and Perceptual Linear Prediction (PLP) coefficients, in 1990 *etc*. Finally, the development of key decoding or search strategy, which has helped large scale continuous speech recognition to be possible, is another historic development.

2.6. Applications of Speech Recognition System

The applications of speech recognition can be classified into three main classes, which include the following:

2.6.1. Cloud-based Call Center/IVR (Interactive Voice Response)

This includes the widely used applications from Tellme's information access over the phone, for Microsoft Exchange Unified Messaging.

2.6.2. PC-Based Dictation/Command and Control

There are a number of dictation applications on the PC. The applications allow you to speak to the computer in form of input, instead of using other input device, like keyboard.

2.6.3. Device-Based Embedded Command Control

There is a wide range of devices that do not have a typical PC keyboard or mouse, and the traditional GUI application cannot be directly extended. As an example, Microsoft's Response Point blue button illustrates what speech interface can do to make the user interface much simpler. Mobile phones and automobile scenarios are also very suitable for speech applications.

2.7. Conclusion

Speech recognition is different from speech understanding. Speech recognition belongs to the field of study called computer auditory/computer hearing, while speech understanding is a combination of computer auditory and natural language processing.

2.8. Summary

Speech recognition has been considered as the main task of computer auditory. It concerns the use of the computer hearing sensor to recognize speech sound. However, there is another aspect of sensory perception on the computer, which is the sensor for physical feeling. This will be discussed in the next unit.

3. TACTILE SENSING

Tactile perception is the sense organ for physical interaction with the environment [3]. In human, it is the skin, which form the physical interface between human and environment. Tactile perception in human allows us to perceive object properties, like size, hardness, temperature, contour *etc*. In a similar manner, tactile perception needs to be implemented on computers, especially robots, so that robots can know when the temperature of its environment is too cold or too hot, size of objects that it handles, hardness of objects that it touches *etc*. Like in human, tactile perception must be implemented on the external surface of robots or its skin.

3.1. Tactile Sensing Explained

Tactile sensing in human serves as reference for tactile sensing in computer agents, like robots. Tactile sensing in computer agents like robots is derived from the human sense of touch. However, there are differences between human tactile sensing and tactile sensing in robots. Tactile sensing in robots can be defined as the process of measuring a given property of an object through contact with the object. Tactile sensor, on the other hand is a device or system that measures a given property of an object through contact with that object [3].

3.2. Justification for Tactile Sensing

The importance of tactile sensing in robotics cannot be over-emphasized. It includes the following:

- Manipulative tasks: Some tasks in robots can be controlled through touch.
- Maintaining stable grasp: Measure of the contact force allows the grasp force control, which can be useful in maintaining stable grasp.

- Compliant manipulators: Grasp force together with manipulators is useful in compliant manipulators.
- Grasp stability: Apart from magnitude, the direction of force is critical in dexterous manipulation, in order to regulate the balance between normal and tangential force, which ensures grasp stability.
- Determination of coefficient of friction: Shear information helps to determine this.
- Determination of useful environmental information: During interaction, robots can determine information about the object, like shape, surface texture, slip can be obtained through the detection of normal and shear force.
- Sensor development: Range of sensors that can detect shape, size, presence, position, force, temperature, surface texture through contact have been developed.

3.3. Types of Tactile Sensors

Different types of robotics tactile sensors have been reported in the literature, which can be embedded under the physical surface of robots. They include the following [3]:

- **Resistive Sensors:** They consist of two conductive sheets that are separated by air, microsphere, insulating fabrics *etc.*
- **Piezoresistive Sensors:** They are made of materials, whose resistance changes with force or pressure. Touch sensing systems use this type of sensors.
- **Tunnel Effect Tactile Sensors:** They are based on Quantum Tunnel Composite.
- **Capacitive Sensors:** They are plate capacity, with the distance between plates or effective area changed by applied force, by shifting their relative positions.
- **Optical Sensors:** They have optical mode of transduction and they use the principle of optical reflection between media of different refractive index.
- **Ultrasonic Sensors:** They use acoustic ultrasonic sensing, which is another technology that has been used for the development of tactile sensors.
- **Magnetism Based Sensors:** They are based on magnetic transduction and they can be used to measure the change that is caused by flux density, which is caused by applied force on a small magnet.
- **Piezoelectric Sensors:** They are made with piezoelectric material that has the property of generating charge or voltage, which is proportional to the applied force or pressure.

3.4. Conclusion

In this unit, you have learnt the meaning of tactile sensing, its importance, and the various tactile sensors as it applies to robotics. The reason for applying tactile sensing to robotics is because robots are the main computer agents that do tactile sensing.

3.5. Summary

Tactile sensing has been applied to robots; however, this is just one of the things that a robot does like a human. There are many other things that robot does. The next chapter will be devoted entirely to robotics and the study and the development of robots.

CONCLUDING REMARKS

The three aspects of sensory perception that this chapter has focused on are computer vision, speech recognition, and tactile sensing. They correspond to the sense organ of seeing, hearing, and feeling, respectively.

REFERENCES

[1]   R. Szeliski, *Computer Vision: Algorithms and Applications,* 2010. http://szeliski.org/BOOK/

[2]   D.H. Ballard, and C.M. Brown, *Computer Vision* Prentice-Hall: Eaglewood Cliffs. New Jersey, 1982.

[3]   S.J. Russells, and P. Norwig, *Artificial Intelligence: A Modern Approach.* Prentice Hall, 1995.

[4]   D. Jurafsky, and J. Martin, *Speech and Language Processing—An Introduction to Natural Language Processing, Computational Linguistics, and Speech Recognition.* Prentice Hall: Upper Saddle River, NJ, 2000.

[5]   C. Lee, F. Soong, K. Paliwal, Ed., *Automatic Speech and Speaker Recognition—Advanced Topics.* Kluwer Academic: Norwell, MA, 1996.
        [http://dx.doi.org/10.1007/978-1-4613-1367-0]

[6]   L. Rabiner, and B. Juang, *Fundamentals of Speech Recognition* Academic Press: New York, 1975.

[7]   S. Furui, *Digital Speech Processing, Synthesis and Recognition.* 2nd ed. Marcel Dekker Inc.: New York, 2001.

[8]   https://www.microsoft.com/en-us/research/wp-content/uploads/2016/02/Book-Chap-HuangDeng 2010.pdf

[9]   R.S. Dahiya, and M. Valle, *Tactile Sensing for Robotic Applications,* 2008. https://www.research gate.net/publication/221787495

[10]   M.H. Lee, and H.R. Nicholls, "Tactile sensing for mechatronics – a state of the art survey", *Mechatronics,* vol. 9, pp. 1-31, 1999.
        [http://dx.doi.org/10.1016/S0957-4158(98)00045-2]

[11]   M.H. Yang, D.J. Kiregman, and N. Ahuja, "Detecting faces in images: a survey", *IEEE Trans. Pattern Anal. Mach. Intell.,* vol. 24, no. 1, pp. 34-58, 2002.
        [http://dx.doi.org/10.1109/34.982883]

CHAPTER 7

Robotics

Abstract: One of the qualities of an intelligent system is the ability to move an object from one place to another. This quality leads to the study of Robotics, which is the aspect of Artificial Intelligence that deals with the study and design of robots. An autonomous robot is a robot that makes decisions on its own, and it shares many things in common with an autonomous vehicle or self-driving vehicle.

Keywords: Autonomous vehicle, Effectors, End effectors, Exoskeleton, Germinoid, Humanoid robot, Manipulators.

1. FOUNDATIONS OF ROBOTICS

Karel Capek, a Czech novelist, was the first to coin the word robot in a play titled Rossum's Universal Robots (RUR) in 1920. The word robot means worker or servant in Czech. The term robot means different things to different people; therefore, many people and organizations have defined robots in different ways. In 1979, the Robot Institute of America defined it as a programmable, multifunction manipulator designed to move materials, parts, tools, or specific devices through variable programmed motions for the performance of a variety of tasks. Another definition of a robot, which is not too general and not too specific, is that a robot is an autonomous machine, which is capable of sensing its environment, carrying out computations to make decisions, and performing actions in the real world. From the IEEE community, it was defined as: "A robot is a machine constructed as an assemblage of joined links, so that they can be articulated into the desired position by a programmable controller and precision actuators, to perform a variety of tasks." Though no definition is perfect, but in any definition of a robot, it must do three things, which are sense, compute and act. A robot senses the world using devices like a camera, sonar, gyroscopes, laser range finders, *etc.* A robot computes using a small electronic circuit, a powerful multicore processor, or a cluster of networked computers [1].

The actions of robots can include movement, combinations of movement and manipulations of things, performing specific tasks, while others can do different things.

1.1. Robot Explained

Every robot senses, computes, and acts in its physical environment. They vary in the way they sense, compute and act. These three functions are performed repeatedly. Robot senses in its environment using sensors, which feed measurements to a controller or computer that computes by processing the measurement from the sensors [1 - 5]. After the computer finishes processing the signal from the sensor, it sends an appropriate control signal to motors and actuators that the robot uses to act. A robot repeatedly performs these actions in a cycle, which people that design robots (roboticists) call a feedback loop, as illustrated in Fig. (**1**) below.

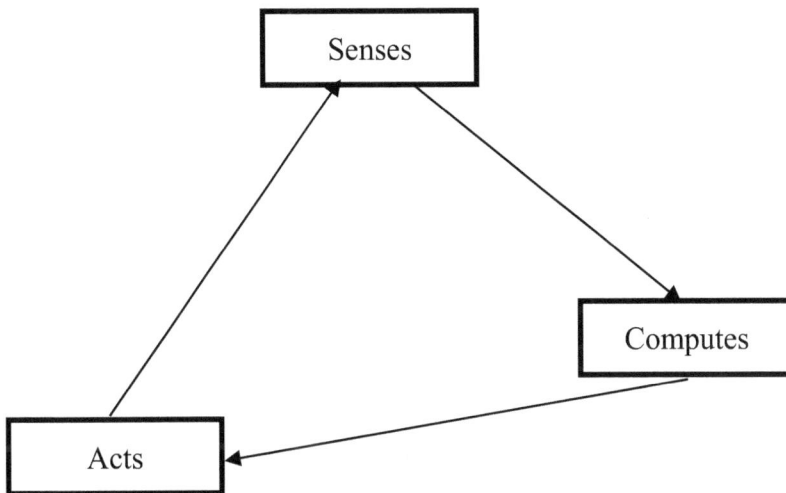

Fig. (1). Feedback loop of a robot.

1.2. Asimov Law of Robotics

Though Karl Kapek was the first to use the word robot in the science fiction publication of the 1920 play, titled Rossum's Universal Robots, the robots in that publication took over and exterminated the human race. However, Asimov envisions the concept of the modern robot in 1930 as a tool for helping the human race, rather than exterminating the human race [6]. Therefore, unlike the early robots that Karl Kapek described, the robots that Asimov envisioned do not threaten the human race. This led to the three laws of robotics, which was invented by Asimov. They are as follows:

- A robot may not harm a human or, through inaction, allow a human to come to harm.
- A robot must obey the orders given by human beings, except when such orders conflict with the first law.
- A robot must protect its own existence as long as it does not conflict with the first or second laws.

1.3. Characteristics of Robot

Three main characteristics can be used to recognize a robot. They are as follows: mechanical versatility, reprogramming capacity, and intelligent capability. Each of these characteristics will be explained briefly.

- **Mechanical Versatility:** This means the ability of the robot to perform different manipulative tasks.
- **Reprogramming Capacity:** This means that robots should have the capacity to be reprogrammed by altering the timing and sequence of the various tasks through software programming.
- **Intelligent Capability:** This means the ability of a robot to recognize its own state and its environment, using sensors and human-like reasoning to update its operations automatically.

1.4. User Level Applications of Robot

Robots can be used everywhere to do dangerous, dirty, and routine/dull tasks that human beings perform. Robots can be used in the following areas:

- **Industry:** Industrial robots can be used in the industry for pick and place, assembly line, machining, inspection, spray coating, spot welding, continuous arc welding, *etc.*
- **Remote Operations:** Robots can be used in a remote or far away location, like undersea, nuclear environment, bomb disposal, law enforcement surveillance, patrol, and in outer space.
- **Service Delivery:** Robots can be used for service delivery in the hospitals, helpmates, handicapped assistance, retail, household servants, vacuum cleaners, and lawnmowers.

1.5. Types of Robots

It may not be easy to classify robots based on types; this is because there are different types of robots, and each type performs its unique function in its unique way. The following classifications are based on the tasks that the robots perform and how they perform the tasks:

- **Aerospace:** This includes all robots that fly in the air and those that operate in space *e.g.*, surveillance drones, NASA robonaut.
- **Consumer Robots:** These are robots that you can buy for fun and help to do household chores, *e.g.*, robot dogs, AI-powered robot assistants.
- **Disaster Response Robots:** These are robots that are used to perform dangerous jobs, like searching for survivors in a disaster situation, like an earthquake and tsunami.
- **Drones:** These are unmanned aerial vehicles, which come in different sizes and shapes.
- **Education Robots:** These are regarded as the next generation of robots, which can be used in classrooms to teach students or help the teacher in teaching.
- **Entertainment Robots:** These are robots that evoke an emotional response and make us laugh.
- **Exoskeletons:** These are robots that help in physical rehabilitation and making a paralysed person walk again.
- **Humanoids:** These are robots that have the exact appearance of a human being.
- **Industrial Robots:** These are robots that have manipulators, which can be used to perform a particular repetitive task in the industry.
- **Medical Robots:** These are robots that are used for medical purposes, like surgical robots and exoskeletons.
- **Military and Security Robots:** These are robots that can be used for ground military operations.
- **Research Robots:** These are robots that can be used for research purposes.
- **Self-driving Cars/Autonomous Cars:** These are vehicles that drive themself, without any drivers. They are robots because they perform the repetitive functions of robots, senses, computes and acts.
- **Telepresence Robots:** These are robots that allow you to be present in a place without actually being there, physically. You log in to the robot *via* the internet, and drive it there. You see what the robot sees, and the people see you. You talk to the people and the people talk to you.
- **Underwater Robots:** These are robots that go the water to obtain information, like videos, pictures and samples of experimental data.

1.6. Components of Robots

Though robots come in different forms and different shapes, however the different components that the different robots are made of will be considered here. They include the following: manipulators, links, base, controller, sensors, actuators, power conversion unit, storage unit, processor, effectors, joints, connectors [5]. Each of these parts or components of robots will be considered briefly.

- **Effectors:** There are parts of robots that it uses to affect the environment. The robots control these effectors in order to affect the environment. Effectors serve two main purpose, which are to change the position of the robot (locomotion) and to affect the environment in different ways, depending on the tasks that the robot performs [5].
- **Actuators:** These are parts of robots that convert software command into physical motion. In order for the effectors to affect the environment, the effectors must be connected to the actuators, so that software commands can be converted to physical motion that will move the effectors, thereby affecting the environment.
- **Manipulators:** These are effectors that robots use to affect the environment through the movement of objects in the environment. Manipulators can be used for rotary movement or prismatic movement. Rotary movement involves rotation of object, while prismatic movement involves linear movement of object.
- **Link:** A link is a rigid body of a robot that can move about.
- **Joint:** Two links meet at a joint, which allow for motion. Illustrating with the human body, the upper arm and forearms are two links, while the elbow and wrist are joints.
- **End Effector:** This part of robot is located at the end of the manipulator. It interacts directly with the object in order to move the object. It can be regarded as the tool that is connected to the arm of the robot, which enables it to perform a task, *e.g.* a gripper, machine tools, measuring instruments,
- **Sensors:** These are tools that robots use for perception. Some sensors can be for sight perception, audio perception, tactile perception *etc.* Each type of perception has its own sensor. This has been considered in detail in the previous chapter on sensory perception. However, robot sensors measure the configuration/condition of robots and its environment. Robot sensory perceptions are more than the five main sensory perceptions of human. Example, robots can have the ability to see in the dark, detect tiny amount of invisible radiation, measure movement that are too small or too fast for the human eye to see.

1.7. Conclusion

This unit has laid a solid foundation for the study of robotics. It has introduced robots, its various types, uses, components, characteristics and the laws of robotics.

1.8. Summary

One type of robots that was identified in this unit is humanoid robot, which is a type of robot that looks like human being and performs tasks that a human being performs. The availability of different humanoid robots today stresses the importance of humanoid robots; therefore, the next unit will be devoted to humanoid robots.

2. HUMANOID ROBOTS

Humanoid robot has been defined as a type of robot that looks like human being in appearance and also exhibits some of the behaviours of human beings and human-like sensing and expressions and other intelligent behaviours of human beings [5]. Humanoid robots have different sizes and shapes; some have the size of complete human being, with all the physical parts of the body present, like head, hand, body and legs. Others have only isolated robotic human head, with human-like sensing and expression. Humanoid robotics, therefore is an aspect of robotics that deals with the creation of robots that share similar motion, sensing, behaviour, appearance and intelligence of human being [7].

2.1. Motivations for Humanoid Robots

The following are some of the reasons that motivate the development of humanoid robots.

• Acting and Thinking Like Human

Since Artificial Intelligence was defined in Unit 1 of Chapter 1 as the field of study the deals with the design of system that act and think like man, therefore, developing a robot that can act and think like man is indeed Artificial Intelligence. Roboticists would like to create robots that share similar physical and intellectual capabilities as in human.

• Humans are the Crown of all Creatures

Humans are endowed with best characteristics features, when compared with other living creatures. These characteristic features include: sound of human voice, appearance of human face, body motion and high level of intelligence. Therefore, by mimicking human characteristics, humanoid robots will achieve some of these great human characteristics in robots.

• Understanding Intelligence

Many humanoid roboticists believe that humanoid robot will help to better understand human. By emulating human intelligence using humanoids, scientists, psychologist and linguist have discovered that there is a strong link between human body and human cognition.

• Interfacing with Human World

Humans have taken time to design our environment to accommodate human form and behaviours. Examples tools that human work with are designed to fit into human hands. Doors, tables and chairs have been designed to accommodate human forms. Therefore, humanoid robots can take advantage of these forms, and simplify the tasks of human, while fitting in the same environment instead of creating another type of environment for it.

• Interfacing with People

People are used to working with people, and many types of communications rely on human forms and behaviours. Some types of natural gestures and expressions rely in subtle movements in the hand and face. Therefore, humanoid robots can take advantage of existing communication channels and effectively interact with human. Furthermore, people have the skill and ability to perform many desirable tasks, like entertainments, such tasks can be transferred to humanoid robots instead of robots with drastically different body.

2.2. Historical Development of Humanoid Robots

Development of mechanical systems with human forms and movements dates back in the 13th century with the design of humanoid automation by Al-Jazari [5]. This was followed by another design of humanoid automation by Leonardo da Vinci in the late 15th century. Significant computing was incorporated into the robots developed in the second half of the 20th century, this was due to advances in digital computing technology. Many of the systems that roboticists developed from that time could sense, move and performed actions that were inspired by human capabilities. WABOT-1 was the first humanoid robot to integrate these functions, and it was developed by Ichiro Kato *et al.* in Japan's Waseda University, in 1973 [5]. The WABOT robots could perform the following functions: visual object recognition, speech generation, speech recognition, bimanual object manipulation, and bipedal walking. In 1996, Honda unveiled the Honda humanoid, P2, which was a full-scale humanoid that was capable of performing stable bipedal movement, with on-board power and processing. An upper-body humanoid was designed by MIT Artificial Intelligence laboratory in the USA. The MIT humanoid robot was a result of the cog project initiated in 1993, inspired by biological and cognitive science. In the early 21st century, many companies and academic researchers have become interested in the development of humanoid robots and many of them are available today.

2.3. Current Trends in Humanoid Robots

Most of the humanoid robots developed today have the following characteristic features:

• Different Forms

Humanoid robots that are available are in different forms and sizes, and perform different aspects of human behaviours. Some have parts of human body, while other parts of the body are absent. Example, some humanoid robots focus on the head and face, while others may have head and two arms, mounted on a wheel.

• Different Degree of Freedom

Degree of freedom refers to the type and direction of movements that robots can perform. Some humanoid robots have focused on some degree of freedom of human beings, while ignoring others. Example, some can generate facial expression like those of human,

• Different Sensors

Humanoid robots use different sensors, which includes the following: laser range finders, cameras, microphone arrays, lavalier microphone, pressure sensors [7]. However, humanoid roboticists can choose a range of sensors and mount them in a way that will mimic human sense organs.

2.4. Locomotion in Humanoid Robots

Humanoid robots that have legs move from one place to another using bipedal movement. This is the same way that human move, which involves moving the two legs forward, one after another. Bipedal locomotion is very challenging, especially on rough surface. Statically stability can be achieved in small humanoid robot by having large feet and small centre of mass. However, humanoid robot with human-like weight distribution and body size can achieve stability dynamically as it walks with the two legs. In order to ensure that humanoid robot does not fall while on bipedal motion, the methods that it uses are based of zero moment point. However, bipedal walking algorithms that are based on zero moment point finds it difficult handling unexpected perturbations, which can occur in uneven surfaces. Furthermore, humanoid robot using bipedal walking algorithms differs from human locomotion. This is because zero moment point do not exploit the natural dynamics of their legs or control the impedance of their joints. However, humanoid robot can fall due to large disturbance, such fall can damage the environment or the humanoid robot. Minimizing the damage or graceful recovery from humanoid fall is an important problem that roboticists are trying to solve.

2.5. Manipulation in Humanoid Robots

The manipulators that humanoid robots use to manipulate or affect the environment are the hands and arms. How each of these manipulators is used to manipulate the environment will be discussed briefly.

• The Arm and Hand

The arm of humanoid robots emulates the arm of human, which has about seven degrees of free, three degrees of freedom at the shoulder, one degree of freedom at the elbow and three degrees of freedom at the wrist. Unlike the human hand, which has about 20 degrees of freedom, four for each finger, the hand of different humanoid robots varies in their design. The hand of the humanoid robot can be regarded as the end effector, which serves the same purpose as gripper that makes direct contact with the object. With appropriate end effectors, humanoid robots can perform tasks like human, which involve rhythmic manipulations. Example of such tasks are hammering nails, sawing through woods, playing with toy, drumming *etc.* Furthermore, people work in cooperation with other people, therefore humanoid robots have the potential to cooperate with human in order to perform some tasks. This type of manipulation in humanoid robot is called cooperative manipulation. Fig. (**2**) shows a humanoid robot cooperating with human in performing a task [7].

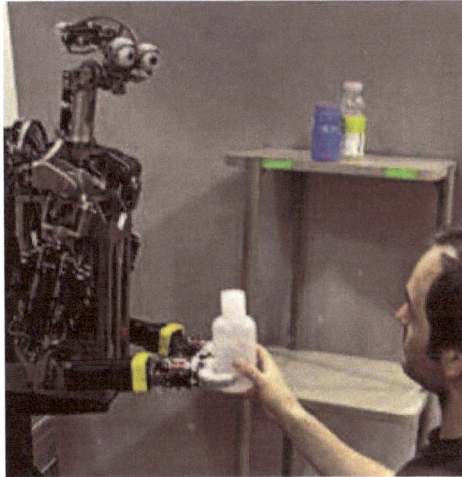

Fig. (2). A Humanoid cooperating with human to perform task.

Learning by demonstration is one of the abilities of human, this quality has been used in humanoid so that humanoid can learn new manipulative tasks by observation and demonstration.

2.6. Communication in Humanoid Robots

Like human, humanoids can communicate with people through body posture and body movement. Example, the hand and arm of humanoid can reach and grasp, point and gesture. Though in human, eye movement can be used for sensing, humanoid robots can use eye movement either for expression or for sensing. Humanoids have been designed with the ability to interpret human expressions. Algorithms for performing the following tasks have been developed and incorporated into humanoids: person finding, person identification, gesture recognition, face pose estimation. Example, in Fig. (**3**), a humanoid called Asimo has used the functions to perform reception tasks by identifying person, recognize gestures for bye bye, stop, come here *etc.* Currently, some humanoid roboticists have developed humanoid robots that have the same facial resemblances, facial expression, same voice, same colour and height as a particular individual [5]. This type of humanoid robot is called Germinoid.

2.7. Conclusion

Various aspects of humanoid robots have been considered in this unit, its motivation, history, current trend, locomotion, manipulation and communication.

2.8. Summary

Over the last decade, the number of humanoid robots developed for research purposes has grown. However, humanoid robots have been extensively used for entertainment in form of competition with toys. The availability of humanoid robots everywhere depends on their preference by customers. However, there are other types of robots that are gaining attention, one of such is robotics cars.

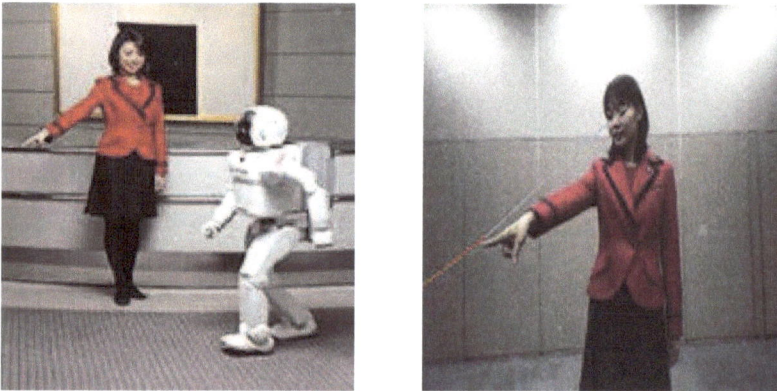

Fig. (3). A humanoid called Asimo performing reception tasks.

3. AUTONOMOUS/ROBOTIC VEHICLES

While humanoid robot takes the form and abilities of a human being, autonomous/robotic vehicles can be regarded as a robot that takes the form of a car. Being autonomous, it means that it makes its independent decisions based on the signals that it receives using the sensors. Being a robot, it means that it performs the three main functions of a robot, it senses, computes and takes action. The actions of an autonomous or robotic vehicle are the intelligent actions of a professional driver. Therefore, autonomous vehicles are robots that take the form of a car, which drives itself. Autonomous or robotic vehicles can be called driverless vehicles, however, some of them have humanoid robots as their drivers.

3.1. Levels of Vehicles Automation

The Society for Automotive Engineers has identified six different levels of vehicle automation [4, 8 - 10]. Each level identifies the significant features available in the vehicles that belong to that level, with respect to vehicle automation. The descriptions of the levels are stated below:

- **Level 0, No Automation**

Zero autonomy, the driver performs all the driving functions.

- **Level 1, Driver Assistance**

Advanced driver assistance system is available, but the vehicle is under the control of the driver.

- **Level 2, Partial Automation**

Advanced driver assistance system is available, but the vehicle has some automated features, like acceleration and steering. However, the driver must be fully engaged with the driving tasks, and monitor the environment all the time.

- **Level 3, Conditional Automation**

Automated driving system is available in the vehicle, which can perform all the driving tasks. However, the human driver must be available to intervene in the driving tasks, whenever the automated driving system needs the intervention of the driver.

- **Level 4. High Automation**

Automated driving system performs all driving tasks in certain circumstances. As such times, the driver may not pay attention to the driving.

- **Level 5, Full Automation**

Automated driving system performs all driving tasks at all times. The human driver will never be involved in the driving of the vehicle [10 - 12].

3.2. How Autonomous Vehicle Technology Works

Autonomous vehicles use the following sensors for vision: camera, radar, LiDAR *etc.* The camera is one of the sensors for vision. Together with an appropriate algorithm, autonomous vehicles can fully comprehend the images captured with camera. Radar is another sensor that autonomous vehicles use for vision, along with camera and LiDA. Its resolution is lower than the resolution of camera and LiDA. LiDA is an acronym for Light Detecting And Ranging. It is a sensor that is located at the top of autonomous vehicles, which spins continuously. Autonomous vehicles use neural network and machine learning algorithm to identify patterns in the images that the sensors captures. This enables it to identify every object around it.

Waymo, an autonomous vehicle developed by Google, which is shown in Fig. (4) works as follows: The passenger determines the destination, afterwards the autonomous vehicle calculates the shortest route, based on real time traffic information. The LiDA on top of the vehicle monitors a 60-meter range in order to create a 3D map of the car's current environment. On the left rear wheel is a sensor that monitors side way movement and determines the position of the car relative to the 3D map. Radar systems in the front bumper and rear bumper of the car calculate the distances to obstacle. Artificial Intelligence system in the car, which is connected to all the sensors collects input from Google Street map and simulates human perception and decision making process using deep learning and controls actions in driver control system and braking system. Though the autonomous vehicle called Waymo belongs to high automation level (Level 4), therefore, a driver will be required to be present in some circumstances [10].

Fig. (4). Google's autonomous vehicle, Waymo.

The following features are available in most level 4 autonomous vehicles.

- Hands-free steering: This helps to center the car.
- Adaptive cruise control down to a stop: This feature automatically maintains a selectable distance between the driver's car and the car in front.
- Lane-centering steering: This intervenes when the vehicle crosses lane marking by automatically nudging the vehicle towards the opposite lane marking.

These features help the autonomous vehicle to drive safely in the midst of traffic, as shown in Fig. (**5**).

Fig. (5). Autonomous vehicles in traffic area. Autonomous vehicle driving in midst traffic.

3.3. History of Autonomous Vehicles

The history of vehicle automation dates back to 1478, when Leonardo da Vinci designed the first prototype. Since then to the end of the 20th century, robotic vehicles have been designed and developed. However, self-driving cars started in the early 2000 with increasing vehicle automation features, which were motivated by its safety and convenience. It started with cruise control and anti-lock brake before the end of 2000. After the dawn of the second millennium, advanced safety features, like electronic stability control, blind spot detection and collision and lane shift warning were introduced. Advanced driver assistance capabilities, like rear-view video camera, automatic emergency brakes, and lane centering assistance were introduced between 2010 and 2016. Partial automation started in 2016 with features like Automatic Cruise Control (ACC) and self-parking ability. However, full vehicle automation is not yet available for public use.

3.4. Benefits of Autonomous Vehicles

Autonomous vehicle optimists have proposed the following benefits to be derived from autonomous vehicles:

• Reduced Stress, Increase Productivity and Mobility

Since the driving task will be taken over from the driver, therefore, it will reduce stress. Reduction in stress will increase productivity. Instead of driving, drivers can be engaged in more productive task or rest. This means that the vehicles can be turned to mobile offices while the vehicle is on motion.

• Traffic Safety and Security

Autonomous vehicle optimists claim that 90% of crash are as a result of human error. They argue that this will drastically be reduced with an autonomous vehicle with a zero tolerance to crash.

• Reduction of External Cost

Autonomous vehicle will reduce external cost, like traffic congestion, car park, pollution emission. This is because autonomous vehicles that are equipped with route guidance system will help to minimize traffic congestion and travel time. Furthermore, green house emission is expected to be low since the vehicle will be powered by electricity or battery, instead of petroleum product.

3.5. Development and Deployment of Autonomous Vehicles

New technology like autonomous vehicles follow an 'S' pattern in its development and deployment [10]. It begins with an initial conception, which undergoes development, testing, approval, commercial release, product improvement, market expansion *etc.*, as illustrated in Fig. (**6**), below. However, autonomous vehicles are currently in the development and testing stages. Many companies have developed prototypes of autonomous vehicles and they are currently testing them. Most of the autonomous vehicles that have been developed are in levels 2 and 3. However, level 4 autonomous vehicles have been developed by many companies, but they are for pilot projects. Before autonomous vehicles can become commercially available, it must undergo thorough testing and regulation standard. Testing and operation of autonomous vehicles are only allowed at this moment in specific highways.

Testing and operating autonomous vehicles require more complex software than aircraft. This is due to the complexity of the roadways interactions. between other vehicles, pedestrians, cyclists, potholes, building *etc.* The production of such complex software is indeed a challenging task to accomplish. Market deployment of autonomous vehicles depends on customers' demand and willingness of travelers to pay for autonomous vehicles mobility [10]. Though the development of level 5 autonomous vehicle is the goal, but that will require more years ahead to accomplish, many have predicted the year, 2040 [10].

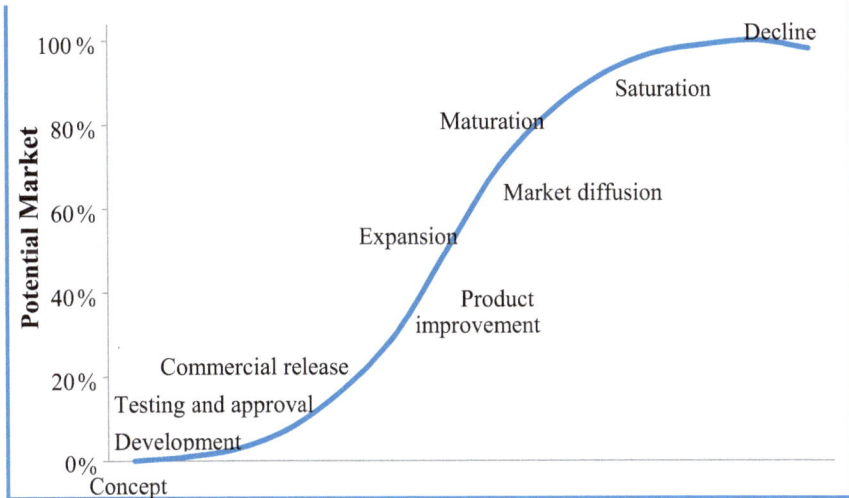

Fig. (6). The 'S' curve of new technology, Autonomous Vehicles.

3.6. Planning Implications for Autonomous Vehicles

Deployment of autonomous vehicles requires adequate preparation, since it introduces paradigm shift in vehicle transportation [10]. The planning will be in the following areas:

• Design of Roadways

New roadways design features may be required for autonomous vehicles, these features include: improved lane marking, electronic signs and sensors, wireless repeaters in tunnels for internet access. Special lanes can be dedicated for autonomous vehicles.

• Vehicle Park Design

Electric autonomous vehicles will require new special vehicle parking facilities, with electric charging stations, vehicle cleaning and maintenance service *etc.*

• Public Transit

Autonomous vehicles can reduce the operational cost of providing transit services, with flexible routes and reduced travel time. Consequently, conventional transit demand can be reduced. It can also support transit by reducing operational cost.

• Passenger Management

Since most autonomous vehicles can be shared among various passengers, therefore, provision must be made for passenger loading and unloading. This can be through the provision of passenger loading areas or on-the-street loading areas.

3.7. Conclusion

Autonomous vehicles have been explored in this unit. The levels of vehicle automation, its history, how the technology works, development & deployment and planning for autonomous vehicles are among the issues considered.

3.8. Summary

Development of any system cannot be completed without appropriate metrics, which will be used to measure the performance of such system. Furthermore, it was defined in Unit 3 of Chapter 5 that tactile sensing in robots is the process of measuring a given property of an object. Therefore, the need to define appropriate metrics that can be used to measure the performance of robots cannot be over-emphasized. The next unit will be devoted to metrics that can be used to measure the performance of robots.

4. METRICS FOR ASSESSING THE PERFORMANCE OF ROBOTS

Robots are designed to perform a specific task in an independent manner. However, the process of performing the task may require planned interaction with human or unplanned interaction with human (intervention). It is necessary to assess how well robot perform the intended task. This can be achieved by defining appropriate metrics (measures) for specific task that robot performs. The aim of this unit is to identify and define appropriate metrics that can be measured in various tasks that robot perform. Emphasis will not be focused on developing the models for the metrics.

4.1. Metrics for Navigational Tasks

Navigational tasks require the robot to move from one point to another, which can be by land, air or sea. The various metrics that can be measured how well the robot performs this task can be classified as follows [13, 14]:

• **Effectiveness Navigational Metrics**

This class of metric measures how well the navigational task is completed, and the following metrics make up this class of navigational metrics: percentage of navigational task completed, coverage area, deviation from planned route, obstacles that were successfully avoided, obstacles that were not avoided but could be overcome.

• **Efficiency Navigational Metrics**

This class of metric measures the time needed to complete the navigational task, and they include the following: Time to complete the navigational task, operator time for the time, average time for obstacle extraction. Where unplanned operator intervention is applicable, the following metrics can be measured: Number of operator intervention per unit time, ratio of operator time to robotic time.

4.2. Metrics for Perception Tasks

Perception tasks in this context involve the use of sensory perceptions with the aim of understanding the environment for applications such as search, surveillance, and target identification. Two basic tasks are involved in perception, they are: interpreting sensed data and seeking new sensor data [13, 14]. Therefore, the metrics for perception can be classified based on the two perceptions as follows: passive perception metric and active perception metric. The passive perception metrics are the metrics that are involved in the interpretation of sensor data, which include: identification, judgement of extent and judgement of motion. Identification measures include: detection and recognition accuracy. The following are the specific metric under each class of metrics:

• **Detection Measures**

They include the following: percentage detected, signal detection, detection by object orientation *etc.* [13 - 15].

• Recognition Measures

Classification accuracy, confusion metric, recognition by object orientation *etc.*

• Judgement of Extent

Absolute and relative distance, size, height, length of perceived object, how long it will take the robot to reach a perceive object.

• Judgement of Motion

Absolute velocity of robot, relative velocity of moving object (Can moving robot meet another moving object).

4.3. Metrics for Management Tasks

When robots are involved in management of tasks, which involve interaction with human, the following metrics can be defined:

• Fan Out

This is the number of robots that a human operator can effectively control.

• Intervention Response Time

This is the time that elapse from the time that the robot needs assistance to the time the assistance was resolved [13 - 15]. Intervention is required when the robot enters into a problem situation. Intervention can be in form of supervisory control or when groups of robots are controlled by human. Intervention response time can be measured from the time the operator first noticed the problem or from the time the robot requested the assistance.

• Level of Autonomy Discrepancy

Robots can be designed to operate with multiple levels of autonomy. A particular level of autonomy may be more efficient to another level of autonomy for a specific task and in a particular environment. Therefore, this metric measures the ability of human operator to accurately and rapidly identify the most efficient level of autonomy and control the robot to operate in such level of autonomy.

4.4. Metrics for Manipulation Tasks

Most of the tasks that robots perform are manipulation tasks. The following metrics can be defined when robots perform manipulation tasks:

• Degree of Mental Computation

This metric measures the degree of mental computation that an operator performs while robot is doing manipulation tasks [13, 14]. Mental computation includes the following tasks: rotation, rate tracking *etc.*

• Contact Error

This is one of the important metrics in manipulation task by a robot. It measures the number of unintentional collision between a manipulator and the environment. It indicates the positional accuracy of the manipulator.

4.5. Metrics for Social Tasks

Some robots are designed to perform social tasks by simulating the social intelligence found in living organism. The following metrics can be measured in such tasks:

• Interaction Characteristics

This metric can be measured by assessing characteristics such as interaction style or social context through observation.

• Persuasiveness

Since the robot is expected to change the behaviour, feeling and attitude of human, therefore, this metric measures the ease with which the robot accomplishes these changes in human.

• Trust

This is an important metric to measure. It measures the extent to which human trust the robot in performing the required task. It determines reliance on complex, imperfect automation in dynamic environment that requires human to adapt to unanticipated circumstances.

• Engagement

Since social interaction is an effective tool for engagement, therefore this metric measures the efficacy of various social characteristics, like emotion, dialogue, personality, *etc.*, for capturing attention and holding interest.

• Compliance

The amount of cooperation that human gives to robots that perform social tasks depends on some social characteristics, like appearance, adherence to norms, *etc.* Therefore, measuring compliance can help to determine the effectiveness of the robot design.

4.6. Conclusion

In this unit, you have learnt the various metrics that can be used to measure how effective robots can perform their various tasks. In particular, the various metrics for the following tasks have been identified and explained, including navigational, perception, management, manipulation, and social.

4.7. Summary

The importance of metrics in measuring how well a robot performs its tasks cannot be over-emphasized. It helps in assessing how well the robot performs its intended task.

CONCLUDING REMARKS

The chapter has introduced robotics by considering its foundations, afterwards, it considers three important and current research area in robotics, which are humanoid robots, autonomous/robotic vehicles and metrics for assessing the performance of robots.

REFERENCES

[1]   B. Williams, "An Introduction to Robotics", *Mechanical Engineering, Ohio University,* 2019.

[2]   J.J. Craig, *Introduction to Robotics: Mechanics and Control.* Pearson Prentics Hall, 2005.

[3]   P. Duysinx, and M. Geradin, *An Introduction to Robotics: Mechanical Aspects.* University of Liege, 2004.

[4]   M. Harb, Y. Xiao, G. Circella, P. L. Mokhtarian and J, L. Walker, "Projecting Travelers into a World of Self-Driving Vehicles",Transportation", https://link.springer.com/article/10.1007%2Fs11116-01--9937-9

[5]   S.J. Russells, and P. Norwig, *Artificial Intelligence: A Modern Approach.* Prentice Hall, 1995.

[6]   C.G. Atkeson, B.P.W. Badu, N. Banerjee, D. Berenson, C.P. Bpve, X. Cui, M. DeDonato, R. Du, S. Feng, P. Franklin, M. Gennert, and J.P. Graff, *15ᵗʰ IEEE-RAS Int. Conf. on Humanoid Robots,* 2015pp. 623-630

[7]   https://www.researchgate.net/publication/226773728_Humanoids

[8]   H. Kyle, *Toyota had the Most Autonomous Vehicle Disengagements,* 2020. www.cnet.com/roadshow/ news/2019-california-self-driving-disengagement-report-baidu-waymo-cruise

[9]   ITF, *Safer Roads with Automated Vehicles?,* 2018. atwww.itf-oecd.org/sites/default/files/docs/safe--roads-automated-vehicles.pdf

[10]   T. Litman, *Autonomous Vehicle Implementations for Transport Planning,* 2020. www.vtpi.org

[11]   E. Papa, and A. Ferreira, *Sustainable Accessibility and the Implementation of Automated Vehicles: Identifying Critical Decisions.* https://bit.ly/2DHjZQz.2018 [http://dx.doi.org/10.3390/urbansci2010005]

[12]   M. Hentschel, and B. Wagner, "Autonomous Robot Navigation Based on Open Street Map Geodata", *13ᵗʰ Int. Conf. on Intelligent Transportation Systems,* 2010pp. 1645-1650

[13]   S.C. Wong, L. Middleton, and B.A. MacDonald, "Performance Metrics for Robot Coverage Tasks", *Proc. Australasian Conference on Robotics and Automation,* 2002

[14]   N.D.M. Ceballos, J.A.V. Velasquez, and N.L. Ospina, *Quantitative Performance Metrics for Mobile Robots Navigation,* 2010. http://www.researchgate.net/publication/2219080282010 [http://dx.doi.org/10.5772/8988]

[15]   A. Steinfeid, T. Fong, D. Kadar, M. Lewis, J. Scholtz, A. Schultz, and M. Goodrich, *Common Metrics for Human-Robot Interaction,* 2006.

SUBJECT INDEX

A

Acoustic signal 290, 291
  encoded 290
Agent 3, 9, 12, 16, 234, 235, 236, 237, 238, 276
  artificial 276
  environment interaction 235
  law enforcement 16
  rational 3
Algorithm 12, 13, 62, 68, 108, 111, 112, 116, 140, 141, 142, 147, 151, 152, 195, 214, 218, 219, 220, 221, 222, 266, 268, 273, 288, 306
  backpropagation 221, 222, 288
  configuration 195
  developed 273
  generalized 266, 268
  ideal 108
  propagation 218, 219, 220
Analyses 13
  diverse data 13
  protected data 13
Analysis 261, 277
  COVID-19 dataset 261
  system 277
ANN 218, 221, 222, 223
  n-layer 222
  one-layer 223
  three-layer 222
  two-layer 218, 222
Application of deep feedforward network 224
Applications 6, 8, 10, 13, 14, 16, 51, 52, 53, 278, 279, 288, 289, 291, 294
  emerging Artificial Intelligence 10, 16
  industrial 8
  machine vision 278
  traditional 14
Applications of artificial intelligence 1, 10, 12, 13, 16, 58, 73, 294
  of Sentiment Analysis 73
  of speech recognition system 294

Artificial Intelligence 1, 3, 5, 7, 8, 9, 10, 16, 38, 39, 44, 245, 246
  and Big Data Analytics 246
  and experimental techniques 3
  applied technologies 10
  birth of 7, 8, 9
  general definition of 1, 16
  funding 8
  programs 5, 38, 39, 44
  research 8, 9
  techniques 245
Artificial neural network algorithm 218
Artificial neurom 205
Artificial intelligence products 10, 15, 16
  emerging 16
Artificial Intelligence systems 3, 6, 7, 8, 10, 16, 18, 310
  developing 6
  significant 7
Artificial neuron 203, 204, 205, 206, 207
  semi-linear 206, 207
Asimov law of robotics 299
Attribute(s) 31, 32, 96, 98, 100, 101, 102, 106, 107, 120, 121, 123, 124, 125, 126, 127, 128, 129, 187, 188, 189, 191, 196, 202, 246, 247, 248
  relation file format (ARFF) 187, 188, 189, 191, 246
  attribute Weapontype 247
  class attribute and non-class 202
  computation of IG for 126, 127, 128
  predicted Regression 196
Automatic 68, 69, 311
  cruise control (ACC) 311
  text summarization 68, 69
Automating logical reasoning 38
Autonomous
  cars 1
  vehicle driving 311
Autonomous vehicle(s) 15, 289, 290, 298, 308, 309, 310, 311, 312, 313, 314
  in traffic area 311

mobility 313
operating 312
technology works 309

B

Bayes 117, 292
  equation 292
  theorem 117
Bayesian theorem 116, 117, 119
Bellman's 239
  equation 239
  solution 239
Big data analytics 246
Binomial probability distribution 171, 172, 175, 253, 256, 257
  function 171, 172, 253, 256
Biological neural network 200, 201, 207, 221, 222
Blockchain 1, 10, 11, 12, 13
  network 10
  technology 1, 10, 11, 12, 13

C

Camera 277, 287, 289, 298, 305, 309
  digital 287
  high-speed 277
  roadside 277
Cluster diagram 101
Clustering 101, 160, 168, 186, 202, 253, 287
  and data visualization 186
  problem 186, 202
  technique 287
Coefficients 77, 196, 294, 296
  agreement 77
  correlation 196
Cognex 278
Cognitive 15, 33
  architecture 33
  artificial intelligence platform 15
Computational linguistics 6, 8
Computer vision 15, 16, 222, 276, 277, 278, 279, 281, 289, 290, 297

applications of 277
algorithms 279, 281, 290
methods 278
problems 279
software 278
Convolutional layer 231, 232
Corona virus pandemic 260
Counter-terrorism 246, 247
  policy 246
  teams 247
COVID-19 242, 259, 260, 273
  dataset 242, 259, 260, 273
  dynamics of 260
  incidents of 259, 260
  restrictions 259
CSV 187, 188, 189, 191
  file 187, 188, 189, 191
  format 187

D

Data 107, 244
  preparation processes 107
  pre-processing stage 244
Dataset 111, 259, 270
  linear 111, 259
  two-attribute 270
Data transformation 104, 105, 106
  techniques 106
Design 6, 304, 313
  artificial intelligence systems 6
  of humanoid automation 304
  of roadways 313
Detection 277, 278, 280, 287, 288, 296, 315
  machine learning algorithms 287
Development 1, 6, 7, 9, 10, 16, 304
  of artificial intelligence 1, 6, 7, 9, 10, 16
  of mechanical systems 304
Digital 11, 280
  currency 11
  image processing 280
Dimensional 170, 283
  affine transformations 283
  linear dataset 170

Distribution function 171, 175, 176, 252, 253, 258
  appropriate probability 176, 253
  discrete probability 171, 175
  relevant probability 252
  simulated probability 252
Dynamic programming 237, 239, 240
  heuristic 239
  method 237

E

Efficiency navigational metrics 315
Electric autonomous vehicles 313
Emotion detection sentiment analysis 73
Engine diagnosis system 22
Environment 35, 36, 234, 235, 236, 237, 238, 239, 295, 298, 299, 300, 302, 304, 306, 315, 317
  dynamic 317
  expert system development 35, 36
  nuclear 300
Error 221
  backpropagation algorithm 221
  propagation algorithm 221

F

Feature scaling method 107
Frequency based technique 69
Fundamentals 51, 104, 276
  of computer vision 276
  of data preparation 104
  of natural language processing 51

G

Generalized ordinary least square method 259
General-purpose vision system 278
Global terrorism database 244, 246, 247, 253
Grained sentiment analysis 73

H

Hardware 205, 278, 293
  degradation 205
  digitization 293
  imaging 278
Hashing algorithms 12
Hearing 2, 3, 6, 276, 290, 291, 294, 297
  computer audition/computer 291
  computer auditory/computer 294
  sense organ of 2, 276, 290
Hidden markov model (HMM) 63
Historical development 9, 10, 293, 304
  of artificial intelligence 9, 10
  of humanoid robots 304
  of speech recognition 293
Human 6, 21
  biological processes 6
  expert reasoning 21
Humanoid 304, 305, 307
  automation 304
  roboticists 304, 305, 307
Humanoid robots 298, 303, 304, 305, 306, 307, 308, 318
  developed 307
  development of 303, 305
  emulates 306
Hybrid 35, 75
  approach 75
  environment 35

I

Image 276, 287, 281
  based modelling 276, 281
  recognition problem 287
  sensing systems 277
Incidents of terrorism 247, 250, 253, 254, 255, 256, 257, 258
  rate of occurrence of 254, 255
Inference engine accesses 30
Information 2, 9, 11, 14, 20, 21, 22, 24, 31, 32, 277, 292, 296, 301
  local shape 277

medical 21
real time traffic 310
Information gain (IG) 121, 122, 123, 124, 125,
    126, 127, 128, 129, 248
Input data 98, 99, 100, 116, 118, 119, 120,
    208, 209, 211, 215, 216, 217
  binary two-digit 209
  dimensional 211
  instance of 116, 119
Intelligence 14, 15, 245, 246, 303, 304, 317
  business 245
  gathering 246
  social 317
  system, emerging artificial 15
Intent detection sentiment analysis 73
Internet 1, 13, 14, 74
  of things (IoT) 1, 13, 14
  sentiment analysis 74
Intervention response time 316

J

Jaccard similarity function 72
Java programming language 44, 50, 255, 270

K

Knowledge 18, 23, 27, 28, 36, 186
  acquisition methods 27, 36
  analysis WEKA 186
  engineering processes 23
  engineer support 28
  modelling methods 27
  representation and automated reasoning 18
Knowledge base 18, 19, 20, 21, 22, 23, 24, 28,
    29, 30, 33, 34, 35
  deep common sense 33

L

Lane shift warning 311
Layer ANN 217, 222
  single 222
Learning 94, 95, 97, 207, 208, 235

process 94, 97, 207, 235
rule 207, 208
theory 95, 235
Learning algorithm 67, 96, 97, 100, 111, 116
    244, 273
  based supervised machine 111
  naive bayes machine 244
  naïve bayes machine 67, 116
  novel machine 273
  novel supervised machine 273
Learning system 97, 236, 238
  reinforcement 236, 238
Least square estimate 116
Least square method 100, 108, 109, 113, 170,
    259
  or linear multiple regression 113
Life insurance company 98
Linear 113, 171, 259
  dataset model 171
  factors 259
  multiple regression 113
Linear regression 100, 108, 111, 192, 194,
    195, 196, 198, 200
  algorithm 111
  machine learning 100
  multiple 108
  problems 200
  simple 108
Linguistic data consortium (LDC) 294
LISP in logic programming 8
Locomotion in humanoid robots 306
Logic 4, 5, 29, 37
  conjunction 37
  disjunction 37
Logical 4, 36, 83, 84, 85, 86
  connectives 36
  expression 85, 86
  functions 83, 84
  positivism 4
  theories 4
Logic function 210, 211, 224, 225, 226, 227,
    228, 229
  output of complex 224
  evaluation 224
Logistic regression 192

M

Machine 2, 7, 27, 58, 66, 116, 170, 253, 278, 287, 288, 298
  autonomous 298
  support vector 66, 253, 287, 288
Machine learning 13, 15, 53, 63, 66, 75, 94, 96, 97, 98, 99, 100, 101, 103, 104, 105, 106, 107, 116, 152, 159, 160, 186, 192, 200, 221, 242, 243, 244, 245, 246, 247, 249, 251, 252, 253, 255, 257, 259, 260, 261, 263, 265, 267, 273, 287, 288
  algorithms 75, 99, 100, 101, 104, 105, 107, 152, 159, 160, 242, 243, 244, 246, 247
  applications 242, 243, 245, 247, 249, 251, 253, 255, 257, 259, 261, 263, 265, 267, 273
  based text classification 66
  component 63
  environment 116
  models 221, 243
  rule 260
  simulation software 221
  system 94, 97, 98, 99, 100, 103, 245
  task 96, 106
  techniques 53, 246, 287, 288
  technologies 15
  tools 13, 186, 192, 200, 242, 243, 244, 245, 251, 252, 253
Machine learning problems 96, 98, 104, 106, 117, 186, 200
  fundamental unsupervised 186
  solving classification 117
  spam detection 96
Machine learning software 67, 186, 245, 246
  open source 67, 186
Machine translation 53
Magnetism based sensors 296
Markov decision process 235
Markovian decision processes (MDPs) 239
Mel-frequency cepstral coefficients (MFCC) 294
Methods 21, 28, 59
  automatic knowledge modelling 28
  hot encoding 59
  probabilistic 21
Microphone arrays 305
Military and security robots 301

N

Naive bayes 198, 242, 243, 244
  algorithms 242, 243, 244
  classification 198
Natural language toolkit (NLTK) 54, 57, 64, 76, 77, 87
Neural network 200, 202, 222, 230, 231, 232, 233, 234, 240, 260, 287
  deep recurrent 233, 234
  traditional artificial 222
Neuro-transmitting chemicals 201
Noise 105, 203, 205
Nonlinear 159, 202
  regression models 159
  transfer function 202

O

Operators 37, 316, 317
  binary 37
Opinion mining process 245
Output signal 200, 203, 204, 205, 206, 207
  approaches 206
Overlapping clustering 160

P

Pairs 115, 152, 215, 216
  training vector 215, 216
Perceptron learning algorithm 214
Perceptual Linear Prediction (PLP) 294
Person 10, 15, 16, 30, 31, 307
  identifying 307
Piezoelectric 296
  material 296
  Sensors 296
Poisson probability distribution function 175, 254, 257

in data analysis 175
Poisson regression 108
Polynomial 132, 142, 145, 150, 152, 156, 259,
 260, 261, 262, 263, 265, 266, 268, 272
 degree of 260, 261
 lower degree 260
 prediction rule of 261, 262, 263, 265, 266,
  268
Polynomial regression 242, 259, 260, 261
 algorithm 259, 261
 model, fitted parametric 260
Probabilistic 160, 207
 approach 207
 clustering 160
Probabilities 101, 170, 171, 180, 186, 251,
 252, 253, 254, 255, 259
 of instances of dataset 101
 distribution functions 170, 171, 180, 186,
  251, 252, 253, 254, 255, 259
Probability theory 35, 117, 235
Process 6, 11, 12, 13, 14, 20, 21, 23, 24, 27,
 28, 34, 35, 54, 60, 94, 104, 106, 129,
 281, 290, 314
 automation 14
 economic 6
 modelling 27
Prolog 8, 35
Propositional logic 36, 37, 38, 39, 43, 44, 50
 atomic statements of 36
 connectives of 36, 37, 39
 operators of 36
 semantics of 37
Python 54, 56, 57, 76, 77, 78, 79, 80, 81, 82,
 83, 85, 86, 87
 codes load NLTK and list 87
 installed 76
Python programming 76, 82, 91, 170, 172
 language 76, 91, 170, 172
Pythonpython 82

Q

Quantum tunnel composite 296

R

Real 277, 278
 time stereo vision systems 278
 time traffic management 277
Region-based recognition 281
Regression algorithm 93, 112, 115, 132, 136,
 140, 142, 145, 147, 150, 156, 159
 multiple linear 112, 115
 non-linear 132, 136
Reinforcement learning 234, 235, 236, 237,
 238, 239, 240
 elements of 237, 239, 240
 methods 239
 problems 236, 238, 240
Reinforcement machine learning 236
Robotics 2, 3, 295, 296, 297, 298, 299, 300,
 301, 303, 305, 307, 308, 309, 311, 313,
 317, 318
 humanoid 303
 cars 308
 laws of 300, 303
 tactile sensors 296
Robot(s) 295, 296, 297, 298, 299, 300, 301,
 302, 303, 304, 308, 314, 315, 316, 317,
 318
 autonomous 298
 components of 302
 moving 316
 surgical 301
 tactile sensing in 295, 314
 senses 298, 299
Root 57, 142, 144, 145, 147, 148, 150, 152,
 154, 156, 157, 158, 159, 259, 260, 262,
 263, 264, 266, 268, 269
 dictionary 57
Rossum's universal robots (RUR) 8, 298

S

Scale-space processing 280
Security agencies 246, 252
Self-driving 15, 301
 autonomous cars 15
 cars/autonomous cars 301

Sensors 13, 14, 23, 25, 276, 295, 296, 299,
    300, 302, 305, 308, 309, 310, 313
  computer hearing 295
Sentiment analysis 51, 52, 53, 65, 72, 73, 74,
    75, 76, 91, 245
  on customer feedback 74
  on customer services 74
Signal-processing module processes 292
Smart computing power 12
Social media 73, 74, 244
    analysis for combating terrorism 244
    sentiment analysis 73, 74
Software 186, 300
    open source Java 186
    programming 300
Solve artificial neural network problem 221
Sound signal 293
  digital 293
Sound wave 291, 293
  digital 293
Spam 96, 97
    detection learning task 96
    detection problem 96, 97
Speech 77, 292
    processing 292
    tagging nltk.tag 77
Speech act 290, 291
  promises 290
  recognizing 290
Speech recognition 276, 290, 291, 293, 294,
    295, 297, 305
    system 291, 292, 293, 294
States Bayes theorem 117
Stochastic 62, 63, 207, 238, 239, 293
    based tagging method/algorithm 63
    processing 293
    solution 239
    tagger disambiguates 63
Synapse 200, 201
Syntax 36, 60, 83, 84
    of Propositional Logic Connectives 36
Systems 8, 15, 16, 18, 21, 22, 27, 28, 29, 33,
    34, 95, 108, 112, 170, 201, 240, 277,
    278, 281, 282, 314
    analysis and design and psychology 27

automated learning 95
computer hardware configuration 8
dynamic 201, 240
gaze tracking 277
geometric 281, 282
license plate recognition 277
medical diagnosis 8, 21, 22

T

Tactile sensor 295, 296, 297
Tagging 63, 64
  previous stochastic 64
Tagging method 62
Tasks 3, 57, 58, 76, 83, 91, 99, 100, 231, 295,
    298, 301, 302, 304, 306, 307, 314, 316,
    317, 318
    computational 231
    lemmatization 57
Techniques 1, 4, 5, 69, 93, 98, 170, 243, 244,
    246, 252, 253, 287
    advanced natural language processing 69
    geometric visualization 252, 253
    quantitative analytic 253
Technologies 10, 11, 12, 13, 14, 15, 16, 68,
    200, 296, 304
    art Artificial Intelligence 16
    digital computing 304
    particular Bitcoin 12
Tellme's information access 294
Terrorism 242, 243, 244, 245, 246, 247, 250,
    252, 253, 254, 255, 256, 257, 258, 259
    battle 245
    counter 246, 252
    fight 245, 259
    suicidal 243
Terrorism dataset 242, 243, 244, 245, 246,
    249, 251, 252, 253, 254, 255, 256, 257,
    259
    analyzed 246
    analyzing 242, 245, 251, 252
    coded 249, 251
    global 243, 253
    multi-dimensional 252

probability distribution of 251, 259
Text 51, 53, 54, 58, 59, 60, 76, 91
    normalization 51, 53, 54
    pre-processing 53, 54, 58, 59, 60, 76, 91
Text mining 244, 245
    lexicon 244
Theoretical relationship 260
Three-dimensional 281, 282, 283
    geometry 281
    transformations 282, 283
Threshold logic unit (TLU) 203, 204, 205,
        206, 208, 209, 211, 212, 213, 214
Tools 5, 27, 35, 104, 189, 244, 245, 298, 299,
        302
    cleaning 244
    data mining 245
    hybrid 35
    mathematical 5
    web scraper 244
Tracking sports action 277
Transformation 62, 63, 282, 283, 284, 285,
        286
    rotate 284
    two-dimensional rotation 285
Translation transformation 283, 284
    two-dimensional 283
Tunnel effect tactile sensors 296
Turing's electromechanical computer 7
Turing test model 1, 2

V

Vacuum cleaners 300
Validating expert system performance 29
Vectors 59, 96, 98, 106, 120, 211, 212, 213,
        215, 281, 282
    augmented 282
Vehicle(s) 288, 289, 301, 308, 309, 310, 311,
        312, 313, 318
    autonomous/robotic 308, 318
    crosses lane 310
    monitors 289
    park design 313
    robotic 308, 311

self-driving 288, 298
    transportation 313
Vehicle automation 308, 311, 314
    features, increasing 311
Vision 3, 6, 276, 278, 279, 309
    spherical 278
Vision systems 277, 278, 279
    for high accuracy measurement 279
    for inspection 279

W

Waikato Environment for Knowledge
        Analysis (WEKA) 67, 168, 169, 186,
        187, 189, 191, 192, 194, 196, 198, 199,
        200, 244, 246
Water/Oil drilling system 22, 126, 127, 128,
        129
Weighted children entropy 126, 127, 128, 129
WEKA 168, 190, 191, 192, 195, 196, 197,
        199
    ARFF viewer 190
    classifier screen 196
    configuration of linear regression 195
    Explorer 168, 191, 192, 193, 197, 199
    launching 192
    to perform k-means clustering on dataset
        168
WhatsApp 244
Wireless networks 13
WordNetLemmatizer 57
Word 62
    pronunciation in text to Speech 62
    sense disambiguation 62

X

Xbox gaming system 278

Y

Yo, predicted value of 156, 159

Z

Zero-layer ANN 223

www.ingramcontent.com/pod-product-compliance
Lightning Source LLC
Chambersburg PA
CBHW050807220326
41598CB00006B/143